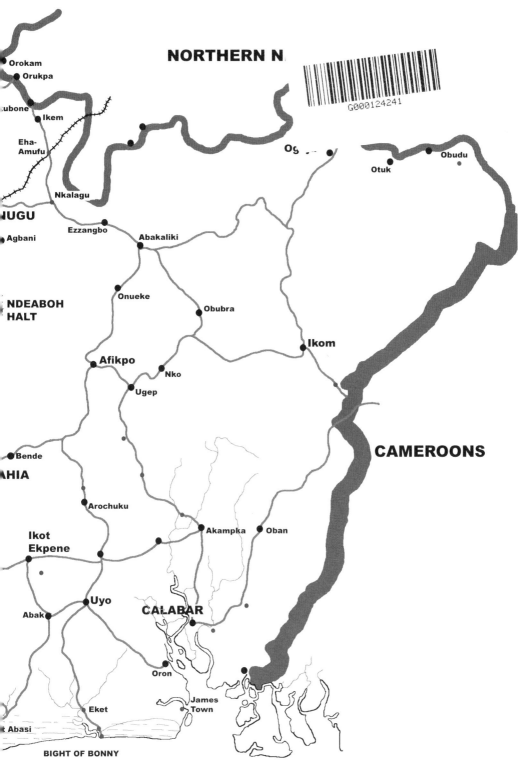

NORTHERN N

Orokam

Orukpa

ubone

Ikem

Eha-
Amufu

Og

Otuk

Obudu

Nkalagu

UGU

Agbani

Ezzangbo

Abakaliki

NDEABOH
HALT

Onueke

Obubra

Ikom

Afikpo

Nko

Ugep

CAMEROONS

Bende

HIA

Arochuku

Ikot
Ekpene

Akampka

Oban

Uyo

Abak

CALABAR

Oron

James
Town

Eket

Abasi

BIGHT OF BONNY

Scale approx. 24 miles to the inch

DUST SUSPENDED

Ahoada at dusk, 1957

DUST
SUSPENDED

A Memoir of Colonial, Overseas and Diplomatic Service Life 1953 to 1986

by

SIR FRANCIS KENNEDY KCMG, CBE, DL

Ash on an old man's sleeve
Is all the ash the burnt roses leave.
Dust in the air suspended
Marks the place where a story ended.

T.S. Eliot: *Little Gidding*

The Memoir Club

© Sir Francis Kennedy 2006

First published in 2006 by
The Memoir Club
Stanhope Old Hall
Stanhope
Weardale
County Durham

British Library Cataloguing in
Publication Data.
A catalogue record for this book
is available from the
British Library

ISBN: 1-84104-109-2

Typeset by TW Typesetting, Plymouth, Devon
Printed by CPI, Bath

For Anne,
who lived it all with me,
and our four wonderful children
who forgave us for all the upheavals that
we caused to their young lives.

The book was written with our grandchildren
and great grandchildren very much in mind –
just in case they are ever curious about
what grandma and granddad
got up to when *they* were young.

Contents

List of illustrations

Foreword

Sir Francis Kennedy's richly fulfilling, exciting and robustly enlightening chronicle of his life and times is a treasure trove of uncommon value. On the surface, it reads like a straight biographical book. It actually encapsulates however the essence of British colonial rule in Africa and the metamorphosis that gave birth to the Commonwealth family, as well as the United Kingdom's international relations in today's rapidly globalizing, technology-driven world.

More specifically, *Dust Suspended* dwells on Sir Francis Kennedy's varied experiences in Nigeria in the different capacities in which he represented Her Majesty's Government. One thread runs through the entire book – the author's unmediated love for Nigeria (and Africa) and his commitment to seeing the emergence of a stable, resurgent, progressive and prosperous Nigeria. This fervour has not dissipated with time.

It is instructive that Sir Francis Kennedy, KCMG, CBE, DL, is a member of the Board of the Pan African Health Foundation (PAHF), a public-private sector initiative aimed at promoting a dynamic new path to health care delivery on the African continent. The work of this Foundation is better appreciated when we consider that sustainable development is feasible in Africa only if we are able to tame the diseases that dis-empower and impoverish our people. The alternative is to allow the continent's disease burden to damage its social fabric, diminish agricultural and industrial production, undermine political, social and economic stability, and contribute to regional and global insecurity.

The fact that Sir Francis can still find time for this kind of committal work is clearly indicative of his lifetime dedication to engendering a fair, just, equitable, harmonious, secure and progressive world order. This singular commitment to global good shines through his entire career, whether in Africa, in the United States of America, or back home in the United Kingdom.

He has remained a committed friend and valued advocate for Nigeria and the African continent.

I feel privileged to have had this good man's path cross mine over the past thirty odd years. It is my fervent hope that this book, *Dust Suspended*, will not just make enjoyable reading but that it will challenge us all to reflect on our own lives' journeys with a view to measuring the 'humanity quotient' of our endeavours.

O.O. Obasanjo
President of the Federal Republic of Nigeria

State House
Abuja   12 April 2006

Preface

If you stand inside the door of Hatchard's bookshop in Piccadilly any Monday around lunch-time you will see people scurrying past from their offices on the way to clubs and sandwich bars. A few enter the shop and make straight for the new releases on the Biography Counter. They have read the reviews in the Sunday newspapers. Most pick up the book and turn straight to the index before slamming it shut and marching out with a frown. One or two find a reference, read a page or two and look at the photographs before replacing the book with a smile. Occasionally, very occasionally, someone goes to the cash desk and actually buys a copy.

There are many dear friends whom Anne and I have known during the years covered by this book whose names do not appear in the index. I hope that they will forgive us. It is not that we have forgotten them or no longer appreciate their friendship; only that in a collection of stories as short as this it is impossible to mention all who deserve it. I also apologize for the inaccuracies in the book. Apart from changing one or two names I have tried to make the narrative as accurate as I could. But at this distance in time memory is a treacherous faculty and despite rechecking the facts where it was possible to do so, I am sure that mistakes remain.

I am most grateful to H.E. President Obasanjo who, despite the extraordinary burdens of his office, found the time to write such generous words in the Foreword to the book. His friendship over several decades and through good times and bad is deeply valued. I thank also Nigeria's distinguished High Commissioner in London, Mr Christopher Kolade, for his patient and invaluable help on a number of occasions.

I thank all the many people who have helped directly or indirectly in the production of the book: Mr Phillips at the Memoir Club, who suggested the project in the first place, and his team who shepherded me along the way to publication. I am especially grateful to Sheila Seacroft, my editor, for her constant encouragement and advice, and to Sir David Trippier, who insisted that the book should be written and urged me on until it was. I am particularly grateful to Miss Terry Barringer of the Institute of Commonwealth Studies for her expert advice and for making available her encyclopaedic knowledge of the history of the Administration of Empire. I thank Anthony Kirk Greene of St Anthony's College,

Oxford, and all involved in the Overseas Service Pension Association Project for their help. Tony is the doyen of Colonial Service Studies and an inspiration to the rest of us. Mary Bone of the Chatham House Library and Dr Mandy Barton of the National Archives have been generous in their advice and in guiding me to the relevant portions of their troves of treasure. Peter Housego, Manager of Global Archive Management at the University of Warwick has been similarly helpful. Without his help in navigating the BP archives, of which he is custodian, I might never have finished the task. The expert assistance of these professionals has made this an altogether more accurate account of some events in Nigeria in the fifties, sixties and seventies, than it would otherwise have been. I am indebted to Mr Frank Wadmore of the University of Central Lancashire and my brother-in-law, Mr Peter Ainsworth, for the Sketch Map of Eastern Nigeria and to H.E. Dr Peter Odili, Governor of Rivers State, Nigeria, for the excellent map of that State.

I would like to thank also John Smith for his wise counsel and patient help; Sir Philip Thomas for the exchange of views on Nigeria as seen from the office of the High Commissioner and on New York as seen from the office of the United Kingdom's Director General of Trade and Investment in the United States; and Chief Emeka Anyaoku for his help with Commonwealth issues and details of the incident in Obosi. I am exceptionally indebted to Sir Brian Barder. The text of the book has benefited greatly from Brian's perceptive suggestions and unerring eye for weak syntax and sloppy expressions. Brian's comments on relations between the Colonial Office and the Regional Government in Eastern Nigeria in the 1950s have been especially valuable because he makes them with the authority of one who has not only served as British High Commissioner in Lagos but who in the early fifties was working as a young civil servant in the Colonial Office in Whitehall. We owe much to our friends Chief Philip Asiodu and his wife Jumoke for leading us to a better understanding of things Nigerian in countless discussions during convivial evenings over many years. I am indebted to my cousin, Cyril Hardman, for reminding me of forgotten details of our Brinscall beginnings and Professor Robert Markus for doing the same for *Humanitas*. I am grateful to my old boss and good friend, Oputa Udoji, who said when I left Nigeria in 1964 that if things did not work out in London there would always be a job for me in Eastern Nigeria as long as he was Chief Secretary. I hope that the book does not disappoint. Finally, I would like to thank the Secretary of Nsukka Municipal Council for reminding me so trenchantly that however large the part other people may play in our lives, it does not follow that we play any part at all in theirs.

Chapter 1

1926: Brinscall

Sir winston churchill was fond of telling people that he had been born in Blenheim Palace, the seat of his great ancestor, the Duke of Marlborough. I have always been glad that I was born in Brinscall and that our address was No. 1 Churchill Road, although it was a disappointment to discover that the Churchill after whom our little street was named was not Winston but his unsatisfactory father, Randolph.

Brinscall is a small village tucked away in a valley on the edge of the Pennine hills between Chorley and Blackburn. You can reach it by road from the west with the glittering sea at your back; or from the north, from the Ribble Valley, where the Romans set up their camp. But when I was a boy the best way to come was from the south, by a little train that chugged its way up the wooded valley from Chorley. In those days the railway crossed School Lane by a bridge half way down Brinscall Hill. Sometimes the locomotive would stop on the bridge to let off steam before entering the station and from the top of Brinscall it looked as though the train had come to rest on Fred Hull's shop.

What you could not do in those days and cannot do today is approach Brinscall from the east. When you climb the last hill from Chorley, there, suddenly, is the village at your feet. Behind it the moor fills the sky like the backdrop of a stage. It is the moor that makes Brinscall special. No one goes to Brinscall by chance or on the way to somewhere else. The only people who go to Brinscall are those who want to.

Brinscall Moor was the last frontier of my childhood. Every summer, sometimes every day, I walked with my grandfather on the moor and in the woods and valleys around. We climbed higher and higher until there was nothing to see but the endless heather and nothing to hear but the wind and the squawk of a startled grouse. But we never reached the end of the moor. There was always another horizon. I used to imagine that the moor had no end. Of the many mistakes I have made in life one of the worst was to go to Brinscall one Sunday afternoon and with a friend and our dog, Hector, to climb the moor. We walked in a straight line across the moor until we reached the busy main road from Bolton to Darwen. In less than two hours we destroyed the mystery of a life-time.

Brinscall Moor is a water catchment area. Water drains off the hills and is collected in reservoirs from where it is piped to the city of Liverpool, thirty five miles away. The water also drains into the valley that runs along the base of Brinscall Moor where it is collected in two lakes that were dammed and deepened to serve the calico print works. The lakes are named Lower Lodge and Higher Lodge. It was the water that brought the calico print works to Brinscall and it was the print works that brought Timothy Kennedy to Brinscall.

Timothy was twenty two years of age when he arrived from Nenagh in Tipperary in 1855. My uncle Bert claimed that Timothy had earlier trained to become a priest at Saint Patrick's College, Maynooth, and that he was the only man in the village, besides the priest and the doctor, who could read Latin. In any event the young Irishman soon rose to a position of responsibility in the newly opened print works.

Timothy had arrived in what was still a tiny rural community. But he would have found plenty of his compatriots in the vicinity working on the extension of the railway from Wigan, a coal-mining town, to Blackburn, already on its way to being the world's greatest manufacturer of woven cotton goods. By 1863 the stations had been built, the great bridges constructed and the track laid. Timothy would have been there when the first train steamed in with ribbons flying.

Timothy soon settled down. Within a year he had met and wooed a girl called Mary Cowburn from the next village. The Cowburns were farming people who later ran a butcher's shop in Wheelton. As yet there was no Catholic Church in Brinscall and so Timothy walked every Sunday to Wheelton to attend Mass at St Chad's church. There, no doubt, he met Mary and there it was that they were married in 1857. There, in the little cemetery behind St Chad's church Timothy and Mary still lie today.

The newly-weds made their home in a little cottage near the top of Brinscall Hill. In that small house, between 1858 and 1882, twelve children were born. The sixth of them, Michael, was to become my grandfather.

Timothy died when my grandfather was twenty one but by then he had secured for his sons employment at the print works. Four of them, including Michael, became foremen. Michael was proud of his skill as a printer. He loved his work. He loved his family and he loved his village. He started work at the age of eight and worked at the print works all his life. He was born in Brinscall and died in Brinscall. Although he spent all his life in that small space he has always seemed to me one of the wisest and most far-seeing of men.

In the late nineteenth century a family called Carey arrived in the village. How the Careys found their way to Brinscall no one can remember. They had two daughters, Elizabeth and Sarah Anne. Sarah Anne, whose name the family invariably pronounced 'Sar'an', made a great impression on Michael Kennedy. Sarah Anne was shy girl with a lovely smile, a rosy complexion and a gentle sense of fun. She and Michael enjoyed a long and happy marriage until my grandfather died in 1939.

Grandfather Carey had been a regular soldier in the British Army. He had fought in the Crimean War and Auntie Lizzie, in a biscuit tin in the bottom drawer of the dresser, kept a number of letters that her father had written during the Crimean War, including one addressed 'From the heights of Alma' on the eve of battle.

Grandmother Carey had been a domestic servant in the officers' mess. She was fond of saying that she had never been to school but had met the scholars. Fifty years later the remark was still being quoted within the family with an admiring shake of the head. Great grandfather Carey moved around the world with his regiment and the family usually moved with him. That is how it came about that his elder daughter Elizabeth was born in Quebec and his younger daughter, Sarah Anne, was born in Winchester. A son, Tom, was also born in Winchester but was drowned when he was twelve whilst playing in a butt of rainwater.

Lizzie had been to secondary school and was considered the more 'refined' of the two daughters. Once at the age of fourteen she had crossed London alone in a hansom cab. This exploit also was recalled with wonderment down the years. In Brinscall Lizzie met and married a quarryman, Jim Halton, who died at a relatively young age of pneumoconiosis. There was a feeling that Lizzie had married below expectations and Jim, who enjoyed a pint, was usually referred to within the family as 'Poor' Jim Halton. After Jim's death Lizzie spent most of the next forty years under a pile of rugs on the sofa, reading novels. One of her daughter Nellie's most important duties was to replenish the stock of novels from the mobile lending library that visited the village each week.

My father, James, was born in 1896 and his brother, Bertrand, in 1900. Father followed in the family footsteps and went to work in the print works. During World War I he served with the Royal Flying Corps in France and later with the army of occupation in Cologne. Uncle Bert took a job with the London, Midland and Scottish Railway and began work in the parcels office in Chorley railway station. In 1919 he qualified as a wireless operator and served with the merchant navy in the Persian Gulf, Singapore and Hong Kong. At the end of his service he returned to Brinscall and the railway. One day he told his father that there were vacancies for well-paid jobs with the railways in India and that he was thinking of applying. My grandfather lowered his paper and remarked: 'Aye, well, if you can't make a success in your own country that's what you'd better do.' Uncle Bert spent the rest of his life working for a negligible wage with the LMS and British Rail.

The young men returning from military service were eager for female company and the girls of Chorley and Brinscall were just as eager to provide it. The young people thought nothing of walking the five miles from Brinscall to Chorley and back for a sing-song round the piano in one of their homes. It was at such an event that Jim Kennedy of Brinscall met Alice Bentham of Chorley. They were married in 1925 and went to live in No. 1 Churchill Road where I was born just as the General Strike was beginning.

There were only three houses in Churchill Road. Mr and Mrs Tin lived next door. Hector Tin was the coal man for Brinscall Co-op. He wore a large moustache and spoke little. According to my mother, Mrs Tin was 'house proud'. From my mother that was high praise. I would often watch Hector and his assistant, Johnny, stabling the horses and settling them in their stalls for the night. Johnny walked with a limp. Sometimes when they were returning home Johnny would give me a ride on the empty cart. Hector would agree only reluctantly but Johnny would lift me up onto the cart and then perch on the shaft behind the horses. During the Second World War when Hector had retired and I had long left Brinscall, Johnny was riding the shafts as usual when the cart jolted and threw him under the wheels. He was run over and killed.

Next door to the Tins lived Jimmy Beaver with his wife and their daughter, Dora. In Brinscall Jimmy was regarded as a bit of a card, raffish and always up to something. He had done all manner of jobs. Once he had been a bookmaker; later he had managed a dance hall. With the advent of sound he opened a little cinema opposite my grandparents' house. He called it 'The Regal'. My earliest memory in life is of standing in the Beavers' sitting room one Sunday morning between the dresser and the table looking into the eyes of the Beavers' collie dog some six inches away. Dora Beaver said that the dog would not bite. Mrs Beaver said that the dog liked me. My mother said 'Don't be frightened'. I was terrified. I could not have been more than two at the time . . .

My second earliest memory was of the incident of the watch. In 1926 my grandfather had been presented with a gold watch by the Calico Printers Association in recognition of over 50 years service. Apparently, whenever I visited my grandparents with my father and mother I would climb on granddad's knee and ask to see the splendid watch. First I would listen to the tick, tock; then admire the inscription on the inside of the back cover. Finally, granddad would open the back so that I could gaze on the breathless beauty of the jewelled movement. I was so enthralled by this ceremony that my grandparents decided that I should have a watch of my own. Granddad went to Blackburn and came back with a real watch. Not a gold watch but a real pocket watch nevertheless. The watch had cost five shillings, a huge sum to my grandparents at the time. The surprise was presented one Sunday afternoon at one of our weekly visits. It is reported that I was suitably delighted. Some time later my mother asked 'Where is Frank? He is very quiet.' I was found in the yard sitting on the stone flags with my new watch and a hammer. Parents and grandparents were aghast. The watch had already been smashed beyond repair. As I was hauled away I tried to explain that I was trying to open the back to see how it worked. Today, granddad's gold watch is kept on a stand on my desk. From time to time I open the back to admire the inscription and gaze at the breathless beauty of the jewelled movement.

Brinscall was a busy place in the 1920s. As well as Woods's print works there was a cotton mill at the bottom of Bury Lane and across from Railway Road was the quarry. A gantry bridge carried a spur of the railway across the road. Each week a little shunting engine would come from Blackburn and shunt a dozen or so wagons up to the quarry. As a wagon was filled it would be released to roll by gravity over the gantry and into the siding. When there were a sufficient number of full wagons the shunting engine would collect them from the siding and tow them to Blackburn.

As well as the print works and the cotton mill and the quarry there were grouse on the moor and a pack of hounds at Brinscall Hall. Last but not least, there was a public indoors swimming pool. Brinscall Baths had been built and donated to the village by a philanthropic textile manufacturer, Mr Parks. It was the only public baths for miles around and was the envy of neighbouring villages. For its location in Brinscall we had to thank not only Mr Parks, of course, but also the water which the moors delivered in such copious amounts.

The sun was shining on the Kennedy family when, in 1928, disaster struck. As part of a scheme to reduce excess capacity in the textile industry Brinscall Print Works was selected for closure. My father had to leave Brinscall and a job which he loved and move to Chorley and a job which he hated. For my grandfather the event was even more calamitous. At 58 he was considered too old to find another job. For the first time in his life he had been earning a decent wage and had expected to have seven more years in which to save for retirement. Suddenly he was out of work and living on a tiny state pension and the rent of a few shillings a quarter from the house in Churchill Road. When my grandmother died in 1941 she was found to have sixpence in her purse, the only money she had in the world.

The family moved to Chorley but for me the links with Brinscall were as strong as ever. Most weekends my father would take me to visit his parents and each Christmas, Easter and Summer I would spend a large part of the holidays in Brinscall. My grandparents lived at No. 5 School Lane where School Lane and Railway Road meet. This was the hub of the village. Immediately opposite was Jimmy Beaver's Picture House. Every Saturday afternoon Grandma and Auntie Lizzie would take their seats behind the lace curtains in the parlour to watch the passers-by and dissect the village gossip. The two sisters would yell in horror when I tried to draw back the curtain to give them a better view.

No. 5 was just as well situated at the rear. My bedroom looked out over the lake to the moors which shelved down to the pine woods in the middle distance. With the sun streaming into the bedroom no one awoke to a lovelier view. Immediately behind the house was the playground on which we spent much of our time. There must have been girls in Brinscall in the nineteen thirties but I do not remember any. Every day I was either walking with granddad or playing with the boys of the village. Alan Owen took me under his wing. He explained to the other boys that I was 'Owd Mike's grandson'. Alan's mother had lost one of her hands in an accident in the weaving mill. She had a wooden arm with a hook at the end of it.

In summer we played cricket all day. Games seemed to start of their own accord. Boys would peel off at meal times and others would take their place. The sides were always England and Australia. The emergency exit of the Baths was the pavilion. The batting side would sit on its steps. When Alan and Jack 'Atky' (Atkinson) were captains they always made a great play of going out to bat. They would adjust imaginary gloves, twiddle their bats, then run down the steps, bat under arm and stride out to take guard. They claimed to reproduce the mannerisms of Bradman and Hammond. Occasionally Jack Atky would announce that he was imitating an even grander and more mysterious character called Victor Trumper.

The left boundary of the playground was the storage yard of Withnell Urban District Council; the right the rear of Brinscall Baths and the boiler house. In front was the Lodge. A hit through the railings of Withnell Urban District Council yard was a two. An off-side boundary was impossible so everyone tried to pull the ball to leg. A straight hit into the lodge was a six. Only the bigger boys hit the ball into the lodge. When that happened the smaller boys, Douglas ('Copper') Wilkinson, Jack

Caddick and myself would collect stones for the bigger boys to throw into the lodge and splash the ball to the bank. I was allowed to collect stones in my school cap for Tommy Small to throw.

To my mother's irritation, the view invariably expressed in Brinscall was that I had arrived from Chorley looking 'peaky'. Auntie Lizzie would explain that I was 'missing my native air'. That remark, my mother would tell father, 'made her blood boil'. Dad would try to glance the ball to leg with the reply: 'Nay, it's only her way.' Granddad kept hens on an allotment and each morning, to remedy the ravages of Chorley life, grandma made me drink a mug of beaten egg, milk and sugar, sprinkled with nutmeg. This mid-morning luxury was delicious but one morning in the middle of an England-Australia game grandma appeared on the sacred turf with egg and milk in hand. I was never allowed to forget the episode. For weeks afterward either Alan Owen or Jack Atky would call out 'Come on Frank for your egg and milk'. The rest of the team would stagger around in exaggerated mirth. I thought that I would never recover from the shame.

Jack Caddick was always running errands. He would slouch across the playground dragging a shopping bag and announce that he could not play today because he had to run an errand. After an exchange of insults he would put his shopping bag behind the stone flag that served as the wicket and join the game, 'but only for one innings'.

Douglas Wilkinson and I were the same age and good pals. Sometimes we played by ourselves in the fields nearby. One day we nagged parents and grandparents to allow us to swim in the lodge. Off we went through the fields for our swim. The water was like ice. 15 minutes later we were back home again, teeth chattering.

Occasionally games more elaborate than cricket would be played. In late summer after harvest time there might be a game of hares and hounds. These were events in which everyone took part. Two or three smaller boys would be the hares and given ten minutes start. Then the pack of twenty or thirty older boys would give chase. The whole village and the hills around became our playground and for those exciting minutes all of it belonged to us. We ran through farm yards, climbed walls, crossed the railway, raced round ponds, through woods, and the grown ups did not seem to mind. Some would shout advice as we ran past. Others smiled encouragement as they recalled the days when they had played hares and hounds. The hills resounded with our cries just as they had for Wordsworth in Cockermouth. I like to think that I know what Wordsworth meant when he wrote:

Fair seed-time had my soul, and I grew up
. . . Much favoured in my birthplace.

What happened to the boys of those idyllic days? Alan joined the Royal Marines and fought in Normandy. I last saw him in 1946, resplendent in his uniform and every inch the soldier. My second cousin, George Lancaster, came back to Brinscall after more than 30 missions over Germany with Bomber Command. He died of tuberculosis a few years after his return. Tommy Small became a labourer with Leyland Motors and played cricket for Chorley. At forty years of age and several stones overweight he was still thumping the ball around on Saturday afternoons. Jack Caddick also played cricket in his twenties and thirties but deserted Brinscall and for some mysterious reason defected to play for our neighbour and rival, Withnell. Douglas Wilkinson I last met in Plymouth in 1945. We were both in the Royal Navy. Douglas lent me 1s 6d to pay for a meal. Douggie now lives in retirement near Fleetwood. From time to time he sends messages through my cousin, Cyril Hardman, reminding me that I owe him one and sixpence.

CHAPTER 2

1930: Babes in the wood

CHORLEY AND BRINSCALL belong to different worlds. You felt it the moment that you stepped off the train. Chorley had always been a market town. By the end of the first world war it was also a textile town and manufacturing centre. If you climbed the Nab and looked back over the town you saw twenty or thirty tall chimneys belching out smoke. However hard the women scrubbed their steps and pumiced–stoned the edges they would be dirty two hours later. Specks of soot drifted down on the clothes as they hung drying on the lines. Every morning from 6.00 a.m. the factory whistles would sound, one after another, calling people to work as church bells had once called people to worship. Everyone knew which whistle belonged to which factory.

My mother, Alice, was the second child of Ralph and Elizabeth Bentham. Lizzie came from an old Chorley family, the Reynolds. Her elder sister Annie married a policeman and went to live in Morecambe. One of their children, Edith, also married a policeman who rose to become the Superintendent of Police in Bury. Edith's elder brother, Frank, was my mother's favourite cousin. I wondered whether she had named me after him. Frank Whitfield was handsome and intelligent. He was also a Communist. One day he came to say goodbye to my mother. He had joined the International Brigade and was going to Spain to fight against Franco. He was killed a few weeks later in the fighting before Madrid.

Lizzie's younger brother, Bob, became the chief engineer at the bleach works at Bircacre. That works also was a victim of the Great Depression. But Bircacre has a mention in British economic history because it was the site of Charnock's cotton mill. This was one of the world's first, custom built, mechanized weaving factory. In 1802 hand-loom weavers from Chorley marched on Bircacre, smashed the looms and burnt down the mill.

Lizzie did not do as well in life as her two siblings. But then she had married Ralph Bentham. The family do not know much about Ralph or where his parents came from. Ralph Bentham was a clogger. The family believed that he made the best clogs in Chorley. But that was not his only vocation. Ralph was the life and soul of any party. He had a good voice and an engaging manner and enjoyed a drink. Ralph was a regular

9

contestant at the Subscription Bowling green and a keen student of the turf. He did not allow clog-making to interfere unduly with these activities.

Between the wars fast food shops were proliferating in northern industrial towns and in 1924 Ralph and Lizzie decided to abandon clog-making and turn their premises into a fish and chip shop. Ralph gave the clog business to his assistant, Ralph Jolly, who opened a shop of his own a few doors away.

Soon after Bentham's Fish and Chip shop opened for business Ralph fell ill and after an agonizing illness died of cancer of the throat. Whilst grieving the loss of her husband Lizzie discovered the depths of her financial predicament. As well as a mortgage on the shop Ralph had left behind assorted trade debts of over £300. To my grandmother this was a fortune. But Lizzie Reynolds told her children that the debts would be paid to the last penny and that their father's good name would be cleared. Her son-in-law, Jim Mawdesley, who was a baker and confectioner, agreed to take over the mortgage which Lizzie would hopefully repay from the earnings of the shop. Lizzie herself went back to work at the cotton mill. Her younger son, Harry, worked at Leyland Motors and helped his mother to run the shop in the evenings.

When Brinscall Print Works closed down father got a job as a fitter at Leyland Motors, Chorley. Jim and Alice were looking for somewhere to live and grandmother who was now over sixty and no longer strong enough to run four looms in a weaving shed, appealed to them to take over the shop and relieve her of the mortgage that had financed its purchase. Reluctantly mother and father moved into the fish and chip shop. They said that they would stay for two years. In the event they stayed for ten and ran the business for twenty.

It was not until many years later that I realized that I came from what are called humble origins. We thought that the people who lived in Queen Street were poor and the people who lived on Bolton Road were rich. But we who lived in Bolton Street thought of ourselves as average; not rich, but not poor. Certainly the people who lived in Queen Street thought that we were rich because Dad worked at Leyland Motors and Mother ran a shop. When father made one of his infrequent appearances at a meeting of the Chorley branch of the Associated Engineering Union, Joe Caterall would mutter, 'Bloody capitalist!' Father would delight in reporting the incident to Jim Mawdesley over their pints in the Joiners Arms. Since Jim ran a confectioner's shop he also was a capitalist.

129 Bolton Street had been a simple weaver's cottage with two rooms downstairs and two bedrooms upstairs. The front room had been

converted into a shop and a brick extension added to the rear to make a kitchen and an additional bedroom. There was a building behind the house that we called the 'back shop'. This was where clogs had once been made and where now potatoes were stored and peeled and prepared for cooking. Family life had to survive the unending din and bustle of the traffic between the shop where the fish and chips were fried and served and the back shop where the potatoes were prepared for cooking. Particularly noisy was a heavy cast iron machine that sliced raw potatoes into chips. The clunk of this machine echoed through the house and into the bedrooms above.

But family life did survive. In addition to all her other work mother clothed the family and cooked their meals. She nursed them when they were sick and in the moments snatched from the tread-mill of the business she read them stories and taught them what was right and what was wrong. She was a qualified music teacher and gave piano lessons to earn extra money. She sang as she worked and each morning would go through a repertoire of songs from Gilbert and Sullivan and the musical comedies of the early twentieth century. I would often be sent to the newsagents to buy the sheet music of the latest popular tune.

I returned from Brinscall one Christmas holiday to find that I had a baby brother, Jack. Two years later my sister Dorothy was born and when I was ten the family reached its final size with the arrival of my brother Michael. By then it was becoming almost impossible to bring up a family and run a business within the confines of 129 Bolton Street. To the relief of parents and children alike the family moved in 1938 to a house at 55 Bolton Road. This house had three bedrooms, a bathroom, two living rooms and a kitchen. To us it was luxury.

When I was four I started school at Sacred Heart Infant School. I sat next to Kathleen Kellett. Our parents were great friends and lived near each other. In the first few weeks Kathleen and I were often called out of class and directed by another teacher in a number of mysterious movements. Then one day we were dressed in white satin and made to walk, hand in hand, on a stage. We gave one performance in a school concert hall and another in the open air theatre in Astley Park. I never had the faintest idea what it was all about. We discovered later that we were the babes in a production of Babes in the Wood. At one point we had to pretend to fall asleep. In the open air production this was impossible because we were supposed to sleep on a real log that Mr Longton had provided as a pillow. Photographs were taken of some of the scenes and 'ooh'd' over by parents. The photos were a source of acute embarrassment to me. At Sacred Heart School boys did not hold hands with girls.

Babes in the Wood. With Kathleen Kellett in white satin, far right. Kneeling rats: on left, Frank Pilkington; second from left, Ken Brindle; fourth from left, William Hoole

Wearing white satin was inconceivable. As the years went by I took to denying any relationship with the little cissie in the satin suit.

In the first two classes we wrote with chalk on blackboards but in the third class we changed to pen or pencil and real exercise books. It was in Miss McEvoy's class of five year olds that I had my first introduction to the vocabulary of sex. I sat next to Cyril Green whom, naturally, we called 'Pea'. As we took our seats after playtime 'Pea' leaned over and whispered: 'Cyril Aston f____d Joan Monks. Pass it on.' So I leaned over and passed on the message to Fred Durkin. I then turned back to Pea and asked 'What does it mean, 'f____d?' 'Oh', whispered Pea, 'it means he put his dicky in Joan Monks's.' I nodded, and with that we turned back to Miss McEvoy's catechism class.

Another incident in that class is indelibly etched in the memory. One afternoon I found myself involved in a dispute with Oswald Gillette. What the quarrel was about I never discovered but Ossie made clear that he was going to 'get' me and that we were going to fight. At that moment the bell rang and we had to go back into class. 'I'll get thee at goin 'ome time,' snarled Ossie. On the class-room wall was a large clock, quite like the one that was to be used in the film *High Noon*. I felt as lonely as Gary Cooper and nowhere near as brave. The word went round the class that there was to be a fight at going-home time. Cyril Green was at pains to inform me – as if I did not already know – that Ossie Gillette was the 'cock of the class'. I thought I was going to throw up. The afternoon seemed never to end. I hoped against hope that Ossie might forget or that it might go dark before school ended. In desperation I even started to pray that the clock might stop as though somehow that might stop time. But nothing was to save me from my doom. The bell rang. The children grabbed their coats and rushed out into the playground and formed a circle.

Ossie and I were pushed into the centre of the circle. We squared up. Ossie murmured imprecations and breathed fire. My heart was pounding so much that I could hardly swing my arms. We shuffled around and vaguely poked fists in each other's direction. We had managed a few pushes and shoves but nothing approaching a punch when to my unbounded relief Miss Wilkinson came round the corner and shooed us all off the premises. There ended The Great Encounter.

After our confrontation Ossie Gillette and I gradually became friends. One summer evening, after school, Ossie invited me to play with him on the waste land behind his parents' house in Princes' Street. I knew that this honour would seal our friendship. I even wondered at times whether the reputation of cock of the class had not been a little exaggerated. But of course friends do not air such doubts.

In the top class of the Infants School I fell in love with Joan Higginson. The Higginson children lived on a farm so far away that if the weather was bad the Headmaster would send them home early. As Joan sat at the other side of the class-room my affection was known only to myself. But at the Christmas party I made the journey across the room and offered Joan Higginson my paper hat. She blushed and ran away.

We lived in the poorest part of town and went to what may have been the toughest of the schools. During breaks the boys' playground was a battlefield. The carnage slackened in spring when every spare moment was spent playing marbles; mysteriously the warfare stopped altogether in early summer so that for a few weeks we could play 'tabbies' with cigarette cards.

One day we received new neighbours. My mother said 'This is Frank Pilkington. He has come to live next door.' When the grown ups had left, Frank said: 'Let's go climbing?' 'Climbing?' I asked. 'Come on,' he said. I followed him into the yard behind his house. Frank climbed to the top of the five foot high black stone wall that separated his yard from that of the Smiths. The stones were very old and the mortar between them had so crumbled that the wall was easy to climb. We stepped along the top of the wall and sat down on the sloping stone roof of Mr Smith's toilet. 'That's climbing', said Frank.

I was seven when Frank arrived. He was two years older. As well as climbing he introduced me to two other activities. Frank explained that if you asked to go to the Library, grown-ups always said yes. This was a particularly useful piece of knowledge if you suspected that household chores were in the offing. We would go to the Reference Room in the Public Library and each request a volume of the Illustrated History of the Great War. These were large books and we turned over the pages looking at the pictures until the library closed at 7.00 p.m. Frank's father had been in the Royal Artillery so he always looked at the pictures of the horse-drawn artillery. My father had served with the Royal Flying Corps so I gazed at pictures of Sopwith Camels and the Red Baron's Messerschmitt.

Frank's third gift was to introduce me to comics. He read variously the *Adventure*, the *Rover*, the *Wizard* and the *Hotspur*. I settled at once on the *Wizard*. The first time I tried to read the *Wizard* it took me an hour to read the first page. It was full of words that I did not know. The first paragraph alone contained the words: 'ordeal', 'hideous' and 'weird'. But eagerness to discover the story behind the illustrations drove me on. It was not long before I was devouring the *Wizard* from cover to cover. The comic was published every Tuesday but I bought it from our newsagent, Jack O'Neil, every Monday lunch-time. For a long time I thought that this was a special, possibly illegal, favour to me personally. The *Wizard* was a major influence on my educational development. For years all my English compositions were 'sexed up', as today's phrase goes, with a liberal sprinkling of the gory *Wizard* vocabulary. Early in 1937 we sat the eleven plus examination. I struggled through the arithmetic in the morning session. The afternoon was devoted to English. The second question invited us to write about our favourite poem. I raced into 'The Charge of the Light Brigade' by Alfred Lord Tennyson. I gave Tennyson the full *Wizard* treatment:

> Half a league, half a league, half a league onwards,
> Into the Valley of Death rode the Six Hundred . . .

What a heinous crime! What a weird blunder! What a hideous ordeal!'

Everybody in Chorley went to church and our family went more often than most. On Sundays we went to mass in the morning and Sunday school in the afternoon. When I was eight I was made an altar boy and then had to attend a Sunday evening service as well. Each day during the week we served at a morning mass. An older boy named Tommy Ince came to teach me Latin. He took the part of the priest and I practised the responses. To my surprise Tommy declared himself satisfied after two or three sessions. 'But when do we learn what the Latin means?' I asked. 'Oh, we don't have to know what it means,' said Tommy. 'We just say the words. The priest knows what they mean.' Luther's point exactly.

Of my brothers and sister, Dorothy has always been the most sensible and Michael the most sensitive. Michael has the most talent musically and the most natural style at games. But of the four children it is generally agreed that brother Jack is the strongest. He never had any problem with the cock of the class for the simple reason that he was the cock of the class. One day our neighbour, Tommy Pilkington, asked the five-year-old playing on the carpet, 'Now, Jack, what are you going to be when you grow up?' To everyone's surprise Jack replied: 'A priest'. To the family's even greater surprise that is what he did become. Jack went on to become a parish priest, a college lecturer and Rector of the English College in Rome and is now Monsignor John Kennedy. Michael also pursued a career in religion. After some years teaching he became a Buddhist and a prominent figure in the Friends of Western Buddhism movement. He writes and lectures on Buddhism.

Many Catholics complain of their experience at school: of the repression, superstition, physical punishment and so on. I have to say that I do not remember experiencing such traumas. Certainly, at Sacred Heart School physical punishment was dispensed on a liberal scale. Canings were an every day event. When William Hoole was summoned for punishment a buzz would go round the school: 'Hey, Billy's got the cane.' He never disappointed. The school would reverberate with his screams. His favourite trick was to jerk his hand away at the very last moment. On a good day this would result in the cane crashing down on Mr Grime's knee. Retribution was terrible but we thought the entertainment worth the price.

On one occasion the class were asked to imagine that they were Police Constables on traffic duty and write down their experiences. The children read out their essays in turn. When it came to Billy's turn he read out: 'I was on duty in Chapel Street when an Austin Seven came towards me driving on the wrong side of the road. The driver had no licence. "Excuse me, Sir, what is your name and address?" "Bernard Grime," said the motorist, "Occupation?" "Teacher." "Follow me", said I. "You are under arrest for dangerous driving and driving without a licence."' The rest was drowned in cheers that could be heard in Buchanan Street.

There was rivalry between Catholics and Protestants in Chorley but none of the bitterness that has sometimes divided communities in other towns in the United Kingdom. Most of the Catholics were from Irish families who had arrived in the nineteenth century and the tensions were probably less religious than social in nature. They were the kind of tensions that arise between immigrant and established communities. I think that religion enriched our lives. The liturgy and music of the Catholic Church were enjoyed by congregations who rarely got the chance to visit a concert hall. Admittedly, the language of some of the hymns that were belted out with such gusto could be startling, even gruesome:

Blood of my Saviour, bathe me in thy tide,
Wash me with water flowing from the side.

Then there were the sermons. My father and Uncle Jim would routinely discuss the previous week's performance in the pub on Saturday night. The views propounded from the pulpit were not always easy to understand. Uncle Bert's daily newspaper was the *Daily Telegraph*. He read books from the Catholic Book Club lent to him by his parish priest. Some of these were right wing, sympathetic to Action Française and anti-Semitic in flavour. They supported Franco in Spain and Salazaar in Portugal. Nevertheless, Uncle Bert invariably voted Labour. Father said that this was because he lived in a Council House. My father on the other hand was a paid-up member of the AEU trade union and frequently fulminated against the 'Lord Tom Noddies' whose only claim to political power was hereditary privilege. But he always voted Conservative on the grounds that you could not trust the other lot to run the country. Look what a mess Ramsay Macdonald had made of it!

On Sundays, I would listen to the parish priest droning on about the dangers of socialism and materialism. I was never quite sure what Father Formby meant by socialism but the materialism bit seemed odd even then. The white faces of the congregation, many of whom were unemployed, betrayed no sign of material wealth. It occurred to me that a bit of materialism was just what they needed.

In 1930 no one in Chorley had electricity and very few had a wireless. The parish was the centre of social as well as religious activity. 'Next Thursday,' it would be announced, 'there will be a Hot Pot Supper organized by the Married Women in the Hut, followed by a Social Evening in the School. Tickets can be obtained from Mr Joe Westby in Worthy Street and Mr Peter Hyde in Lyons Lane.' These were exciting events. After a supper of Lancashire Hot Pot and pickled onions we would be entertained by a series of 'turns'. Sometimes there would be a conjuror and usually someone would recite a monologue. But without fail, at some point in the evening, to deafening applause, Mary McFadden would give a rendition of 'The Rose of Tralee'.

One Saturday afternoon in 1937 I learned to swim. It was a hot summer day. So with costume and towel rolled up under my arm I went by train to Brinscall to swim in the Baths. As he was leaving, the only other person in the pool told me that there were some pennies on the bottom at the deep end. This caught my full attention. After several unsuccessful attempts to retrieve the coins by jumping in I began to dive. As I dived further and further towards the middle of the pool I scrambled back by a mixture of breast stroke and crawl. One by one I recovered the pennies. I was sitting on the side of the pool reflecting on what had been a satisfactory afternoon when Alan Owen, fully dressed, suddenly appeared by my side. 'Tha's passed t'scholarship,' he said. 'No, I haven't,' I replied. 'Tha's passed t'scholarship,' he insisted. 'It's in t' paper.' I had forgotten all about the 11 plus examination taken six months earlier. I got dressed and went round to No. 5 School Lane. Granddad was sitting at the living room table with the *Blackburn Northern Telegraph* spread out before him. 'You've won a county scholarship.' he said. 'It might be a mistake,' I pointed out. 'It's no mistake,' intoned Granddad. 'Sacred Heart School, Chorley:' he read, 'Eugene Mary Dickinson. Mary B. Duffy. F. Kennedy.' I finished my tea and Ryvita biscuits and caught the train back to Chorley.

CHAPTER 3

1939: There'll be no war

Preston catholic college was a grammar school run by priests of the Jesuit Order. The school was squeezed in awkwardly amongst commercial and residential property in the centre of the town but there was a swimming pool in the basement and playing fields a short distance away on the bank of the river Ribble. The school was run on public school lines. The boys were divided into houses. Discipline was maintained by prefects with the 'ferula' as the ultimate deterrent.

I travelled the nine miles each day from Chorley to Preston by train. Other 'train boys' were James Cornwell and Ken Brindle who had preceded me from Sacred Heart School, Chorley, and who were to remain life-long friends. (James was to marry Kathleen, my white satin companion in the Wood.) Another train boy was Leo Baxendale. Leo and I were the same age and sat next to each other.

Our introduction to the new and exciting world of the College was eased by the fact that our Form Mistress, Miss Martin, was also new and also came from Chorley. I was agreeably surprised to discover that despite coming from a tough school in a poor part of town I was comfortably ahead of most of the class in Arithmetic and English. These remained my favourite subjects and I have always been grateful to our Primary School teacher, Mr Grime, for the start that he gave us.

The central event of the lives of my generation was the Second World War. When asked, as he often was, whether there was going to be a war my grandfather would take out his pipe and say 'There'll be no war'. For him this proved to be true but only because he died in May, 1939. I was sent to stay with my grandma in Brinscall for three nights until the funeral. As I did my homework by the light of an Aladdin oil lamp I noticed for the first time how absolutely silent the village was once darkness fell. Grandma Kennedy now came to live with us in Chorley. She lived out the last sad years of her life in a strange town without the man on whom she had depended totally for fifty years. With the death of my grandfather my childhood came to an end. From then on I went to Brinscall only as a visitor. I never again woke up to that lovely view.

One Thursday afternoon my father was called to one side by Peter Penny, the foreman at Leyland Motor Works, and sent home. The following morning, 1 September, he came downstairs dressed in his best suit. I watched in silence as he polished his shoes, resting each foot in turn on the slop stone. Eventually I said: 'Never mind, Dad, it can't last forever.' He looked at me for a minute and then replied 'No, it can't, Frank.' He walked to the railway station and caught a train to Aldershot. Four days later he was in France.

Father had been persuaded by mother's brother, Uncle Harry, to enlist in the Army Supplementary Reserve. Harry had deployed two arguments. The first was that Hitler, though evil, was not a stupid man. Nothing could be more stupid than a Second World War. Therefore Hitler would not start a war. The second argument was that the sum due each quarter to Chorley Borough Council – which both Father and Harry had great difficulty in scraping together – was almost exactly equal to the amount paid four times a year to anyone who enlisted in the Army Supplementary Reserve. The second argument prevailed.

School did not reopen for several weeks after the outbreak of war and when it did reopen I had my first tussle with the school authorities. In the first form we had been taught French and in the second form we were taught Latin as well. We had also been taught elements of Chemistry and Physics and I was an enthusiastic student of these subjects. When we were given timetables for the new school year I discovered to my surprise that in Form 3A we were to be taught Greek as well as Latin and French but no Chemistry and no Physics. I was indignant. I marched home and told my mother that I did not want to learn any more languages. I did want to learn science. She asked me what I wanted her to do. I said that I wanted her to write to the Head Master, Father Grafton, and ask him to transfer me from Form 3A to Form 3B where, instead of learning Greek, I would be allowed to continue with Chemistry and Physics as well as French and Latin. Mother wrote the letter.

I am told that Father Grafton was a good Head Master. The only contact I ever had with him had been during my first week when I was walking across the school yard. A voice behind me bellowed 'You, boy, pick up that paper.' I looked round to see the formidable figure of the Head Master pointing to a piece of paper blowing across the yard. The Head Master did not summon me to discuss my mother's letter nor did any teacher mention the subject. After some days Father Grafton's reply arrived. It was short. 'At Preston', wrote the Head Master, 'clever boys go into A Forms and learn Greek. Frank is a clever boy. That is why he is in Form 3A. It would be unfair to the other boys to transfer him to Form 3B because he would then win all the class prizes.'

I was outraged at the priest's disregard of any wishes the pupil or his parents might have in the matter and of the relevance of the subjects of study to any future career that the pupil might wish to pursue. I told my mother that I should not be forced to study subjects that I did not want to study and prevented from studying those that I did. They could keep their prizes. They were no good anyway, I said, since they were remaindered books that had been left unsold at a local bookshop. I argued that if mother threatened to remove me from the school Father Grafton would give way.

Mother found it all very difficult. Her husband was in France. She was running a business as well as a house. She was looking after her mother-in-law and bringing up four children. Secondary school education was a world she had never visited. I knew that she wanted to support me and wanted to back my judgement. But she wanted to do the right thing in a matter that she knew was important but did not understand. She kept repeating 'If only your Father were here!' Since the beginning of the war, Uncle Bert, father's brother, had made a practice of calling on Sunday afternoon. It was decided that Uncle Bert should be consulted.

The following Sunday Uncle Bert arrived as usual. The problem was explained to him. He was shown a copy of Mother's letter and the reply from Father Grafton. He pondered the matter for several minutes. I waited in the dock for the judge to deliver his verdict. Finally he looked up and spoke: 'Alice, the J's know best.' That was that. I went back to school and started to learn Greek.

Had Uncle Bert supported me instead of Father Grafton, my career would have followed a quite different path and I might not be writing this memoir. Some fifty years passed before I was prepared to concede that Uncle Bert may have had a point. Teaching classics was what the Jesuits were good at and there is no doubt that they provided education of a much higher quality in those subjects than in others. I came eventually to appreciate the value of a classical education. But I remain convinced that no child of thirteen should be denied the choice of an education in science. I also believe that the dispute was not unconnected with wider educational and cultural issues that have been debated for over a century and that our country has still to resolve.

At the end of April 1940 an ominous note arrived from father saying that he was leaving the base workshops of the British Expeditionary Force in Nantes in Brittany to be attached to an infantry brigade in North West France. A few days later Germany swept into Holland and Belgium. There was no further word from father. Each day the reports were ever more alarming as the British fell back towards the sea. Neighbours would ask whether mother had heard of the latest calamity and whether there was any news from Jim. They would leave shaking their heads. Uncle Bert, who worked in Manchester, called to say that he had seen reports of disasters so bad that the newspapers dare not print them. Finally, on 1 June, a telegram arrived. Dad was safe on English soil. He had been evacuated from Dunkirk. Two days later he was home on week-end leave. On the Sunday we visited Uncle Bert. The Sunday newspaper said that the French Premier, Paul Reynaud, had appealed to President Roosevelt for the immediate delivery of fighter aircraft. I wore long trousers for the first time: grey flannels with a sports coat.

A fortnight later two friends and I went for a lunch-time walk in the sunshine in Preston's Avenham Park. A newspaper bill board announced: 'France capitulates'. We sat and stared in sickened silence across the valley. I could not imagine worse news. The French Army, the finest in the world according to Uncle Bert, had capitulated. The first lesson in the afternoon was Greek history. We asked the teacher, 'Tubby' Craven, whether he had heard the news. He hadn't. When we told him he grinned: 'Well, at least now we are on our own and don't have to bother about allies.' I could not believe my ears. How could such an idiot be appointed to teach history? From that moment I never listened to a word he said.

My father was discharged from the Army in 1941. When he arrived home my mother presented him with the rent book for the premises of the shop. The mortgage had been cleared and all Ralph's debts finally repaid. At the end of the war the shop was sold and mother was invited by an aunt to take over the Reynold's children's clothing business in the centre of town. She accepted with alacrity, delighted finally to escape from the drudgery of the fish and chip shop. My sister, Dorothy, later helped mother to manage the new business. Lizzie no doubt would have been pleased that her brother and his wife had helped to bring to an honourable conclusion the saga of her husband's debts.

The family moved to a different parish in a different part of town. Shortly afterwards the little shops and ancient cottages in Bolton Street were demolished and the cobbled streets torn up. The 'mountains' climbed with Frank Pilkington and the waste land explored with Ossie Gillette disappeared forever. An estate of single storey council houses was built in their place.

In the fifth form one young teacher tried to interest me in the classics. He introduced a group of us to Homer and Cicero and even some Hebrew. I conceded that Greek was a more appealing language than Latin and that Plato was actually quite interesting. But I had set my face against the ancient languages for the reasons already described. There was a choice of two courses in the sixth form and on principle I opted for Moderns rather than Classics, although I could not see anything very modern about a syllabus of Latin, French, and History.

Father Grafton had long since retired when I resumed my struggle over the school curriculum. I discovered that a boy in the year ahead of me was taking a subject called English Literature instead of Latin and was being coached by another Jesuit priest who had recently arrived at the school, Father A.C. Stephenson. This seemed to me light at the end of a tunnel.

I pleaded with the Head Master to be allowed to study English Literature. If he insisted I would continue with Latin provided I was allowed to drop Roman History. The Head Master said that Father Stephenson had a full teaching load and could not teach another subject. He remarked that I seemed bent on courting failure in the Higher School Certificate examinations.

I went to see Father Stephenson. Tall, pale and tired-looking, the young Jesuit listened in silence as I made my appeal in a sparsely furnished room in the presbytery across the road from the school. Finally he reached behind him and from a bookcase took down a volume of Matthew Arnold's *Essays in Criticism*. He asked me to read the first essay and come back in a week's time.

A week later I returned and gave an account of what I thought Matthew Arnold had written. Father Stephenson said that he would not teach me. If I wished to go ahead he would be willing to read any work that I might produce. That was all. I knew in my bones that that would not be all and jumped at the offer. The Head Master agreed that I could drop Roman History and take Latin only to subsidiary level. As far as the new-fangled subject of English Literature was concerned, I should be on my own and he disclaimed any responsibility for what he termed a foolish course of action.

Father Tony Stephenson taught the Sixth Form Religious Doctrine. He would march into class and scatter cyclostyled foolscap sheets of comments on subjects such as causality and the existence of God, Charles Darwin and the argument from Design and Kantian distinctions of a priori and empirical knowledge. The pages sparkled with phrases like 'harmonious reciprocity,' 'a subtle adaptation of means to ends.' I had not come across language as exciting since that first dip into the world of the *Wizard*.

Like Gerard Manley Hopkins Tony Stephenson kept his interest in poetry separate from his life as a Jesuit. Whilst at Cambridge he had published two closely argued pieces on Shakespearean imagery in *Scrutiny*, the magazine run by F.R. Leavis and his wife, Queenie. Most of his fellow priests knew nothing of these articles. When he wrote out a list of books that I might read during vacations, *Revaluations* by F.R. Leavis was near the top.

I was made to face the rigours of practical criticism. The first exercise that I attempted was an appreciation of a poem called 'The Builders' by a writer that I had never heard of. I sweated for hours over it. A week later the essay was handed back. At the bottom of the last page in tiny handwriting was the single word: 'promising'. ' Is that it?' I asked myself. '*Promising!*' But I tried even harder at the next attempt. Once I rashly described the sentiment in some lines of poetry as 'artificial'. The page came back with a question mark in the margin followed by the comment: 'artificial' < 'ars facio'. Poetry is *art*. Art is *made!*'

As the war went on and more and more of the staff were called into the forces the standard of teaching at Preston declined. Father Stephenson was the outstanding exception. He had a major influence on me. Ironically, he might have exercised an even stronger influence if I had opted for classics instead of moderns because at that time he was teaching sixth form Greek and Greek philosophy. But he had not arrived at the school when I had had to make the choice.

The Head Master acquiesced in my eccentric ways and made me Captain of the School. In subsequent years the school offered English Literature as a subject for sixth form study. Whilst I was in the lower sixth the school was inspected by government inspectors. The inspectors, I was told, gave a generally favourable report but, to my delight, expressed dissatisfaction at the absence of science from the curriculum in the higher forms. In my last year the school was compelled to introduce a subject for sixth formers called 'Outlines of scientific knowledge'. The lessons were no more than an educational fig leaf but I grinned smugly from the front row as, Mr Carty, lesson notes in one hand and chalk in the other, struggled through the unfamiliar territory of Newton's theory of optics.

For some reason, in the middle of the war, the government encouraged the formation of youth clubs. Maybe they were Britain's answer to the Hitler Youth Movement. Some of us thought it very fortunate that the formation of youth clubs should come just in time to help us through adolescence. We had been segregated by gender when we entered secondary school. Youth Clubs reintroduced us to the girls that we had known at primary school and introduced us to the girls that we would have known had we attended other primary schools in the district. The Youth Clubs organized bike rides and hikes and amateur dramatics and debates and lectures but above all they organized dances. We learned to dance the Quick Step to the strains of 'Amapola' and the Slow Foxtrot to

'Whispering Grass'. Every dance hall in those days had a live band. Ours was the New Astorians led by Charlie Thomas on clarinet. Charlie played like Artie Shaw. He also sold the tickets at Chorley Cricket Club on Saturday afternoons in summer. He would kick off with a number like 'Cherokee', à la Charlie Barnett but the band would really hit its stride with the first number after the interval. This was always Glen Miller's 'In the Mood' and might be followed by 'Song of India' or 'Tuxedo Junction'.

One day when I went to collect the sugar ration the grocer, Mr Brereton, placed a tin on the counter and said: 'Tell your mother – only one tin for each customer.' That was our introduction to the delicacy of chopped ham delivered from the United States, courtesy of Lend Lease. As it happened the brand name on that first tin was not 'Spam' but 'Prem'. Either way it was delicious.

Suddenly, it seemed overnight, there appeared in Chorley tall, young men in strange uniforms. They were men of the US Army Air Force. They queued at bus stops, attended church on Sunday and played baseball in the park. They packed the cinemas and the pubs. When they visited friends they arrived with chocolates and cigarettes: not packets but *cartons* of cigarettes; with fragrant smelling tobacco and names like Chesterfield and Philip Morris. They built a camp on the edge of the town and called it Washington Hall. They opened a café in the high street and called it Stars and Stripes. It sold coffee and doughnuts and Coca Cola to these heroes from across the ocean. The GIs turned out in force for the Saturday night hops. After the interval, Charlie Thomas would allow a young American boy to take over the drums for Gene Krupa's great solo in 'Sing, Sing, Sing.' When that happened everybody stopped dancing and crowded round the band, clapping in time to the music of the Drummer Boy.

I sometimes hear people criticizing the Nigerian Police for their corruption and incompetence and I often hear people, myself included, criticizing the US for the policies of their government. The criticisms are often well-founded. But we are all the prisoners of our experience. When I go to Nigeria I cannot look at a Police uniform without a memory trickling back of an occasion deep in the Nigerian bush when a dozen men dressed in those grey shirts and khaki shorts came running round a corner in the nick of time in what was the most welcome sight of my life.

If the worst day of the war was the Fall of France the best, for me, was the day that the United States entered the conflict. As Churchill said, from then on the outcome was never in doubt. Whatever our disagreements with US, people of my age can never forget the comradeship of World War II and the difference made to the fortunes of our country by the arrival of the US forces. Of course, that was a different army fighting in a different war but it is difficult for me to meet an American service man without a subliminal memory of those young men in brown uniforms who suddenly appeared on the streets of Chorley in 1943. Some may have misbehaved, and some may have taken away our girls, but that is not what I remember. Young conscripts from every part of the US, they brought excitement and optimism at a time when these were in short supply. My only grouse was that British boys were not allowed to use the Stars and Stripes café in Market Street. I found this especially galling since it was our girl friends who were actually serving the GIs their coffee and the doughnuts.

When I left school Father Stephenson also left Preston. He moved to a school in Glasgow and then to a seminary in North Wales. We exchanged letters for a time. He wrote from Wales suggesting that after the war I should train to become a doctor. He said that I had a good bedside manner.

Some time later Father Stephenson took up a post at the University of Toronto. In the nineteen fifties I read in the *Sunday Telegraph* a review of a pamphlet by him called 'Anglo Catholic Fallacies'. This was a riposte to the publication of an essay called 'Roman Catholic Fallacies'. The correspondence debated the validity or otherwise of Anglican Orders and the argument turned, as I remember, on the validity of the ordination of Archbishop Parker.

I never heard of Father Stephenson again and presumed that he was still in Canada, until in the nineteen seventies I learnt to my surprise that the publication of Anglo Catholic Fallacies was by no means the end of the story and that Father Stephenson had come round to the view that in fact the Anglican orders *were* valid and that the Vatican's position in the controversy was untenable. He resigned his position in the Jesuit Order and left the Catholic Church to become an Anglican. But later still, so I was told, like Cranmer in reverse, Stephenson retracted his conversion and re-entered the Catholic Church. But by now he had no means of support, either from the Anglican Church or the Catholic Church, and in particular had cut himself off from the Jesuit Order. Without financial support from anyone, he ended his days in loneliness and poverty in a small town in Wales. He was killed at a railway station when he threw himself under a train.

The tragedy still shocks. Tony Stephenson is one of the persons in life to whom I feel most indebted. I would like my children to have met him. Yet when he was in despair we were abroad, oblivious of his plight. Better to have died on a pyre in Oxford than a railway platform in Wales.

CHAPTER 4

1944: Junior probationer for electrical mechanic

I T HAS BECOME CUSTOMARY for our children to take 'a year off' between school and university. I had two wonderful 'years off'. In November 1944 I was called up into the Royal Navy and given the grand title of Junior Probationer for Electrical Mechanic. At last I was going to become an engineer! But then I was sent on an officers training course.

On frosty winter mornings we would march up and down the parade ground of HMS *Raleigh* in Devon and as dawn broke look across the valley at the little parish church silhouetted on the horizon. Some days we would practise rowing in Devonport harbour. Other days we would be instructed in torpedo and mine warfare in HMS *Defiance*, an ancient wooden sailing ship. As we marched between the stone walls of the little country lanes it was easy to imagine that Drake and his captains might have come that way. The fields and hills cannot have looked much different to Drake's men four centuries earlier.

Devonport harbour in those days was packed with ships of all shapes and sizes, flying flags of every nationality. There were battleships, cruisers, destroyers, frigates and landing craft. Every type of ship, I think, save aircraft carriers. They had already left to join the American Pacific Fleet off Okinawa and Japan. The ships that we saw had been part of the armada that had sailed to France on 6 June. According to Sappho, some men say that an army of ships is the most beautiful thing on this black earth. It is difficult to imagine that anyone will ever set eyes on a greater fleet of ships than that assembled in the southern ports of England in 1944.

After HMS *Raleigh* some of us were posted to the training cruiser HMS *Dauntless* which was based in Rosyth in Scotland. Every Monday morning we lined the forward deck as *Dauntless* sailed under the Forth Bridge and every Friday evening we sailed under the bridge on our way back to port. During the week the Navy tried to teach 20 raw cadets the elements of seamanship, navigation, signalling and gunnery. We were taught how to sail the ship and how to fight the ship. We took turns on the bridge and in the engine room. We fired the Oerlikon anti-aircraft guns. An aircraft towed a drogue for us to fire at. I was the first in the group to step up to the platform. I groped for the trigger whilst searching for the target whilst a Petty Officer bawled in my ear 'Shoot, shoot'. I narrowly missed shooting at the plane instead of the drogue. We took turns to fire the great six-inch guns. When you pressed the firing button a cloud of yellow smoke belched forth from the gun's mouth. Seconds ticked away before the smoke cleared and a column of water shot up as the shell splashed down on a target six miles away.

I enjoyed my time in the Royal Navy. Except, that is, for the dreadful February morning when we were ordered aloft to keep watch in the crow's nest. I was allotted the period 8 a.m to 10 a.m. Members of Ship's Company had left us in no doubt of the terrors to come. Ship's Company were the regular sailors whose job it was to sail, and if necessary, fight the ship despite the havoc caused by cadets. One of them had stressed that the cold would be unbearable and that we should wear every scrap of clothing that we possessed.

Unfortunately I followed the advice. Over the ordinary underwear I pulled on the special woollen long johns and vests that had been issued in case we had to sail in Arctic waters. Over the tunic I wore my greatcoat. Over *that* I squeezed into an oil-skin waterproof. With gloves on hands and naval cap tied under chin I looked and felt like a Michelin India Rubber man. I could hardly bend my knees and could only totter about stiff-legged, like Boris Karloff in a Frankenstein film. I was just about to start discarding excess clothing when I heard my name bawled out.

It was a raw winter's morning and still very dark. Visibility could not have been more than a hundred yards. The ship was lurching through a heavy sea at about fifteen knots. I tottered past the Commander (T). I never found out quite what this officer was supposed to do. He strutted up and down the deck, hands behind his back like Charles Laughton doing Captain Bligh. From time to time he would look up at the rigging, or the bridge or a gun platform and shout 'Smack it about up there'. I saluted him and commenced the ascent of my naval Everest.

The first dozen feet were manageable because the bridge and foc'sle offered some protection from the wind. Then the nightmare began. The mast was not perpendicular but slanted backward. The wind tore at the oil-skin coat ballooning out behind me. I seemed to be carrying several stones of surplus clothing. Despite the cold a rivulet of sweat trickled down my back. I was hanging on to the metal rungs of the ladder by my fingertips and already wondering how long it would be before these were prised open by the combined force of wind and weight. I glanced down and saw, not deck but sea. Another darting glance and swinging through my vision was a brief passage of deck followed by more sea. As the ship rolled from side to side the upper mast sailed through the air like a mad trapeze. I made a wild guess at the chances of hitting water rather than deck in the approaching catastrophe. The odds on becoming a bit of squashed meat within the next few seconds were unpleasantly high. I bridled at the fatuity of it all. With Radar and Asdic and all the other gadgets who needed crow's nests anyway? On the previous course a cadet had been killed when a cable had snapped. These things happened. The Commander would probably report to the Captain: 'Cadet fallen from main mast. Poor bugger lost his footing.' The Captain would reply 'Oh, bad show! Carry on Commander, Hard to Starboard.' Perhaps they would shovel me over the side and consign my remains to the deep.

The weight was getting worse at every rung. In a desperate attempt to hang on I threw my arms round the ladder and hugged it to my chest, grasping the iron rungs from behind. This made progress even slower but it did take some of the weight off my fingers. At long last, at exhaustion point, I reached the yard arm and was level with the crow's nest. The crow's nest was a ridiculous little barrel attached to the front of the mast like the firework attached to the stick of a sky rocket. Two eyes under a sailor's hat peered over the rim of the barrel. The eyes belonged to fellow cadet Blanche.

'Can't see a f___g thing,' said Blanche, by way of greeting. 'Yeah, yeah,' I replied. 'Just get out of that thing so I can get in.' 'No,' said Blanche. 'You get off the ladder so I can get on it.' The horror of what the man was suggesting suddenly struck home. He was demanding that *I* should stand on the yard arm so that *he* could cling to the mast whilst swinging round to the ladder on the other side. The ship was still lurching and rolling and we were still swinging on the mad trapeze from one side to the other. This was no time for argument. Blanche was ensconced in the barrel and I was hanging on to the metal rung by my fingertips. I had no option but to grab the cable and take the dizzying step out on to the yard arm whilst Blanche inched his way round to the ladder. Blanche's head disappeared down the mast with remarkable speed as I flopped into the barrel. I reported my arrival to the bridge. Through the voice tube came the Captain's voice: 'Carry on Crow's Nest.' 'Aye, aye, Sir.' I replied.

It was still half dark. My eyes were streaming. I looked through the binoculars. I might have been swimming under water in a pool of cotton wool. As Blanche had said, you could not see a f___g thing. I bent my knees and slowly, slowly sank until my eyes were just below the rim of the barrel.

Suddenly the voice tube barked into life. 'Bridge to Crow's Nest. What's going on up there? Ship on Starboard beam.' I jerked to attention and looked out. My God, it was almost daylight. The sun was breaking through the clouds. I must have been in the barrel for half an hour. I looked at the watch. Twenty to nine! There was a ship on the starboard beam not three hundred yards away. There was a ship on the port bow. There were ships all over the place. The Captain had deliberately steered us into the busy shipping lane at the mouth of the Firth. I began to report ship after ship. 'Crow's nest to Bridge.' 'Come in Crow's Nest.' 'Ship on port bow bearing 120 degrees to port.' Each time I called, the Captain had to acknowledge the report and repeat the bearing. I began to detect a growing impatience in my Master's voice and he turned the ship to starboard as we moved further into the North Sea. Unfortunately I had not the sense to stop when I was almost even.

As I gazed around through the binoculars I saw something floating on the surface about two hundred yards away. At least I thought I did. Anything afloat in the heavy sea bobbed in and out of sight with each heave of the waves. It was then that I made the fatal mistake. 'Crow's Nest to Bridge.' 'Come in Crow's Nest.' 'Unidentified Object Starboard Bow. 5 degrees. Distance 250 yards.' It was as though I had tossed a hand grenade onto the Bridge. The place screamed into action 'Double starboard lookouts!' shouted the Captain. 'Double starboard lookouts.' came the reply. ' Man starboard anti-aircraft guns!' 'Man starboard anti-aircraft guns!' If there was one thing that alarmed the management of a training cruiser in coastal waters it was an unidentified object. It might be the periscope of a German U-boat. The lookouts reported one by one. No one could see an unidentified object. But none of them were as high as me or could see as far as me. No one could actually contradict me, but there was no mistaking the tide of scepticism rising all around me.

In the midst of the kafuffle I noticed what looked like part of an orange box. It might have been chucked overboard with the garbage from one of the ships. It bobbed up and down a couple of times before disappearing astern. I was not sure whether to report this or not and whether to do so would be a winning or a losing card. The Captain continued to ask again and again whether I could still see the UIO. I reported finally that the object had disappeared. I suggested that what I had seen must have been flotsam that had now sunk. The Captain sounded far from satisfied but relapsed into silence.

At that precise moment the face of my relief, Cadet Cornish, appeared above the rungs of the ladder. Wide-eyed, he suggested that I get out of the nest so that he could get in. 'Get on that b____y yard arm,' I screamed. 'And think yourself damn lucky you were not up here two hours earlier.' He did.

By the first week in May the war in Europe was coming to an end. Allied armies were sweeping across Germany. On the evening of the 7th I listened to one news bulletin after another. I was very anxious that the war should end on the 8th and not on the 7th or the 9th of May. On the 8th, Starboard Watch would be granted leave. On the other two days, Port Watch would be the lucky winners. Late in the evening the news came through. The war would end at midnight. I turned in around 1 a.m.

I was woken around 4 a.m. by someone violently shaking my hammock. I looked up to see the fatuous face of Cornish, who had a depraved taste in practical jokes. 'Get up, get up,' he said, 'You are wanted on deck immediately. A German sub has sunk a ship.' 'Piss off, Cornish,' I replied. 'The war's over.' 'If you are not on deck in five minutes,' screamed Cornish, 'you're on a charge. It's chaos up there.' Behind Cornish I now made out the outlines of another figure that looked like Blanche. 'He's right,' said the figure. I was out of the hammock, dressed and on deck in four minutes.

Dauntless was drifting in a heavy mist off the Southern shore of the Forth: engines switched off; all lights extinguished. A German sub had torpedoed a merchant ship off Methil on the Northern shore of the Forth. I was given a large torch and told to stand on the prow of the ship. I was to switch on the warning light whenever another ship approached us. A procession of tugs and other small boats had been crossing the bow of our ship to pick up survivors. I did not see any ships but could hear the sound of their throbbing engines grow louder and then recede. After two or three had passed there was no sound at all except the lapping of the waves against the ship's side. As dawn began to break I leaned against the forward gun turret and cursed the U-boat commander who had broken the peace and imperilled Starboard Watch's chance of celebrating victory ashore.

But we did celebrate the victory. When the mist cleared, instead of returning to Rosythe the Captain made for Leith harbour, just a few miles from Edinburgh. By noon I was sitting down to a free lunch served by nice Scottish ladies in the Victoria League Centre on Princes Street. The party lasted all day long and all night long. When darkness fell a vast crowd occupied Princes Street from one end to the other. We sat side by side, boy girl, boy girl, along the curb side. Bands played. We sang. We danced. We cheered. At around 1 a.m. I walked five miles to Portobello where I collapsed on the floor of a school and slept for two hours. At 7 a.m. I made my way to Leith Harbour to rejoin HMS *Dauntless* in Leith in time for Port Watch to have their day ashore. I had had only four hours sleep in the two previous days. But the King had given the order 'Splice the Main Brace' and the Captain had ordered 'Hands to Make and Mend'. I drank my rum, slung my hammock and sank into the sleep that 'knits up the ravelled sleeve of care'.

A few days later our course ended and one by one we paraded before an Admiral. The Admiral told me that the Royal Navy would not after all be requiring my services as a commissioned officer. He asked me whether I wished to say anything. The thought of an unidentified object on the starboard bow flashed briefly across my mind. On balance, better follow the golden rule. 'No, Sir,' I replied. When I left the wardroom to return to midships, who was pacing the deck but Commander Bligh? Surely, I thought, we are not going to go into the 'Smack-it-about-up-there' routine? On the contrary, the Commander was friendliness personified. He particularly wanted me to understand that although we would no longer be ship-mates we were still in this thing together and still had a job to do – 'to finish off the Japs.' Until that moment I confess that thoughts of Emperor Hirohito's navy had not crossed my mind. I presumed that the correct nautical response was 'Aye, aye, Sir,' but as this sounded ridiculous I thanked the Commander and gave him one of the especially smart salutes that I reserved normally for admirals.

I did not mind too much leaving *Dauntless* because I was looking forward to resuming my career as a Junior Probationer for Electrical Mechanic. It was a great disappointment to be told on reporting to barracks that with the war in Europe ended not only were my services as an officer not needed but the Navy did not need any more Junior Probationers for Electrical Mechanics either – at least not the kind who were going to leave the Navy as soon as their training was finished. Thus, alas, my scientific and technological ambitions were once again thwarted.

In December 1945, with my chums Brian Marsden, Gus Burton and Paddy Reeves we sailed on the carrier HMS *Victorious* to Australia. We sailed twelve thousand miles and at each port of call the union flag or white ensign flew from the mast at the harbour entrance. At Sydney we tied up alongside the carrier HMS *Formidable*. The carriers *Indefatigable* and *Implacable* were also in the harbour. These aircraft carriers had replaced the battleships as the core of the strike force of the British Pacific Fleet. Several had taken part in the battle for Okinawa.

In 1945 Australia seemed to us a kind of paradise. It was literally a land of milk and honey. Sydney was, and I believe still is, a great place to be young in. We swam and sunbathed. We surfed on the beaches. We ate steaks in Silvers' restaurants and guzzled Peters ice cream by the gallon. We dodged the military police in Kings Cross and danced in the vast Trocadero ballroom. We drank Aussie beer and were introduced to the Penfold wines. Although the Aussie males never addressed us as anything but 'Pommie B____ds' the Australians could not have been more generous or more welcoming. They invited us into their homes and helped us in every way they could to enjoy their wonderful country.

We were stationed in a camp on the outskirts of the city called HMS *Golden Hind*. One day I bumped into a sailor from Chorley called John Harrison, who had once tried to teach me how to be a fast bowler on Ranglets Recreation Ground. John had organized for himself a remarkable arrangement. With the help of friends in the records office he had managed to have his name erased from all roll calls except that for pay. He was living with a girl in Sydney and after pay parade would climb the barbed wire fence and catch the train into the city, returning only the day before the next pay parade. Friends would telephone him if anything exceptional arose that might require his presence.

At *Golden Hind* I met a young Education Officer who had read English at Cambridge and had been at Downing College. The Sub Lieutenant thought Leavis 'bonkers' and begged me not to take a degree in English. He said that an MA English Honours was useless currency in the job market. He urged me to study law or medicine or economics – anything that had a purpose and a use. Sure, it was fun to study literature but you needed to get a decent job. You could always read poetry and novels in your spare time. In later years I came round more and more to the point of view of the Sub Lieutenant but that was not how I saw it at the time. I chose the fun.

There were lots of places to go to in Sydney on Saturday night. On Sunday evenings opportunities were more limited. But we found a church hall near Circular Quay where you could dance to music provided by a drummer, an accordion and a base violin. Brian Marsden, Gus Burton, Paddy Reeves and I were regular visitors. At one of these Sunday evenings I met a charming young girl who lived in Manley and said that her brother was studying to become a Christian Brother. The next time we met, Barbara said that her parents wished to invite me to tea in their home in Manley and it was agreed that I should go the following Sunday afternoon.

It had never occurred to us that our days in paradise were numbered. Suddenly, without warning, we were given our marching orders. I was posted to the British East Indies fleet in Ceylon. Brian was sent to join a sloop in the Pacific. Gus was sent to the UK to get medical treatment. I sent a message to Manley saying that sadly I would not be able to come to tea.

Sydney Harbour staged marvellous farewells when the great ships sailed. A band played on the quayside. Sailors lined the main deck and the lower decks and waved at the friends, relatives and sweethearts on the dock-side below. The crowds waved back. Most had come armed with paper streamers. Each sailor held one end of the streamer and a friend the other. There seemed to be two thousand friends and one thousand, nine hundred and ninety nine streamers. As the ship pulled away to the haunting notes of the Maori Farewell, one by one the streamers broke. In films, the soldier always spots the girl just as the train is pulling out of the station. In real life things do not always turn out that way.

Fifty years after *Indefatigable* sailed from Sydney, British Airways held their Annual General Meeting in the Barbican in London. BA owned twenty five per cent of Qantas and had concluded a commercial agreement with that company. I sat on the platform with the rest of the board as shareholders asked questions and offered comments. One lady took the microphone to say that she was Australian and a shareholder both of BA and Qantas. She complimented the Board on the performance of the company. Following the meeting an attendant came to say that a lady was asking to see me. Her name was Barbara Vickers but on her card she had written in brackets 'Simmons.'

Barbara was a widow with a grown up family. Her Christian Brother brother had just retired. She had become a first-class swimmer and had visited the UK frequently over the years but this was the first time that she had attended a BA board meeting. The Annual Report contained photographs of the Directors and she said that she had recognized me when she had covered the top part of the picture where the hair had been! Barbara said that when she had received my message fifty years earlier she had gone down to the Harbour in Sydney to look for HMS *Indefatigable* but the ship had already sailed. I cannot think of anything as empty as a dock from which a ship has sailed.

When I was not dreaming of Australia I spent the afternoons on HMS *Indefatigable* trying to understand a Penguin book by Susan Stebbing called *Philosophy and the Physicists*. We landed in Trincomalee and a few weeks later I was transferred to a base engineering storage centre at a place called Veyangoda, half way between Colombo and Kandy. In August I went to Kandy for the great Buddhist festival, when the Buddha's tooth is carried in procession, preceded by ninety sacred elephants.

Later in the summer of 1946 I was posted back to Portsmouth, as I thought, to be demobilized. I sailed back in the aircraft carrier HMS *Formidable*. Instead of being demobilized I was sent to HMS *Fort York*. Some said that this was a camp near Gosport. Others said that it was a camp on the way to Havant. It turned out to be a minesweeper in a dry dock in Portsmouth harbour.

HMS *Fort York* had been launched in Montreal in 1941 by the wife of Malcolm Macdonald who was at that time British High Commissioner in

Canada, and was now being used as a Fishery Protection Vessel. Our job was to prevent Belgian and other European trawlers from fishing illegally in UK coastal waters. The difficulty was that the trawlers were faster than *Fort York* and by the time we caught up with them they had usually hauled in their nets. The Captain would call them over a loud hailer: 'MV *Petanque*, you have been fishing within the three mile limit'. 'Oh, noh, mey Cepitaine,' would come back the reply in 'Allo, allo' accents, 'We 'ave not been feeshing.' 'Oh well, just be careful in future.' 'Oh, yes mey Cepitaine.' Pause. Then ' I say, *Petanque*, could you spare a few kilos of fish?' Over the side would come a dozen buckets of fish. For days afterwards the ship would stink of fish.

We spent the late summer and autumn patrolling the South coast of England. It was a lovely way to pass the time. We would call at Brixton, Torquay, Fowey, and Fishguard. Sometimes we would make a sortie to Guernsey or Jersey and spend a few afternoons in the sunshine off the Cherbourg Peninsula. When we visited Brighton we would enter the Brighton-Hove canal at Shoreham. At one point you could jump down from the moving ship and catch a red double decker bus on the road that ran alongside the canal.

The captain of the ship was an RNR officer who was looking forward to imminent retirement. His policy, a policy enthusiastically endorsed by his crew, was to avoid like the plague all ports with a naval presence. The theory was that if reminded of our existence the authorities might issue us with fresh orders. The policy had one big disadvantage. Portsmouth dockyard was not only the place from which we were given orders; it was also the place from which we drew our stores. After a week or two at sea we would run out of food. Hence the fish. When the German Chancellor, Bismarck, was in his sixties he is said to have lost three stones by going on a diet of herrings. He had herrings for breakfast, herrings for lunch and herrings for dinner. It was a bit like that on HMS *Fort York*.

I was in charge of the naval stores and had frequent arguments with my superior officers. Contrary to all regulations, the Captain had crammed a child's pram in the forward naval store, which he was taking home for one of his grandchildren. The First Lieutenant had a motor-cycle lashed to a bollard amidships. This was always the first item winched overboard when we docked. Small wonder that we sought to avoid naval ports. There were large discrepancies between quantities in the stores and the amounts shown in the ledgers. I used to warn the Chief Engineer that if ever there were an audit of the ship's stores he and I would be walking the plank. His invariable reply was: 'Don't worry about it, Jack.' By the time the authorities tried to reconcile the documents with the stock, said the Chief, he and I would long since have been demobbed.

Most of the time life on board *Fort York* was fun. But in bad weather it was unbearable. The tiny vessel would pitch and yaw and roll until everyone was ill, whether or not they actually vomited. It would be impossible to cook. The cook would be forced to shut down the stoves for safety. Cutlery and plates would fly around the cabin. Once we were caught in mid channel in a gale that raged for twelve hours. When the storm abated everyone was exhausted. Ironically the principal sufferer was always the Sick Bay Artificer. Whatever the weather, he was sea-sick as soon as the ship left harbour. As we prepared to sail he would open his little medical store and lay out in a line all the basins and receptacles he possessed for his own emergency use. Then he would go up on deck and sit behind the mast wrapped in a great coat. He refused all food and all drink and unless he received a direct order from the bridge would not budge from his post until lights out and he could sling his hammock. After a week the poor man would look like a walking ghost.

One weekend we put into Portland Harbour. Portland was indeed a naval port and as far as I could see nothing but a naval port. The town was some four miles away on the other side of the island. In the afternoon I decided not to go ashore. Instead I slung my hammock and took down a book from the tiny book-case we called the ship's library. The book was a copy of Thomas Hardy's novel, *The Well Beloved*. It was about a place that in older times had been called the Isle of Slingers. One night during a terrible storm a shingle of stones had been cast up by the sea to form a causeway that now joined the island to the mainland. I read the first chapter describing some of the characters and the chalk quarries in which they worked. Then I turned back to the illustration at the beginning of the book. It was an engraving of an island and a causeway of pebbles joining it to the mainland. I leaned out of the hammock and looked through the porthole. There before my eyes was the very same scene pictured in the book. I was on the Isle of Slingers! This was a coincidence too powerful to be ignored. I jumped down, stored the hammock and ran ashore in search of Thomas Hardy.

One day a parcel arrived for me courtesy of the British Fleet Post Office. Inside was a book with a note from Brian Marsden on his sloop in the Pacific. The note said: 'This book is just up your street. Read it and send it back.' The book was a collection of stories written by Beverley Nichols about French Canadians in World War I. One, called the Airy Prince was about a girl who lived alone with her grandfather and her cat in a remote farm in Picardy. She would read stories to the cat, especially one about a fairy prince who appeared from the sky and rescued his Cinderella. So when an Allied airman with engine trouble landed his biplane in a nearby field she knew that her Prince had arrived. Alain de Botton tells us that reading Proust can seriously change your life. I suppose that you might say the same about reading Homer or Virgil or the story of the prince or the story of the story. When I had finished the book I returned it, as instructed, to Brian in his sloop in the Pacific.

Towards the end of 1946, as winter approached, the good times came to an end. The Admiralty caught up at last with HMS *Fort York*. We were ordered out of the English Channel and told to protect the fishing trawlers based on Lowestoft. They did not seem in much need of protection to me. We patrolled the dreary North Sea and occasionally put into Lowestoft. I only once went ashore there. It rained all afternoon and all evening. Soon we received our final orders. We sailed first to Harwich to deliver valuable stores and then to Sheerness to pay off the ship. I packed all the ledgers and ships documents into sacks and delivered them to a vast storage hangar. 'HMS *Fort York*,' I reported. 'Over there,' ordered the Petty Officer. I threw the sacks on to a mountain of similar sacks that would have taken an army of auditors years to check.

The Chief Engineer tried to persuade me to stay on in the Navy for a few extra months. He promised me promotion and an interesting job but I was eager to get on with the next phase of my life. We left HMS *Fort York* tied up in a creek alongside three other minesweepers. After serving for two years and one month Rating PMX 259736 reported back to Portsmouth Dockyard and was demobilized. I changed into civilian clothes and caught the train to Chorley.

CHAPTER 5

1947: Surely, you do not think I am doing this for the money?

THE WINTER OF 1946/7 was one of the coldest on record. Snow, piled high under the hedgerows, was still frozen at the end of March. It was thanks to this weather that I got a job for a time as a teacher. One day in February an official from the Local Education Authority knocked on the door and asked if I would stand in for a teacher who had slipped on the ice and broken a leg. That was how I came to teach in a small school in the village of Wheelton in the early months of 1947. The school building was a bit like the one in the film *Ryan's Daughter*. When I looked through the classroom window I could just see a corner of the cemetery. In that cemetery lay my great grandfather and great grandmother and my grandfather and grandmother.

I enrolled at Manchester University in October 1947 but I felt that I already knew something about the university thanks to a friend who a year previously had completed the course in English Honours that I was about to begin. Kathleen[1] had been helpful to me in various ways and had passed on several of the course text books in Anglo Saxon and Middle English. More importantly, she had presented me with copies of the first two issues of a new magazine published by the Manchester University Press. Through her I met two of the students on the magazine's editorial board, John McCabe[2] and Louis Levy,[3] both of whom became dear friends. Later I got to know the other students involved in the production, especially the magazine's Secretary, Robert Markus, and the editor and driving force behind the paper, Walter Stein. We have been friends ever since.

Humanitas was remarkable both for the quality of its writing and for the fact that it was a student initiative. Its editorial board consisted of a small group of brilliant students assisted by one or two members of the academic staff, notably Michael Polanyi and Dorothy Emmett, who were both professors at the university. One of the themes explored by the paper was the tension between the values of the Renaissance and the Enlightenment

---

[1] Kathleen Maher. Kathleen went on to marry Frank, the elder brother of my friend, Ken Brindle.
[2] John entered the Order of Preachers and became the Reverend Herbert McCabe OP.
[3] Louis later changed his name by deed poll to Louis Allen.

37

on the one hand and religious faith on the other. An early editorial warned:

> The world is full of people who want to believe but cannot. Many want to believe in God. Vastly more want to believe in lesser things, such as the existence of plain truth, of elementary moral obligations, and particularly in freedom. They feel that the pruning knife of scepticism, which for centuries has slashed away so much error and released so much creative energy, has also struck at our essential beliefs.

I frequently read how drab the immediate post-war years were in England. They seemed anything but drab to me. It is true that Manchester at that time was still pretty grimy and dilapidated. The great cotton metropolis had been heavily damaged by the Luftwaffe in two raids in 1942. Swathes of the city remained empty. Food and clothing were still rationed. The Halle Orchestra played in a temporary home in the Belle View Amusement Park. Manchester United football team shared the home of their rival, Manchester City. The cotton industry, on which Manchester's wealth had been based, had resumed its long-term economic decline.

I was too excited by university life to be bothered by these things. I had found digs in a large house in Slade Lane, Longsight. The back of the house looked on to the main Manchester-London railway line and our landlord, Mr Capper, was a retired railwayman. I shared a room first with Peter Tyrer and later with another friend, Arthur Alston. We paid a rent of thirty-five shillings a week with breakfast and evening meal provided. We were very comfortable and found the food more than acceptable.

Then as now, Manchester University was highly regarded as a centre of academic excellence. Many of its teaching staff had international reputations: Namier and Cheney in history, Blackett in Physics, Ashby in Biology, Michael Polanyi in Chemistry and Dorothy Emmett in Philosophy. The great, but tragic, Alan Turing was working on the first prototype computer (though at the time I do not think that any of us had heard of Bletchley Park and Turing's wartime achievements there.) The Deputy Head of the English Department and one of the reasons for my going to Manchester was L.C. Knights, the assistant editor of *Scrutiny* and disciple of Leavis. No sooner had I arrived than Knights, much to my annoyance, departed to take up a newly established Chair of English at Sheffield.

But it was less the quality of the teaching staff than the liveliness of the student body that made the late forties a special time to be at university. The undergraduate population was older and more mature than its pre-war predecessor. Many students had returned after several years in the forces, in which they had seen active service and travelled widely. Manchester's Jewish population had been augmented by families escaping from Nazi persecution. The children of some of those families were now entering the university. They brought with them a cultural depth and resonance that enriched the intellectual life of the student body. After the isolation of war the flow of ideas between Britain and the neighbouring countries of Europe had been resumed. We heard for the first time of new trends and fashions: and new names like Sartre and Camus in France and Heidegger and Jaspers in Germany. Some of us had difficulty in understanding what the philosophy of some of these writers actually amounted to but it seemed wonderfully exciting to hear people arguing that philosophy was not just about thinking and knowing but about doing and choosing.

Whilst I was immersing myself in student life in Manchester, brother Jack, and his friend, Tony Kenny, left the seminary in England to continue their studies at the Gregorian University in Rome. Many years later my brother was to return to Rome as Rector of the English College. I mention these things because the transfer to Rome was as broadening and exciting for my brother as my experience in Manchester was for me.

Although we usually attended lectures, our group spent a vast amount of time in the university cafeteria drinking coffee and putting the world to rights. We took it all very seriously. The cold war was at its most intense and quite a few students believed that we would not finish our degree course before we were recalled into the armed forces at the outbreak of a Third World War.

Of the plethora of student societies I joined the English Society and the Catholic Society. The English Society produced plays and poetry readings and for some reason ran a soccer team. We lost most of our matches. The Societies often sponsored distinguished visitors to speak at lunchtime meetings of the Student Union. One year I was Secretary of the Catholic Society. The Committee decided that Evelyn Waugh would be an entertaining speaker and I was told to arrange the visit. I had no clear idea how to do this but wrote to Waugh and to my surprise he replied agreeing to come to Manchester and give an address. He said that he would speak on the novels of Graham Greene and François Mauriac. I reported back to the Committee, expecting a pat on the back if not a round of applause. The Chairman was a student named Steve Tarpey. His only comment was, 'How much?' 'How much?' I said. 'No one mentioned "how much" when I was asked to get this man. It is too late to start talking money now.' Tarpey was unmoved: 'Ten pounds is all we have in the kitty. Anything above that comes out of your own pocket.' That, I knew, was a fiscal impossibility.

In great embarrassment I wrote again to Evelyn Waugh. After waffling around the subject I made some idiotic reference to honoraria and prevailing rates thereof. Waugh replied immediately by postcard: 'Dear Kennedy,' he wrote, 'surely you do not think I am doing this for the money? I am giving this lecture as a Lenten penance. A room at the Midland and a dozen oysters will be quite sufficient. Yours ever, Waugh.'

And so it was. I met the great man at the railway station and conveyed him to the Midland, where a dozen oysters were waiting on ice. I left him to pay for his own champagne. The visit was a huge success. Waugh had the students helpless with laughter, whilst not so much as the suspicion of a smile crossed his own scowling face. When it came time for questions Bob Bolt asked whether Scobie (the adulterous hero of Greene's novel, *The Heart of the Matter*) had gone to hell. 'Of course,' said Waugh. I wondered whether Greene himself would have replied so unequivocally.

The dominant literary figure in those days was T.S. Eliot. We admired Yeats and Auden and Frost and Wilfrid Owen and Dylan Thomas but Eliot, both as critic and poet, was in a class apart. If Eliot coined a phrase like 'dissociation of sensibility' or 'objective correlative' we undergraduates suddenly found it impossible to write an essay without plastering the term on every page. Eliot compared Milton's verse to the Great Wall of China and we all lined up, Leavis included, to say how unreadable we found Paradise Lost. We all tuned in when Eliot, in his thin voice, read from his poetry on the BBC. When the Four Quartets were published in their entirety John MacCabe, Tony Benson and I used to meet on Sunday evenings in Robert Markus's little flat in Moss Side. We were later joined by Eric John and Margaret Bullen. We would each read a passage aloud and then try to work out its meaning and merits. Robert always opted to read from Little Gidding because he thought that the best of the four. He was right.

People do not seem to read Eliot so much these days. When I travel by train I often see students with heads deep into books by Camus or Simone de Beavoir but rarely by the man who was our maestro. I suppose that it is not be surprising that someone who described himself in politics as a monarchist and in religion as an Anglo Catholic should be out of fashion. He has been attacked for the treatment of his first wife and accused of anti-Semitism; and of course he has never been forgiven by fans of D.H. Lawrence for savaging their hero. Despite the criticism I continue to regard Eliot as one of our greatest poets. His lines have given me pleasure for more than half a century.

I graduated in 1950 with an Upper Second degree. I had hoped that I might sneak a First but given my dismal performance in the Anglo Saxon and Middle English papers knew that this was unlikely. The result may have helped my entry into the Colonial Service. During the nineteen eighties Anne and I had a ground floor flat near Belgrave Square in London. Our landlady, who lived in the basement, was the widow of the great Ralph Furse, who for many years had been in charge of recruitment policy in the Colonial Office.

We and Mrs Furse had a number of disagreements, not least over the question of noise during what are called unsocial hours. Mrs Furse was quite deaf but loved music. Unfortunately she was also a poor sleeper. We were frequently startled out of sleep in the middle of the night by Beethoven's Ninth Symphony blaring out from the basement flat. Anne took to keeping a broom by the bed. When the earthquake erupted she would bang on the floor and Mrs Furse would turn down the volume. Mrs Furse was not happy at having her musical freedom curtailed in this way. One morning as I was leaving the flat Mrs Furse was entering the hall to collect her mail. 'Ah, Sir Francis,' she said, 'I understand that you were once a member of the Colonial Service?' 'Yes, I was.' I replied. 'You know', continued Mrs Furse, 'my husband, Ralph, used to say that he always tried to avoid recruiting into the Colonial Service people who were very clever. They would not fit in, you see. No, much better to have people from army families or the Church!' And with the sweetest of smiles she disappeared, like Alice, down the steps to her basement.

I made wonderful friends at university and most of those friendships survived the decades and distances that followed. Many of them went on to great things. John McCabe became a member of the Order of Preachers and as Father Herbert McCabe was an authority on the philosophy of Thomas Aquinas. Walter Stein became a senior figure in Adult Education. Robert Markus, who married Margaret Bullen, the girl who used to read Eliot with us, is Professor Emeritus of History at the University of Nottingham and member of the Institute of Advanced Studies at Princeton. He is an internationally recognized expert on the thought of St Augustine. The late Louis Allen was for many years Deputy Head of the Department of French at Durham University and is highly respected both as a Japanese scholar and a military historian. His books on the war in South East Asia were among the first published in the English language to draw on Japanese as well as British and American primary sources. Alasdair McIntyre is teaching at Notre Dame University and is one of the most exciting philosophers on either side of the Atlantic. A possibly even more distinguished philosopher is Sir Anthony Kenny, the young student who accompanied my brother to Rome. A former Master of Balliol, Tony Kenny has been one of the most brilliant and prolific writers on philosophy in this country for almost half a century. I suppose that the member of our student circle who became most famous in later life was Robert Bolt. He became an author and playwright and wrote the scripts for some of David Lean's greatest films, including *Lawrence of Arabia* and *Dr Zhivago*. The rest of us have been dining out on the connection ever since. When one of the films is mentioned we usually let it slip that we were students together at university.

Tony Benson, a physicist who used to humour me by talking about Susan Stebbing when he would have preferred to discuss poetry, became head of the Department of Building Science at Liverpool University. Eric John also became a university teacher. My old friend and flatmate, Arthur Alston, settled in Berkeley in California where he worked for an oil company and also did extension work for the University of California.

I am sometimes asked how I came to be a diplomat. The answer is, 'Because of John Rushton.' John was a colleague in the English Hons course at Manchester. He played left back for the English Society soccer team to Arthur Alston's right back. Having taken our degrees, several of us were training to qualify as teachers. One Saturday morning we were drinking coffee as usual in the university cafeteria. Most were poring over the vacancy columns in the *Daily Telegraph* and the *Times Educational Supplement*. I was just drinking coffee. John who was sitting on the opposite side of the table called across to ask my date of birth. Then my address and so on. After a time he pushed across a piece of paper: 'Here, Ken, sign this,' he said. 'It would not do for me but it is just up your street.' I did as he said and John sent off a completed application form for a competition for graduate entry into the Executive and Administrative Branches of the Civil Service. A few weeks later I was invited for an interview, then to a series of competitive examinations and eventually I appeared before a final board. The Chairman asked me why my application was for entry into the Executive Branch rather than the Administrative Branch. I said that applicants for the latter had to be under 25 on 1 January of the following year. He suggested that I might consider the Colonial Administrative Service which had no such age limit. I said that I would.

Some weeks after the end of term I received a letter saying that I had been successful in the competition and was to be appointed as an Accounts Officer in the Royal Ordnance Factory, Chorley. Thus began a career that would never have happened if it had not been for John Rushton. I have tried without success to get in touch with John to whom I owe so much.

My debt to John Rushton is great but not nearly so great as that to another person that I met at university. Towards the end of my course in

Manchester I met the lovely, young, blonde girl who was to become my wife. I still remember the summer morning when I saw her approaching in the sunshine down Oxford Street in a smart black suit and yellow blouse. Anne was studying Domestic Science. Her brother had also attended Preston Catholic College and had been Captain of the School a few years after me. Her parents were farming near Southport but later moved to Mawdesley, a village a few miles from Chorley and the next village to Eccleston where, as it has turned out, we have been living happily for the last fifteen years.

CHAPTER 6

1951: They aren't still sending *them* out, are they?

THE ROYAL ORDNANCE FACTORY in Euxton near Chorley had been constructed immediately before the Second World War and was reputed to have been the largest munitions factory of its kind in Europe. The Accounts Department was divided into Financial Accounts, Cost Accounts, Capital and Store Accounts. I was responsible for the latter. Large quantities of materials and components were entering and leaving the factory each day. Store Accounts had to keep track of the number and value of these movements of stock. The total stock was usually around £3.5m and a high proportion of this was turned over each quarter. Every six weeks the account was balanced. The individual ledger totals would be added and compared to the total in the master ledger. They ought to agree. In my time they rarely did.

The physical arrangement of the Accounts Department was still Victorian in style. The desks of the clerks were arranged in long rows. The Officer in Charge sat at a desk facing the row of clerks, like a teacher in a class room. No one in the Royal Ordinance Factory had ever before seen a graduate entry Executive Officer and no one seemed quite sure what to make of the creature. I reported to an Accounts Officer who in turn reported to the Chief Factory Accountant. Both were as helpful as they could be but when I entered my department and looked down the long row of desks there was no mistaking the scepticism in the faces staring back at me.

After a few days I was told that we had come to the end of a six week accounting period. Our instructions were to balance the book to a penny within four working days. The first trial balance showed that there was a discrepancy of over £15,000. Two weeks later we still had not balanced. Whilst we were struggling to balance, none of the deliveries and despatches of the new accounting period were being posted. When I suggested that we should work overtime to resolve the issue one girl burst into tears. She said she had to meet her boyfriend outside the Plaza cinema at 7 o'clock and could not possibly work overtime. Another lady said that she had to care for an ailing relative and could not countenance any additional stress.

As we went into a third week the outstanding amount had been reduced to some £34.00 but we still had not balanced. Some of the clerks thought that the fault must be in the calculation of the balances. I knew that the fault was human, not mechanical. The one thing we could be sure of was that the machines had not made a mistake in addition or subtraction. But of course the machine would not know if a clerk posted as a credit what was in fact a debit or if a clerk typed £72 instead of £27. Sometimes a counter error was made which disguised the size of the underlying error. On top of my accounting worries I ran into the problem of draughts.

Very few people went home to lunch. Some ate in the canteen. Others ate sandwiches at their desks. People whiled away the break reading newspapers. Some played cards. One day when I returned from the canteen one of my team, Eddie Bolton, called out, 'Game of draughts, Frank?' '*Draughts?*' I repeated, 'No thanks.' But Eddie would not give up. I struggled through two games and lost both. I was saved by the bell from further punishment.

The next day was Friday. I returned from lunch to find the Accounts office more crowded than usual. 'Bert, here, would like a game, Frank,' called Eddie. Bert King was an old sweat in charge of Capital Assets. He read the *Manchester Guardian* and walked with a limp.

The first game lasted about forty seconds. We each made two or three moves and then suddenly Bert went plonk, plonk, plonk, and swept three of my men off the board. By some fluke I managed to blunder through the second game to a draw. The third was another wipe-out. Glances were exchanged, smiles suppressed. I tottered back to my corner and looked up at the accounts staff. We were into the third week and still had not balanced.

I spent the weekend playing draughts. I found a book called 'Opening moves in chess and draughts.' I read and re-read one of the chapters until I had memorized the basic moves. I returned from the canteen on Monday lunchtime to find the office packed. There were people from Accounts Department, Contracts Department and even Wages Department. The first game was heading for a stalemate when I made a slip. Bert pounced. Game to Bert. The second game was a draw. The third game I won.

Hostilities were resumed on the Tuesday. Bert would resort to fancy little tricks. He would 'accidentally' brush the board with a sleeve or distract attention by suddenly turning round. Slowly I began to grind him down as I got the hang of his game. We played all lunchtime Tuesday and again on Wednesday. One or two games ended in draws. The rest I won. When I returned from the canteen on Thursday Bert's head was buried in the *Manchester Guardian*. A grunt from behind the paper indicated that he had no interest in draughts. Nor, it seemed, had Eddie. The draughts shoot-out was over.

Four of us worked overtime all weekend. It was Sunday afternoon when Arthur Woods finally located the last recalcitrant item that had been incorrectly posted. After four weeks and two days we had balanced the account. When the next accounting period closed we balanced the ledgers in two weeks and following the closure after that in less than a week. Thereafter the ledgers were routinely balanced in two or three days as they always should have been.

I got on with my colleagues and enjoyed the work. But I could not see myself doing that sort of job indefinitely. Once you had balanced the ledgers and won the draughts the stimulus began to leak away. I considered taking a qualification in Cost and Works Accounting but I sensed that if I were to take a professional qualification it should be as a Chartered rather than a Cost and Works Accountant. My immediate boss, Peter White, was a quiet and considerate man and he was a qualified Chartered Accountant. But what struck me about Peter was that he seemed always to carry around an air of sadness. I used to look at Peter White and ask myself whether that was what I wanted to be in twenty or thirty years time.

One day in Market Street I bumped into my old friend from elementary school, William Hoole. Bill told me that he was *en route* to Trinidad where he was training to become an Agricultural Officer in the Colonial Service. I told him that I was in the process of not becoming a Cost and Works Accountant in the Ministry of Supply. Bill suggested that I should apply for a post as an Administrative Officer in the Colonial Service. I had no knowledge whatever of the Colonial Service and had never met anyone who had, but I remembered that the Chairman of the Civil Service Board had made a similar suggestion the previous year. The following day Bill supplied me with a brochure about the Colonial Service together with an application form. I told my colleagues in the ROF what I planned to do. The Chief Factory Accountant thought that it an excellent idea to transfer to the Administrative Class but crazy to go out to the Colonies.

On the way to London for the interview I studied the brochure given to me by Bill Hoole. I took a particular interest in a table which indicated the conditions of service and starting salaries in the different colonies. Levels of pay seemed to be highest in Hong Kong but Hong Kong was less generous in frequency of leave than the African Colonies. After considering the differentials for a few minutes I decided to opt for Nigeria as choice of colony. When I got to Nigeria I soon found out that in reality the pay was nothing like as munificent as it had seemed. But I was not disappointed about the leave, which really was extraordinarily generous.

Had I taken the trouble to learn more about the various colonies I might have chosen differently. But I did know that Nigeria was the largest of our colonies and I had the idea that the larger the colony the greater the scope a career in that colony might offer. There may have been something in that.

When I appeared before the final selection board I recognized the Chairman as the same person who had chaired the civil service board before whom I had appeared the previous year. Of course he did not recognize me. After a few preliminary exchanges he asked me why I had applied for the Colonial Administrative Service. I said that some time ago I had appeared before a similar board and the Chairman had recommended that I should make such an application. So I had taken the advice of that distinguished Chairman. The penny finally dropped. 'Yes, yes, thank you very much, Mr Kennedy, that will do. Next candidate please.'

On the Devonshire Course at London University we studied a number of subjects thought to be relevant to the work of a Colonial Administrative Officer. We studied law and economics at LSE, anthropology at University College, imperial history at King's College and a language at the School of African and Oriental Studies. The pace was leisurely, the atmosphere relaxed. The course Director was Angus Robin, an Officer on temporary secondment from Eastern Nigeria. Robin kept a fatherly eye on us all. Several of us stayed in a British Council Hostel in Hans Crescent in Knightsbridge. The hostel provided a temporary home to a hundred or more students from all over the Commonwealth. One Monday in September I made my way to the London School of Economics for our first lecture. I sat next to a student who introduced himself as Ian Orchardson. We became friends and have so remained ever since. Sadly, Ian died in 2005.

The Devonshire Course may have tried to cover too wide a ground. We did a bit of this and a bit of that. We had seminars on local government and colonial administration and were encouraged to read Hailey's Colonial Administration and Margery Perham. Much of this is now lost to memory but it seemed important at the time. I was much impressed by the quality of the lectures and the quality of the text books in Law and Economics. Cheshire and Fifoot on Contracts, Anson on Tort and Kenny on Criminal Law: for me these books opened up a new world and I remembered no precise equivalent in the English Honours course that I had completed at Manchester. Samuelson's Economics was another masterpiece of a text book. A young Mary Douglas taught us some anthropology at University College. She has since written a number of widely admired books on witchcraft and similar themes. But it was the law and economics that I found most interesting at the time and that I have found most helpful since in my colonial and subsequent careers.

We spent an enjoyable and instructive few days at Wye Agricultural College where we were given a brief introduction into Agricultural Economics and some of the agricultural issues that we were likely to encounter in the field.

Whilst the Devonshire Course gave us an excellent introduction to the principles of English law, we might perhaps have benefited from some more practical instruction on how to find our way round the legal Statutes of the particular country in which we were going to serve. But that is a personal view, influenced no doubt by my early blunders in the Native Courts in Nsukka. I also felt that those of us destined for a difficult language area really needed more intensive instruction and practice in the language than we received. The contrast between the cadets who arrived in Northern Nigeria speaking passable Hausa and those of us who turned up in Eastern Nigeria hardly able to get beyond 'ndeewo, ee de kwa mma?' ('Hello, how are you?'), was painful. Igbo is a tonal language. To achieve the same level of proficiency as the Hausa student I believe that the English speaking student of Igbo needed to devote at least twice the number of hours to its study and practice. Today of course the techniques of language instruction are far more developed than they were in 1953 but I also think that our approach to language learning should have been more disciplined.

When we came to the final examinations of the Devonshire Course my proficiency in Igbo was still lamentable. The evening before the examination I wrote out an account of what my journey to Nigeria would be like and what I would do when I got there. It ran along the lines of: 'I shall travel from Liverpool to Lagos by ship and then from Lagos to Enugu by train. Nsukka is 44 miles from Enugu. The farmers in Nsukka grow yams. In Nsukka there is much palm oil.' and so on. I then got one of my Igbo friends in Hans Crescent to translate my story into idiomatic Igbo and spent the rest of the evening learning by heart his translation. The first task the following morning was to translate what to me was a largely unintelligible piece of written Igbo but the second question said: write an essay on the part of the country to which you have been posted. I was away. When the marks were distributed, the tutor said that the examiners had been puzzled by my paper, which seemed to consist of wretchedly inadequate answers, interspersed with pieces of surprising brilliance. I agreed that it was puzzling.

When I arrived in Nigeria I discovered that once you had passed the language examination you received a small rise in salary. I applied at once to take the exam. My colleagues wisely took the view that before taking the examination, it was sensible first actually to learn some of the language; I was undeterred by such considerations. I crammed for the exam by reading each night to my steward from some booklets for school children that I had bought from the Church Missionary Society bookshop in Onitsha. These were traditional stories written for small children. What the snake said to the lion would be a typical story line; perfect for passing away a moonlit evening looking after children in the dry season, less useful in discussions of government and what we liked to think were other grown-up subjects.

I drove to Enugu to sit the examination in a Teacher Training College. I struggled through the written examination; it was the oral that was a nasty shock. The invigilator, a British Education Officer, announced that he was going to invite a person selected at random to come in and converse with me for ten minutes. I watched through the open window as he stopped first one passer-by then another. Each looked at him as though he were barking mad and hurried along. Finally he approached a labourer who was sweeping the road. I could see the man hesitate but part of the deal was that the volunteer would be paid ten shillings for his pains. This was four times a labourer's daily wage. Looking nervously around, the man shuffled in as though entering a cell for the condemned.

This was a desperate situation. A glance at the Education Officer persuaded me that he probably knew little more Igbo than I did. Anyway that was how I had to bet. As slowly as I decently could, I went through the traditional greetings. 'Hail,' I said. 'Hail,' he replied. 'I see you have risen from sleep,' I said. At three o' clock in the afternoon, I realized too late, this was a pretty stupid remark. The man's eyes widened as they darted from me to the Education Officer. 'Do you have children? I do not have children.' The labourer mumbled a lengthy and, to me, totally unintelligible reply. The Education Officer fixed me with an unfriendly stare. 'The soup is in the pot,' I said. This was my all-time favourite Igbo saying: 'Ofe de n'ite' said in deep bass tones. Unfortunately it convinced my interlocutor that he was dealing with someone mentally unhinged. He made for the door like a hunted animal. 'Come back, I beg you. I beg you,' I cried in my best Igbo. Eventually we managed to get my friend sitting again. I leaned forward and in a confidential tone said 'Enugu is forty four miles from Nsukka. They grow yams in Nsukka.' That was the final straw. My man took his money and ran.

After paying off the terrified conversationalist, the invigilator, by now quite a cross invigilator, turned to me and said that he did not know what all that had been about. Regrettably, he said, his Igbo was not quite good enough to fail me, which was very much what he would prefer to do. With those charming words ringing in my ears I got in the car and drove back to Nsukka. Still, I passed and started to receive the language allowance.

Newton said that we are dwarfs, able to see so far only because we stand on the shoulders of giants. I came to think that in the African colonies the giants on whose shoulders we stood were our predecessors in the Indian Civil Service. The BBC Reith Lectures delivered that year by Lord Radcliffe had impressed me as much as anything taught on the Devonshire Course. Radcliffe deliberated on discussions of power by such as Plato, De Toqueville and the authors of the American Constitution. But it was his lecture on India that caught my attention. Radcliffe quoted Macaulay on the emergence of the Indian Civil Service out of 'the Corruption, Licentiousness and Want of Principle' of eighteenth century India and his reference to 'the spotless glory of Elphinstone and Monro':

> They are men who after ruling armies, after dictating peace at the gates of hostile capitals, after administering the revenues of great provinces, after residing at the courts of tributary Kings, return to their native land with no more than a decent competence.

Monro, the son of a Glasgow merchant and too poor to pay for his passage, had worked his way out to Madras as an ordinary seaman. Years later Sir Thomas Monro wrote to his Directors in London:

> You have much to bring to your subjects, but you cannot look for more than a passive gratitude. You are not here to turn India into England or Scotland; . . . and when in the fullness of time your subjects can frame and maintain a worthy government for themselves, get out and take the glory of the achievement and the sense of having done your duty as the chief reward for your exertions.

A hundred years after Monro had died of cholera in Madras, a revenue officer noted that you had only to say that some rule had been laid down by Monro to end all argument upon it.

Radcliffe did not touch upon the efforts of his contemporaries 'to end honourably what these men had honourably begun' but I never forgot his comments on the sense of service and the idealism which at its best had informed that service. So many soldiers, sailors, civil servants have remarked as Radcliffe did: 'Nor do these incurious islands care greatly for what is done in their name beyond their sight.' There were families, said Kipling, who served India generation after generation, 'as dolphins follow in line across the open sea.'

In July 1953 I sailed across the open sea from Liverpool to Lagos on the Elder Dempster liner, MV *Aureol*. Anne and her friend, Anne Bagnall, waved from the quayside as the Liver Building receded in the background. The fifteen new cadets then enjoyed thirteen days travel in what seemed to us the utmost luxury. The senior passenger at the Captain's table was Major Godfrey Allen, Resident of Rivers Province. He wore a monocle, dressed immaculately and sat stiff-backed in his white dinner jacket. My partner at deck tennis was a senior District Officer who was returning to Eastern Nigeria after five years secondment in the Pacific. One evening as dusk was falling the passengers gathered on deck for their first sight of Africa. We looked at the low, dark silhouette on the horizon. My partner said: 'Mm, Africa. Need to be in good health. To serve there, er, takes, ah, well, yes, some courage.' Six months later he was invalided home after a nervous breakdown.

In Lagos Ian Orchardson and I stayed with a hospitable Officer in the Commerce and Industry Department, named Peter Clayton. We went sailing in Lagos harbour on Saturday afternoon and before leaving for the railway station on Monday morning Peter took us for breakfast in the Ikoyi Club. We were joined at the table by two senior officers. One of them, resplendent in white uniform and shiny brass buttons, was the Director of Customs. Peter introduced us and said that we were ADO cadets, newly arrived. To which the Director replied, 'Christ! They aren't still sending *them* out, are they?'

CHAPTER 7

1953: No white man worked here

THE ROAD FROM Enugu climbed the dizzy spirals of Milliken Hill and headed west towards Onitsha. At Nine Mile Corner we turned north towards Nsukka. For twenty miles the Nsukka Native Authority Kit Car groaned up the red, laterite hills and bounced down the dead straight road through valleys of oil palm and scrub. At the back of the truck were a trunk and a packing case. These we called 'loads'. Also in the back was a cook whom I had recruited in Enugu. The driver's name was Kenneth. Kenneth was a man of few words. He wore a khaki shirt and a maroon beret. Each time we passed a man or woman walking along the side of the road in the village at the top of Milliken Hill, he would lean out of the cab and scream: 'Wah wah!' After a while I summoned up the courage to ask what 'Wah wah' meant. 'Bush men,' Kenneth replied. 'Dey no wear cloth.' We bounced along in silence for another dozen miles.

In Nsukka I reported to the District Office. The DO had left a message that I was to go to his house. I walked the hundred yards or so to the residence along a pebbled path between stones neatly painted white. The house looked out across the plain towards the Northern Region. Although it was by now almost ten o'clock in the morning the escarpment was still wreathed in morning mist. The scene seemed more like the film set of *Wuthering Heights* than tropical Africa. The DO's wife, Jean Lewis, appeared at the door of the thatched house. Wearing a cotton dress with a cardigan draped round her shoulders Jean welcomed me graciously. 'Would you like coffee? I am having a cup of Ovaltine myself,' she smiled. I thought that nothing could have been more English. Greer Garson herself could not have played the part of DO's wife more perfectly.

Along the ridge of the Nsukka hill, the station consisted of four mud walled houses each with a thatched roof; first the Resident's Rest House, then the DO's house, then the ADO's house and finally the house of the Doctor, Albert Zahra. Each house had a fine view and a little garden in front with vividly coloured shrubs: frangipani, hibiscus and bouganvillia. There were also canna lilies, portulacca and harmattan lilies. Just below the houses were two tennis courts and below them, the District Office. Nearby were the Native Authority Offices, the Prison and the Post Office. In the dry season the hillside was ablaze with harmattan lilies.

Between the DO's house and the tennis courts a little path ran over the crest of the hill and down to a spring called Asho. Every morning before they went to school children with buckets on their heads would pass back and forth fetching water from the spring. In the evening Toby and Jean Lewis, usually accompanied by Augustine their steward and Whisky the dog, would often take a stroll round the station. They would stop and exchange gossip with the families of the office staff and of the police and prison warders. There was always banter with the family of the warders because the other wives maintained that the Chief Warder's wife had a crush on Toby. The exchanges showed what a happy atmosphere prevailed in Nsukka at that time. But nothing is ever perfect and Toby and his wife had suffered one or two unfortunate experiences as they walked along the path that led to the spring.

One day a notice appeared on a tree by the side of the path. The notice was signed by John Nwodo, Sanitary Inspector, and addressed to the Secretary of Igbo-Etiti Native Authority. It read:

> Would you please warn the Court messengers to stop from messing up the Court Compound and adjacent road with excrement?
>
> Also boys and girls who fetch water from Asho should refrain from defecating promiscuously near the District Officer's residence.

A Native Court Messenger, in khaki shorts and shirt with a little maroon pillbox hat came to my office and saluted smartly. He said that his name was Hyacinth and that he was my orderly. I met the other members of the office staff and visited the prison, of which I discovered that I was the Assistant Superintendent. My office was newly white-washed, spotless and empty. There were two letters in the in-tray. One was a letter inviting the DO to a local school event. I took the best part of an hour drafting and redrafting a three line reply.

Toby and Jean very kindly put me up for the first four days. Then after the relative luxury of the DO's house I moved into my own house and entered the real world of a new ADO. The first meal served up by the cook I had chosen at random in Enugu was roast chicken and boiled rice followed by fresh fruit salad. The chicken tasted like boiled string. For the next two months the menu did not vary except that every second week, when a cow was slaughtered in the market, some scraggy beef would be substituted for the chicken. When I left Nigeria it was many years before I could be persuaded to eat chicken. I did obtain some relief over the dessert. After thirty or forty consecutive offerings I pushed back the plate of fresh fruit salad and said, 'today, no jungle juice.' Cook did not say a word. Within minutes he plonked down a plate of banana fritters. They were sprinkled with sugar. I thought they were delicious.

Nsukka Division was roughly the shape of a triangle. The base ran some eighty miles from the Uzo-Uwani area along the Anambra River in the west to Eha-Amufu in the east. Eha-Amufu was a stop on the railway line that ran from Kafanchan in the north to Port Harcourt on the Niger Delta. Beyond Eha-Amufu was Abakaliki Division. The two sides of the triangle formed parts of the border with Makurdi Province in the Northern Region. Instead of Igbos they were settled by Igala and Idoma people. The central part of the triangle was a plateau some thousand feet above sea level. It was this elevation that gave Nsukka its pleasant climate.

In those first few evenings I would sit on my canvas chair and watch the magnificent sunsets and ask myself what I was I doing there, three thousand miles from Chorley in a country that I knew virtually nothing about. According to Radcliffe we were there to end honourably what had been honourably begun. Unfortunately, along the West Coast from Freetown to Luanda the white man's relationship with Africa had begun anything but honourably. The slave trade has cast a shadow that still troubles relationships between white and black and may do so for many years still to come. But that was not what I worried about as I gazed out over the Nsukka plateau.

In his wonderfully honest book: *No Telegraph to Heaven*, Malcolm Milne described what he saw as the difference between the pre-war British administrative officers and those of my generation. The difference, as Malcolm put it, between those who had been to prep school and those to grammar school. Malcolm was from the kind of family who for generations had gone out to serve the Empire 'as dolphins follow in line across the open sea.' I did not feel that I was coming to serve the British Empire. I just hoped that I might do something useful for the people of Eastern Nigeria, but it was not obvious what that something might be. The officer at my final interview had asked me how long I expected to serve in Nigeria. 'Ten years,' I replied. 'What then?' he asked. 'Then,' I said, 'Nigeria will become independent and I will finish my career in Hong Kong or Kenya or some other colony whose political development is ten years behind that of Nigeria.' The officer nodded in what I took to be agreement.

What worried me was, what could I possibly do that could not be done just as well by a Nigerian? On Sunday I sat in church in the middle of the congregation and offered a silent prayer that however unlikely the possibility might be, I might make some modest difference. Whilst thus engaged I was interrupted by one of the officials: 'Father says no sit there. Please to come, sit in front.' 'Oh, no thanks. I am perfectly happy here,' I replied. A few moments later I was startled by the sight of the parish priest stomping down the aisle. An irate Irish voice boomed out: 'Will ye do as ye're told and git out o' there. Aren't ye sittin' in the middle o' th' wimmin?' I looked round and for the first time noticed that all the men were on one side of the church and all the women, with a solitary white face in their midst, on the other. There was no doubting the difference.

On my second day at work Toby took me with him to hear cases in Itchi Native Court. One or other of the parties had appealed to the DO against the verdict of the Native Court. If still dissatisfied, that party would be able to appeal against the DO's decision to the Resident. The fee for a review was ten shillings. Alternatively the aggrieved party could proceed by way of appeal. The cost of an appeal was two pounds and two shillings. The rules for an appeal were more formal and at any stage the appellant could request that the case be transferred to the magistrate's court. From the magistrates court the case might be appealed all the way to the House of Lords. All land cases had to proceed by way of appeal.

Most of the cases were either dowry cases or cases of trespass or petty theft. In the dowry cases the family of a divorced bride were usually disputing the value of the bride price that had to be returned to the family of the bridegroom. I was baffled by the whole process. Igbos seemed to be born litigants. I would listen intently as an appellant delivered a presentation that I found wholly persuasive. But then the defendant would step forward and deliver an equally convincing presentation that contradicted in every particular that of the previous speaker. Toby got through the cases at a brisk rate. He would listen to one side and then the other and suddenly announce 'I find for the defendant,' or 'I dismiss the appeal and confirm the judgment of the Native Court.' I had no idea how he reached his conclusions. Mid morning, we took a break. Toby had brought along a thermos flask of coffee and we each smoked a 'Bicycle' brand cigarette with our coffee. Toby said 'I'll give you a tip. When you write up your judgments keep them short. The more you write the more excuse you give the Resident to overturn your verdict.' It was a canny piece of advice and not just for work in Native Courts. Toby also said that in all land cases without exception you should insist on inspecting the land in person. That advice I faithfully followed all my days in Eastern Nigeria.

The following morning was one of the most traumatic I have had to face. I went round in the five-ton truck to collect Toby for the eleven mile journey to Itchi. Toby did not appear. Instead Jean came to the door. She said, 'The DO is not well. He is staying in bed this morning and says that you should go to court without him.' I gaped at her, rooted to the spot, but Jean just turned on her heels and went inside.

The knowledge that this was Toby's idea of throwing me in at the deep end was no comfort whatsoever. I walked slowly up the centre of the

Court with my heart in my shoes. The Sergeant called the court to attention and everyone stood in silence until I took my seat. The mud-walled, zinc-roofed building was packed. Late-comers leaned in through every opening. The court sessions were a form of theatre much enjoyed by the local community. Money changed hands. Parties would offer 'dash' to the Court Clerk and perhaps to the Interpreter. In some courts the officials would return the dash or half of it to the losing party. But with fees at ten shillings a time justice was still cheap at the DO's court. One feature that drew the crowds was the fun of seeing whether the white man would get at the truth or make a complete ass of himself. In many cases the only person in the room who did not know what had happened in a case was the DO. Still, the DO must have got at the truth in a fair number of cases for the system to have been embraced so readily by the communities which it served.

To the ADO in Itchi Native Court that Tuesday morning the truth seemed a long way away. I called the first case. I listened to the plaintiff, then to the defendant. Then to the plaintiff again. One was as convincing as the other. I recalled the defendant. The Interpreter, Mr Okechukwu, raised his eyes to the ceiling. I adjourned the case. I called the second case. The evidence in this case was just as confusing as in the first. I adjourned that case also. Then I adjourned the session and in a tiny cell-like room at the back of the court, drank my sweet coffee and smoked two Bicycle cigarettes, one after another. At the rate I was going, the session might last for weeks, even years. When we resumed I managed to find a case in which I could make a judgment with some confidence. I then went back to the first two cases and after further endless questioning declined to upset the judgments of the Native Court. So I struggled through to the end of the afternoon and we adjourned for the day. When we left the court I made sure that I took with me the records of the outstanding cases.

I spent all evening studying the records. I tried to work out possible lines of questioning that might lead to the truth; ideally to a question that only the person whose story was true would be able plausibly to answer. I entered Court next morning much better prepared and slightly more confident. I even managed to finish the first case in forty minutes. By Saturday morning I had finally got to the end of the cases outstanding in Itchi Native Court. I was anxious to get back to Nsukka but the Chief who was Chairman of the Court insisted that I visited his house for some refreshment. He lived in a lovely traditional house in a clearing in the village. It was a beautiful sunny morning. I was offered the traditional bitter kola nut and then Chief treated me to a beer and generally did his best to put the green young ADO at ease.

Back in Nsukka, Toby called Mr Okechukwu to his office and asked how the ADO had performed. Apparently Mr Okechukwu said, after a pause, 'Very thorough, very thorough.' Toby took that as a compliment. I did not enlighten him. Anyhow, the following week I was sent to review cases in Enugu Ezike and then in Eha Amufu. I still remember one extraordinary case in Enugu Ezike. A man had been sued by the Chairman of a Church Committee for chopping down a mango tree that was the property of the Roman Catholic Mission. I could not fathom what was at the bottom of the dispute and in the end said that I would inspect the scene of the crime. I found that the tree had been standing in the middle of the school football pitch. A new and cowering Head Master admitted to me that he had ordered its removal, never dreaming that it would cause such a fuss with the elders on whose property the school had been built. The unfortunate defendant was an innocent father who had given the boys a hand in carrying out the wishes of the Head Master. I dismissed the case.

Later I went to Eteh near the northern border of the division and it was there that I made the worst mistake of my career. The rules of the Native Court were that Native Law and Custom was to be upheld in all cases except when it conflicted with natural justice, e.g. in a case of judicial murder or witchcraft. One of the cases which I was asked to review concerned the custody of a five-year-old child. The father of the child had died and by the customary law of that area his senior brother had inherited the property of his brother, including the wife and child. The senior brother was much older than the young woman. He was also a chief of his village. The family of the young woman and the family of the deceased all agreed that the woman and child should remain with the senior brother. I assumed that the woman's relatives did not wish to face demands from the senior brother for the repayment of part of the original dowry. But the young woman ran away from the senior brother and wanted to take the child with her. The senior brother insisted on keeping the child. The Native Court rejected the woman's application for custody. It was a heart-rending case because the child was clearly desperate to return to the mother. I adjourned the hearing and discussed the case at great length with the elders. They were adamant that their law required that the claim of the senior brother be upheld. Eventually, I resumed the hearing and told the plaintiff that although I had every sympathy with her claim I was bound to follow the law and custom of the community and uphold the judgment of the Native Court. I ordered the child to be returned to the senior brother. As soon as I pronounced the judgment the young woman flung herself at my feet, clutching my ankles and begging me to help her. 'DO, bikho, bikho.' 'DO, I beg you, I beg you.' I cleared the Court. It was a long time before the sound of her cries ceased to reverberate in my mind.

When I got back to the District Office I took down the set of volumes of the laws of Nigeria in Toby's office and started to read through the provisions of Chapter 42, something I should have done on day one of my arrival, if not during the Devonshire Course in England. Eventually I came across the relevant provision governing the provenance of the Native Court: Native Law and Custom must be upheld in all cases except (a) those in conflict with natural justice, e.g. those involving cannibalism or witchcraft and (b) cases involving the custody of children, in which cases the welfare of the child shall be paramount. '*The welfare of the child shall be paramount.*' So I knew that somewhere in Eteh a young woman and her child were suffering agonies of separation not because of an inhumane legal system but because of the incompetence of a British ADO. I carried around with me a sense of guilt that was alleviated only when I got to Onitsha and worked in the office of the acting Resident. At the first opportunity I looked up the records of appeals to the Resident from Eteh Native Court in Nsukka Division in 1953. I soon found the case. The Resident, Brian Thwaites, had heard the case on appeal. He wrote simply: 'It is clearly in the best interest of the child that she should be with the mother. I set aside the judgment of the ADO and award custody to the mother.' So, despite the blunder of the ADO, the system had worked as it was supposed to work.

Three weeks after arriving in Nsukka I succumbed to malaria. I had not noticed any mosquitoes but one Saturday evening I became terribly sick and spent all night, first sweating, then shivering. In the morning my neighbour, Dr Albert Zahra came to see me. I said that I thought that there must have been something wrong with the Beck's beer that he had given me the previous lunchtime. He was indignant. (A bottle of Beck's cost two pence more than a bottle of Star.) There was nothing wrong with his beer he said. What I had was malaria. He gave me mepacrine tablets to take but I could not keep them down and spent the night crawling to the toilet and back under the mosquito net. On Monday morning Albert brought the much loved Sister Doctor from the Catholic Mission Hospital, Sister Cabrini, to see me. She confirmed Albert's diagnosis. Albert then injected mepacrine into my blood stream and gave me something to stabilize my stomach. He stayed and nursed me through Monday night and by Tuesday I began to get better. I was extremely fortunate to have such care. Toby turned up on Wednesday with six half bottles of Guinness to help with the convalescence; which they certainly did.

The colonial system was not democratic but in rural Nigeria, at the time that I am describing, it certainly operated with the consent of the governed. One of its features was the practice of holding daily surgeries at which anyone in the District could see the DO with any complaint or request. These surgeries we called 'Petition Time'. In Nsukka we held petition time from 11 a.m. to 12 noon each day. They were a great resource for the ordinary man who had to struggle with a baffling bureaucracy. Often people walked many miles to see the DO. One Saturday as I was about to leave the office the clerk said that a man wished to see me. He had walked over twelve miles. I declined pointing out that it was almost 1.00 p.m. and that I had held petitions from 11 o clock. A few moments later the clerk came back to say that the man had a nail in his head. I rushed outside to find the man sitting on the curb side in much distress. He had indeed a nail in his head, one of the terrible practices sometimes inflicted in violent disputes in communities in the area. I had the man rushed to the Mission Hospital where he was operated on and by some miracle survived.

Nsukka taught me an early lesson in brand development. Outside the office were always one or two petition writers. For a fee they would summarize in writing the request or complaint that a petitioner wished to make. The DO did not require such summaries but many believed that they would help their case. One morning I stopped to chat with one of the petition writers. He was sitting with neat sheets of white paper on his lap and two bottles of Quink Ink. A notice by his side read: 'Petitions: 5s or 2/6s.' I asked what the difference was. The Writer explained that petitions written in black cost two shillings and six pence. Those written in blue black cost five shillings. I still did not get it. 'Well,' said the Writer, 'if your petition is in black the DO will answer within three weeks but if your petition is in blue black he will give you a reply within one week.' 'Ah', said I, 'then you are making Ju Ju against me.' 'Yes,' said the writer. Hoots of laughter from the onlookers.

Although the Kit Car driver and I were never on the same wavelength I got on famously with the driver of the Divisional five-ton lorry. Since the DO usually claimed the Kit Car, the lorry was often my mode of transport. Sylvanus Eke came from Ukehe, seventeen miles away on the Enugu road. Ukehe happened also to be the home town of John Nwodo, our Sanitary Inspector, who was shortly to become a member of the Eastern House of Assembly and later a Minister in the Regional Government. I was an admirer of Sylvanus. He had fought in Burma with the West African Frontier Force. He was intelligent and a natural leader. He repeatedly urged me to visit his village and inspect a partially completed community development project there. So one evening we went. His people had begun to build a road to connect the village to the main road. About a mile of road had been cut through thick forest and all the labour had been provided by volunteers from the village. One bridge and one culvert had been completed but there was still a mile to go and a half finished bridge required completing and two more culverts needed building. The Obas and the villagers gathered in the village square. I congratulated them on their work. The Chief Oba dashed me a chicken and then began to speak with the eloquence that all Igbos seemed naturally to command. 'DO', said the Chief, 'We have cut down our oil palms and spoiled our crops and now our faces are covered in shame because for five months nothing has happened. The other villages have all been idle whilst we worked. Now they are mocking us and ridiculing us.' I promised them cement and the services of a mason to finish the job.

At the end of August I received my first month's salary. After deductions, the sum came to £29 15s. That evening I spent a long time on the patio trying to work out how I might survive on £29 15s. I had a cook, a steward and a 'small boy' or apprentice steward. I made two decisions. First, I would ration myself to one case of Star beer and one bottle of whisky per month. Second, I went inside and sacked the 'small boy'. In the event I survived the three months without difficulty for the simple reason that on the DO's orders I spent so much time on tour. Not only was there little opportunity in the bush to spend money, but a touring officer received an allowance of ten shillings per night away from the station.

It was about this time that I received a wonderfully thoughtful letter from my old Manchester physicist friend, Tony Benson, now at the Department of Building Science, Liverpool. Dear Frank, he wrote, I expect that as you are no doubt touring the bush on Her Majesty's business you may be short of reading material. If you will send me a modest sum of money – I suggest £5.0.0. – I will see what I can do.' I sent off the money as requested and two months later received a tea chest full of second-hand books painstakingly collected by Tony. They were a carefully chosen selection ranging from a full set of Proust to a book of instructions on how to repair a motor car – all acquired at rock bottom prices. They were a marvellous present because in the rural areas I visited farmers got up at dawn and went to bed soon after dusk, except in the dry season when everybody celebrated the new harvest far into the night. I read a great deal by the spluttering light of a Tilly lamp.

I was spending more and more time preparing for elections; first for local government, then for district councils and county councils, and finally for the regional and federal government. Constituencies had to be delineated, voters registered, candidates nominated and finally the elections held. I spent many weeks touring the Uzo Uwani area along the Anambra River, trying to explain to puzzled villagers what it all meant.

One Sunday afternoon I set out at four o' clock to register voters in a town called Mbu some twenty miles from Nsukka. This was a second attempt. No one had turned up on the first occasion and we were lagging behind schedule. I sat in the back of the truck with Hyacinth and five clerks. Mr Okechukwu was sitting, stony-faced, with the driver. He was not pleased at having to forfeit his Sunday evening in this way. Despite the jolting and swaying of the truck Hyacinth managed to fall asleep. After ten miles or so a mattress in a corner of the truck began to smoulder and then burst into flames. Someone had dropped burning cigarette ash on it. There was a great to-do as everyone started to beat out the flames. In the middle of the hoo-ha Hyacinth woke up. In a flash he had dived, head first, over the tail board of the moving vehicle with terror on his face and clutching my brief-case in his left hand. The truck screeched to a halt and I ran back. I thought that Hyacinth might be dead. He was spread-eagled across the road. Blood was pouring from a wound in his head. We carried him back to the truck and turned back to Nsukka. At the same time I sent a message to Mbu that we would be late but were still coming. We delivered Hyacinth to the Mission Hospital and set out yet again.

It was beginning to go dark by the time we got to Mbu and we had to finish the registration by the light of hurricane lamps. By this time Mr Okechukwu was in a filthy mood. 'Name!' he would shout. Silence. 'Kadu afia?' 'Er, yes, what?' the startled villager would reply. 'Name, name, name! What is your *name*?' The exchange began to take on a distinctly 'wah-wah' tone. After all, Mr Okechukwu came from Onitsha and everyone knew that the schools and colleges of that town had supplied the Region with most of its lawyers and doctors. To make matters worse every second voter said that his or her name was either Okonkwo or Okeke. It drove Okechukwu to distraction. But we finished the register and got back to Nsukka before midnight. Hyacinth had already been discharged from hospital. The following morning he was in the office bright and perky as usual with a patch on his head but otherwise no worse for wear.

My favourite view in the division was of the Nkpologu Hills from the Nsukka road. To get to Umulokpa in those days you drove north for a dozen miles and then veered west to climb the palm-clad hills of Nkpologu which stretched to the horizon before dropping down to the Anambra River. In Nkpologu Native Court I once heard a case about a girl of fifteen who complained that she had been forced into prostitution. The complaint was dismissed. The Court ruled that by the customary law of that community the priest of the ju ju shrine always came from a certain quarter of the village. The people of another quarter of the village were 'Osus' or slaves. These Osus had always to supply a young female to act as a sort of vestal virgin. She tended the shrine and lived under the command of the priest. So much was agreed by all the members of the Native Court. I could hardly believe what I was hearing. After all, this was the middle of the twentieth century. I adjourned the hearing to inspect the shrine which was set in a sort of rocky grotto. The priest, a man in his sixties, showed me round. The young complainant quietly continued her domestic chores. There was no dispute about the facts. The priest agreed that the girl's services to the ju ju included those of concubine. I upheld the appeal.

The centre of the Uzo Uwani district was a town of some twelve thousand people called Omor. Omor was the last town in the Eastern Region that could be reached only on foot. When touring there, the lorry would drop me, my orderly, the District Interpreter and all our pots and pans and camp beds and mosquito nets at Umulokpa where District Clerk would negotiate with the local chief for the hire of porters. Once a price had been agreed the long column would set off in time-honoured style down a narrow path which led to Omor. Mr Okechukwu and I rode ahead on hired bicycles. Behind trudged the porters, huge boxes swaying precariously on their heads.

I loved touring Omor and the nearby villages. I knew that I was visiting communities whose way of life had hardly changed for many hundreds of years. I also knew that once the bridges that we were building were completed and the road reached the town, that way of life would be swept away. It was a privilege to be among the last to visit such towns before they were changed for ever.

By the entrance to Omor town was a sacred grove and every day sacrifices to the spirits would be left there. To get to the grove you passed through a great arch made of bamboo. From the cross piece of the arch fluttered what looked like hundreds of coloured rags. They were coloured, I was told, by dried menstrual blood. The villagers would be up and about very early in the morning when the air was fresh. The young men would leave for the farms and the women to the nearest market. The children would sweep the village square and sprinkle fresh sand around the entrances to their mud and thatch houses. The old men would attend the meetings of their societies and the young girls would spend hours decorating each others' bodies and fixing each others' hair.

I became friendly with a young Chief of Omor called Madumele and in the early evening would often call for a chat. He much enjoyed these visits and would have chairs arranged in a circle for my arrival. A large group, including his wives, would form around us and everyone would settle down to enjoy the exchange of views. One evening as we were talking a small plane could just be seen on the horizon making its way across the sky. It was the afternoon flight from Enugu to Lagos passing over the Niger at Onitsha. 'Ah,' said the Chief, 'there is something I wish to ask you.' 'Of course', said I. 'Well,' said the Chief, 'there are some foolish young men in this town who say that there are living people inside that thing in the sky. I have told them that that is foolishness. How could a living person fit into such a small thing? But they will not listen to me and I want you to tell them.' All eyes turned in my direction and several voices grunted an approving 'Hah, Hah.' I said that I too had heard these assertions and they did seem difficult to believe. But I reminded the Chief (Descartes would have been pleased!) that the further away you placed an object the smaller it seemed to be. I then extricated myself by suddenly remembering that I had another meeting at my tiny rest-house.

Some years later I was posted to the Regional capital, Enugu, and there our second child, Mark, was born. One day the steward announced that Chief Madumele had come to greet me. My friend had come all the way from Omor to Enugu to congratulate my wife and me on the birth of our first male child. He had heard the news from the ADO in Nsukka. The Chief presented me with two fine cocks. He would not stay very long but was happy to meet my wife, Anne, our little girl, Sarah, and our baby son, Mark. We shared two bottles of Star beer and talked about old times. Then he left and I never saw him again.

Sometimes I would hear land cases on the border with the Northern Region in Idoma or Igalla country. This would usually necessitate a meeting with our opposite numbers from the northern side of the border. I noticed that there was always a certain gravitational pull for each Administrative Officer to side with his 'own' party to the dispute. When my opposite number was Brian Stafford we managed to keep in check these tendencies. With others it was more difficult. I got off to a terrible start with one colleague who introduced himself rather stiffly as 'ADO North'. 'Glad to meet you,' I said, offering my hand: 'ADO South.' 'Very funny,' came the riposte. It turned out that the officer's name was North.

I found it depressing that during the Biafran war so many British Administrative Officers who had served in Nigeria instinctively supported the area of the country in which they had worked. At that time I was working in Whitehall. Every second Monday a group of ex-Nigeria hands used to meet for lunch in the Royal Commonwealth Society. The lunches invariably ended in passionate disagreement between those who had served in the East and those who had served in the Northern and Western Regions.

Teachers often say that they remember most clearly the first class that they taught. That may be why I remember so well those days in Nsukka. But it *was* a lovely division and the mid-nineteen fifties *were* a special time. It was a place and a time in which the British colonial system was possibly seen at its best and for almost the last time.

Admittedly, we were performing on the tiniest of stages. There were no large towns in Nsukka. There were no metalled roads, no telephones, no electricity, no supplies of piped water. There were no businesses of any size and no industry whatever. The only drilling taking place was by a small team from the Balakhani Black Sea Oil Company that moved slowly round the Division drilling boreholes for village water supplies. We were serving a simple, peasant society still dependent upon subsistence agriculture for its living.

Radcliffe believed that the British often overprized their institutions and set too little store by the character of their people. It may be that whatever success we achieved in Nsukka was due not to any merits of the system but because the system was operated by such decent men and women. For Toby Lewis being DO of Nsukka was a labour of love. He was a father figure. He commanded the loyalty of his staff and enjoyed the respect of the people. They believed that he had their interests at heart and that despite their mistakes and miscomprehension, he and his British colleagues meant well and acted without any thought of personal gain. The leaders of the missions who built and ran a large number of the schools in the area, and Sister Cabrini and her team of nuns who ran the Division's only hospital, also regarded themselves as part of Toby's family, and it was much to his credit that they did. These young men and women were working far from home all the hours that God sent for negligible or no remuneration because they believed that what they were doing was good.

Of course there were many prophets of doom, many people, like the white-uniformed Director of Customs, who predicted that the rush to self-government would end in tears. But we younger people tended to be optimists. British and Nigerian civil servants alike believed that we were embarked jointly on a great adventure. Emerging politicians like John Nwodo and Robert Okuta were also part of the family. They would routinely call on the DO to brief him on doings within the main political party in the East, the NCNC, and swap views on the latest developments. The nineteen fifties were a time of hope and a time of innocence.

They were golden days but they were also the days before the deluge; before the failure to manage the oil reserves, before the raging inflation, before the flight from the countryside, before the population explosion in the urban centres and before the terrible war. These forces unleashed a tidal wave that swept through the country and changed forever the lives of its people.

In the aftermath of these disasters and twenty five years after Jean Lewis had offered me the cup of Ovaltine I revisited Nsukka. Driving up from Enugu I remembered that I was passing through the village of Ukehe that I had first visited with Sylvanus Eke. I stopped and on the off-chance knocked on the door of what had been the house of John Nwodo. A house boy answered the door and said that master was at home but was sleeping. Ten minutes later he entered the room. Much older but still unmistakeably John; still the same warm smile, the same engaging voice. He told me about the horrors of the war. The Federal Army had attacked from the north and for a time the front line had passed through Ukehe. For some weeks he and members of his family had hidden in the bush. Several of his relatives had been killed in the battle.

I also tracked down Hyacinth. He had recently retired. He had risen to the position of Assistant Superintendent of the Nsukka Market. He was living in a village outside Nsukka with an attractive young woman who was his third wife. At first Hyacinth was overjoyed to see me and we chatted happily about the times we had spent together. But suddenly his mood changed and he fell silent. 'You should not have come,' he declared. 'Why on earth not?' I asked. 'Because,' he said, 'when we knew ourselves we were young and our lives were before us. But look at us now. We are old.'

I went to Uzo Uwani in search of my friend the Chief of Omor. A concrete highway slashed across the countryside from the Anambra to Nkpologu. A vast cross-over was under construction at Umulokpa. Our little community development bridges had long since disappeared. But the Chief was no longer alive. After the war he had adjudicated in a land dispute in Omor. He had delivered a controversial verdict. The young man who had lost the case had fought in the Biafran army during the war. He went back to his compound and dug up a rifle and ammunition that he had hidden at the end of hostilities. He killed my friend with a single shot.

The government station at Nsukka had changed beyond recognition. The market encroached upon the area from one side and the University of Nigeria from the other. I could not find my old house. Eventually I did manage to find what had been the District Office. It was now the office of the Municipal Council of Nsukka. But it was still the same old wooden structure with the zinc roof. The DO's room was now the office of the Secretary of the Municipal Council of Nsukka. I knocked on the door and receiving no reply entered. The Secretary was writing at the desk. He was probably as old as Toby Lewis had been when he worked in that room. As bureaucrats tend to do, he went on writing. I went on standing. At last he lowered his pen and raised an interrogative eyebrow: 'Yes?' I explained that I was a visitor and would be grateful if he could tell me where I could find what had been the house of the ADO during the time of the British administration. I might have been talking double Dutch. He looked at me blankly. I tried again. I said that I had lived in Nsukka in the nineteen fifties and had worked in the same building. My DO, Toby Lewis, had worked in that very room. The Secretary of the Municipal Council of Nsukka put down his pen and leaned forward across his desk. Fixing me with his gaze, he said with quiet finality: 'No white man worked here.'

In the end I found the house. I stood on the patio and looked out once more to the horizon; no longer across an open plain but now over a sea of houses and the academic buildings of the University of Nigeria. I was beginning to understand what Voltaire had meant when he said that history is the tricks we play upon the dead. I had always known of course that the Nsukka that I had remembered so fondly over so many years no longer existed. What had not occurred to me until that moment was that for most people, including most of the town's present inhabitants, it had *never* existed.

CHAPTER 8

1954: Sorry old man, bit of a shambles

THE IDYLL DID NOT LAST. I had taken it for granted that I should remain in Nsukka until the end of my tour. But suddenly, after six months, I was yanked out of Nsukka and ordered to change places with the ADO, Onitsha.

The Federation of Nigeria at that time was divided into three regions and the Federal capital of Lagos. Each region was divided into a number of provinces, each under the control of a Resident. The provinces were in turn divided into divisions, with a District Officer in charge of each. That was the simple structure by which the Colony was governed. Onitsha Province was made up of Onitsha, Awka, Awgu, Udi and Nsukka Divisions. The province stretched from the River Niger in the West to the railway in the East. The Regional capital, Enugu, was located within Udi Division. The Resident, Onitsha Province, took the view that ADO cadets were there to be trained and moved them around accordingly. The wishes of the cadets themselves did not greatly concern him.

In those days Onitsha was a town of about 70,000 people. Today it is many multiples of that figure. Thanks to its location near the junction of the Niger and Anambra rivers and the fact that it was one of the highest points on the river navigable all year round, Onitsha had been a major commercial centre since the nineteenth century and even earlier. Its market was famous throughout West Africa. It was the main crossing point for east–west traffic. North of Onitsha road builders faced the added barrier of the Anambra; further south the Niger began to feed into the many tributaries of the Delta.

Onitsha was a centre of educational excellence. Secondary schools of exceptional quality had produced many of the region's doctors and lawyers, some of whom became the country's first generation of political leaders. Nnamdi Azikiwe was born in Zunguru, a rail centre in the Northern Region. But his family home was the Inland Town, Onitsha. Every second Monday, the father of the future President, a retired railway man, used to come to the District Office to collect his pension. It was by his wish that he collected it in person.

Throughout the nineteenth century and the early decades of the twentieth, the river was the favoured mode of commercial transport. The most prosperous and educationally most advanced areas in what became the Eastern Region tended to be found along the rivers. With the advent of roads this pattern was reversed. Riverside towns like Aguleri, Anam, Osomari and Atani had a palpable air of receding gentility. Signs of past prosperity and educational attainment were everywhere but also unmistakeable was the undertow of the receding economic tide.

The classic portrayal of life in an Igbo village before the arrival of the British is Chinua Achebe's in his novel *Things Fall Apart*, but for a description of the actual arrival of the white man it is difficult to better that given by my old boss, Jerome Udoji, in his book, *Under Three Masters*. In a few evocative pages he describes the arrival of the British in Ozubulu in 1905 and the *Itiji Egbe* or 'destruction of arms' that followed. Thanks to the patronage of the British major one of the elders usurped the traditional authority of the others. Impressed by the power of the white man one of the other Obi's set out for Onitsha to find his own white man. He soon came back with a white man, whom he installed in a well-sited house on a bluff overlooking a valley with good spring-water. What he had not understood was that he had brought back, not a British political officer, but Father Duhaze, a French missionary from Alsace Lorraine.

The District Officer to whom I reported was Freddie Cobb. Freddie was assisted by two ADOs. The other and more senior ADO was Ntieyong Akpan. NU Akpan later became Chief Secretary in the breakaway Biafran regime. Ntieyong was in charge of the part of the division south of Onitsha and I was responsible for the northern portion. The Resident at the time was Peter Gunning, who later became Sir Peter Gunning and Deputy Governor. The ADO, Resident's office, was my old friend Ian Orchardson.

The DO was almost permanently on tour so Ntieyong Akpan and I were left pretty much to our own devices, which suited us splendidly. I enjoyed touring the northern part of the division, especially the protected area between the Anambra and Niger rivers which still contained plenty of game, including elephants. It was fun touring by river. The District Office had its own launch. Three hoots on the siren meant 'District Officer entering harbour'. On one occasion I went to stay at Nzam on the Niger where there was a government rest house. By an extraordinary coincidence, as I came round a bend in the river the rest house in which I was to stay collapsed before my eyes. The brick walls crumpled in on themselves and the zinc roof slowly settled on the rubble. A column of dust rose in the sky from the debris. Fortunately, Shell BP was drilling for oil in the vicinity. That was the first time that I had come into contact with oil exploration. The Tool Pusher in charge of the drilling rig, an

Australian named Ernie Beaver, kindly invited me to stay in one of their portable cabins. I enjoyed three nights of air conditioned luxury as a result. Ernie was not impressed by the quality of government building.

A town I visited frequently was Aguleri on the Anambra River. Aguleri and its neighbour Umuleri had quarrelled for generations over the precise boundary of the land between them. All was quiet when I visited the area and I was saddened to read in a newspaper two years ago that fighting had flared up in Nigeria between Aguleri and Umuleri people and that some three hundred people had lost their lives.

The Chief of Aguleri was King Idigo II. Whenever I visited Aguleri the first duty was a courtesy call on King Idigo, who would spend hours explaining to me the history of his people. Nearby lived an old priest known to his parishioners as 'Fader Joe'. Athough there had been missionaries in Aguleri for more than a hundred years few people in the area had become Christian before the arrival of the Irish Holy Ghost missionaries. Father Joe Delaney was credited with converting to Christianity the wife of the first King Idigo. She had once delivered twins and she was said to have been the first woman in Aguleri to have had twins who survived. Igbos traditionally believed that twins were an abomination and that only the animals had multiple progeny. One of the two children was usually suffocated by one means or another soon after birth.

By the time that I met him, Joe Delaney was in his mid-eighties. He had arrived in Nigeria before the British flag was first raised above the Resident's Office, Onitsha, and he lived to see it lowered for the last time. Joe had toured the interior of Igbo land and had entered villages that had never before seen a white man. In one village near Aba he claimed that the chief had ordered that his bicycle be tied to a tree so that it would not go back to summon help for the missionary.

Joe's pride and joy was a great church that he had built in Aguleri. It had taken many years to raise the money and several years to build. He had been assisted by a faithful catechist called Martin. The church was finished just before the Second World War. A great feast was planned to mark the official opening and the Bishop and guests from all over the country were invited. The last job to be done was the extension of the cemetery. As they were toiling to finish, Martin leant on his hoe and said that the first person to be buried in the new cemetery would be him. A few days before the consecration of the new church Joe was called away to visit a sick person on the other side of the Anambra river. When he got back to Aguleri he found that Martin had died of pneumonia. Joe had wept inconsolably over his friend's death. When he died, Joe would tell me, he was going to be buried in the new cemetery between Martin and the woman who had been his first convert to Christianity.

When I visited Aguleri again many years later, I went to the cemetery on the deserted hillside that looked out over the river Anambra but I could not find the grave of Fader Joe and his two friends. I went back into the town and after a search found Martin's son who was now headmaster of the village school. He confirmed that his father had died suddenly from pneumonia after being exhausted by the long hours of work on the new church. He said that when Father Joe had died the parishioners had planned to bury him, as he had wished, in the cemetery next to his father. But the Bishop had come from Onitsha and said that Father Joe was too big a man to be buried there. He had to be buried in the church. A plaque in the wall of the church commemorates the frustration of Fader Joe's dearest wish. So Martin and Father Delaney's first convert lie side by side on the bluff overlooking the river with an empty grave between them.

There is a noisy bustle about Nigerian towns that you do not meet anywhere else. Onitsha was typical. It was a town of traders, all of whom seemed to be shouting at once. The shouting and the laughing and the scrambling typify both the *joie de vivre* and the relentless fight for survival that an Igbo youngster in an urban environment faces each day from morning to night. Onitsha embraced on the one hand the quiet dignity of the Inland Town and on the other the mad chaos of the market. At the foot of the market flowed the great river on which its existence depended and after which the country had been named. On the edge of the market was a store owned by the Unilever subsidiary, UAC. On a slate outside the store were written in chalk the buying and selling prices of a bale of cotton drill. Three times every morning and three times every afternoon a clerk went into the market to check the prices at which the cloth was trading. UAC then rubbed out the chalk figure and adjusted the price accordingly. I have never come across competition more perfect than that in Onitsha.

For several months in 1954 an ostrich walked down Market Road each morning and took up a position on the traffic roundabout near the CMS bookshop. No one knew from where the ostrich had come or why it chose to stay in that particular spot. But it was a unanimous opinion that ostriches are very bad-tempered birds that are not to be disturbed. Everyone took care not to disturb the ostrich.

One of the nice things about my transfer to Onitsha was that I was reunited with my friend Ian Orchardson, who was at that time working as ADO at the Resident's office and whom I was to replace when it came time for Ian to go on leave. I also met again my old friend William Hoole, also sadly deceased, who had suggested to me the idea of a career in the Colonial Service. Bill was working at an agricultural experimental farm some 20 kilometres away.

One of the pleasures of city life was the cinema. Onitsha had a cinema called the Rex. It was owned by a nice Lebanese man called (if memory serves) Albert Farah. The cinema was a tiny affair. The back ten rows were protected by a 'pan' roof. The rest were open to the skies. When it rained there was a mad scramble out of the cheap seats into the protected area. The programme was changed three times a week. If a film was applauded it might be kept on for a few extra showings. If it was booed it was taken off at once. There was great audience participation in the cinema shows, much booing and cheering and 'Look out! He's behind you. No! *Behind* you!' If a film flopped, Albert would announce in the morning paper: 'By popular request the Rex Cinema brings you a return of the great film, *Hamlet*, with Laurence Olivier. Or, alternatively: 'the great film, *Samson and Delilah*, with Victor Mature and Hedy Lamarr.' These were Onitsha's two favourite films. So popular were they that Albert kept two copies of them permanently in reserve. The front rows would chant out the dialogue with Olivier, not because they had read a word of Shakespeare but because they had seen the film so many times. By the time we reached the sword fight in Act V the front rows would be out of their seats in excitement. There would be a similar frenzy when Victor Mature wrestled the lion to win the heart of the delectable Hedy Lamarr.

Another leisure attraction was the Onitsha Club. We ADOs were careful about spending too much time in the club because we could not afford to buy the beer that we were dying to drink. But we played a lot of tennis and some cricket and occasionally a few games of liar dice. On one memorable evening, after many beers, the young manager of the British Bank of West Africa (which later became part of the Standard Charter Bank), after a long series of wrong calls in a game of liar dice, bet his car on a single throw. He lost, threw the car keys on the table and walked home. I gazed on speechless, mouth agape. The manager was posted back to England shortly afterwards. His replacement, Geoff Higgins, was a fast bowler and the captain of our cricket team. Whilst Geoff was at the helm we beat Enugu, Port Harcourt and all the other teams in the Region. Sometimes I used to tease Geoff about banking. How could it be right to make money by lending more in loans than you had received in deposits? etc. One day Geoff suggested that I should join the bank. He thought that I would be good at it. I found this a tempting offer because I knew that our days in the colonial service were numbered and banking seemed to offer an interesting career. But Geoff said that I would be sent to the Netherlands for six months training. I could not see how I was going to finance yet another period of training and did not pursue what may have been an attractive career opportunity.

No sooner had I settled into my job in the northern part of the Division than I was told that I had to swap with Nteiyong Akpan and become ADO, South, whilst he became ADO, North. South of Onitsha there were attractive towns along the Niger that one reached by river, such as Osomari and Atani, but there were also a number of important inland towns including Ogidi, Obosi, Nnewi and Ihialla.

In October 1954, for the first time, elections were held by universal adult suffrage to select members for the Federal House of Representatives. I was appointed Electoral Officer for Onitsha South. Voter registration had already been completed. All that remained was the actual poll.

I set up polling stations in the main towns, about eight in all, and arranged for the training of the polling staff. All the polling centres but one were located in schools, which would be closed for the day. In Nnewi I made the polling centre the Nnewi Town Community Centre. This was a newly constructed, two-storey building with a veranda running along the front both on the ground floor and the first floor. From the verandas a series of louvred doors opened into a large hall on each floor. At each of the four doors upstairs and the same downstairs I sited a table at which two registration clerks could check the identity of the voter before issuing a voting paper. The registers had been compiled in manuscript in hard-back, ruled, foolscap books. Once identified, the voter passed inside the hall to cast his or her vote in one of the booths and then left by a staircase at the rear of the building. That was the plan.

I knew that the only place that I was likely to experience any problems was in Nnewi. That was partly because registration had been heavy in that town but more because the NCNC candidate was L.P. Ojukwu, later Sir Phillip Ojukwu, who was a Nnewi man. L.P. Ojukwu was a successful Igbo businessman who had built up a large transport business. He was a major contributor to the finances of the NCNC and was said to exercise influence on the party leader, Dr Nnamdi Azikiwe. The Resident, Peter Gunning, had sent me additional resources for Election Day. One was a body of fourteen police. I sent a Police Constable to act as a token presence at eight of the polling stations. The other six I sent to Nnewi. Two senior British Administrative Officers had also volunteered to help. One was Ray Coatswith, soon to become Permanent Secretary to the Minister of Health, and the other Ian Jackson, a senior DO, who had written a book on Community Development. I asked both these officers to go to Nnewi early on polling day and hold the fort until I arrived.

On the morning of polling day I left Onitsha at six o'clock and drove to Ihialla some forty miles away. Ihialla was close to the border with Owerri Province and was the farthermost polling station from Onitsha. From Ihialla I worked my way back calling at each polling station in turn. In all the posts voting was taking place in a calm, orderly fashion, with long queues of people patiently waiting their turn to cast their votes. For the women especially, this was a novel experience. There were the occasional outbursts of irritation as when a polling officer discovered that voters were placing their voting papers on top of instead of inside the ballot boxes. If one person made the mistake, others tended to follow like sheep. But by and large the poll was proceeding satisfactorily. When I had visited all the other polling stations I turned the car and made for Nnewi.

When I reached the outskirts of Nnewi, about half a mile from the Community Hall, I was waved down by an agitated Electoral Candidate and a group of his supporters. LP was wringing his hands. 'You must do something DO. This is terrible. No one is voting. Every thing is confusion. I am going to lodge an Appeal. My people have been here since daybreak and are still not able to vote.' Although I had no idea what he was talking about, I told Mr Ojukwu not to worry. Every thing would be fine and everyone would be able to vote.

I still remember the scene of chaos that awaited me at the Nnewi Community Hall. Hordes of people were milling around in front of the polling station. Crowds of angry voters were mobbing the registration tables. The polling clerks were overwhelmed. In the noise and confusion they were hardly able to find a single name in the registers. Voting was virtually at a standstill. A crowd of women descended on me complaining that they had been there since six in the morning and still had not voted. The Police were nowhere to be seen. On top of everything else a truck was careering around the place with a group of youths in the back dressed as cowboys and waving a banner that read 'The Nnewi NCNC Youth Cowboys.' They were making an unbelievable din. One Cowboy was banging a bass drum, another blared out a trumpet every two minutes whilst yet another was discharging into the air blank cartridges. You could hardly hear yourself think. I ploughed through the yelling mob to the building and climbed to the first floor. With elbows on the veranda rail and smoking cigarettes, Ian Jackson and Ray Coatswith were leaning forward as they contemplated the mayhem below. Ian turned to me with the immortal words – that is to me they have been immortal – 'Sorry, old man. Bit of a shambles. Sent in Police at 9 a.m. Spent force by 9.30.' 'By 9.20,' corrected Ray. 'By 9.20,' agreed Ian. As the Americans say, I was fit to bust. I knew that come six o'clock Ray and Ian would get into their cars and drive back to Enugu. As Electoral Officer Onitsha South I would be left with the mess. I was not concerned by what the Resident would say or for that matter L.P. Ojukwu. But that such a mess should happen on *my* watch in *my* patch was insufferable.

The situation was certainly desperate. So I decided on desperate measures. First I asked if there were a Secondary School nearby. There was. I sent a note to the Headmaster saying that if I could have the services of 16 of his smartest sixth formers for five hours, I would pay them 10 shillings each for their work. I knew that sort of money would bring them running. Within 30 minutes a school vehicle arrived with a group of 16 young men, smartly dressed in white. Some looked more like teachers than students but that suited me all the more.

Secondly, I called for the leader of the Cowboys. I explained that until we restored order no one would be able to vote and the great NCNC candidate, Mr L.P. Ojukwu, would be deprived of a large number of votes and Nnewi would be covered in shame in the eyes of its neighbours. I said that I needed the assistance of the NCNC Young Cowboys to restore order and help the Police to maintain it. The man under the Stetson and false beard could hardly believe his luck at this unexpected empowerment. Like the poacher who had always known that his real vocation was that of gamekeeper, he actually jumped to attention. '*Yes, Sah!* What are my orders, sah?' he asked. 'Clear the compound,' I replied. And the Cowboys set about whooping and clearing the Hall and its approaches. I announced to the crowd that voting would be suspended for 15 minutes until the Hall was clear and new polling staff had taken up their positions. There was some chuntering but I insisted that when voting resumed everyone would vote and no one would have to stand in a queue for long. First we would bring the operation to a complete stop. Then, after 15 minutes, we would start again and do the job properly.

Thirdly, I committed what I am sure was a serious infringement of Electoral Regulations. I took each of the hard-backed foolscap registers in turn and tore it down the spine into two pieces. Instead of eight registers I now had sixteen. I allocated one sixth former and one trained clerk to each of the new registers. I now had sixteen polling stations instead of the original eight.

I first reopened the ground floor. I stationed a Police Constable and reserve Polling Clerk at the head of the queue to direct each voter to the appropriate table. Within half an hour the stream was moving quietly and at a steadily increasing pace. I then repeated the exercise on the first floor.

In the middle of all the noise I received an urgent telephone message from the Resident, Peter Gunning. LP had no doubt been on to him. I took the call in a nearby Post Office. Peter gave me authority to keep the poll open beyond the scheduled closing time of 6.00 p.m. It had never been my intention to do other than keep open until the last voter had cast his vote, but I told him not to worry. He could be assured that everyone in Nnewi qualified to vote would have the opportunity to vote.

By now it was well into the afternoon and very hot. The bearded Cowboy approached. He and his men were drenched in sweat. Law and Order work was harder than they had expected. The leader asked permission to retire. I thanked the Cowboy so profusely that he gave me the quizzical look of one unsure whether his pocket has been picked. The Cowboys climbed wearily on to the back onto their truck and with a last honk on the trumpet and an apology for a whoop they drove off into the Nnewi sunset. They had done their job. The din had subsided. Order had been restored. L.P. Ojukwu had recovered composure. At around 6.30 p.m. we closed the polling station. Following the procedure in the vineyard described in St Matthew's gospel I paid off the Assistant Polling Clerks recruited from the Secondary School. I glued back together the sundered registration books. We sealed the ballot boxes and piled them into a lorry. The little convoy set off for Onitsha under its police escort.

The following day we counted the votes. LP was the father of Emeka Ojukwu, who later became known to the world as the leader of Biafra. It was ironic that LP should be campaigning for a seat in the legislature of the Federal government from which his son a few years later would so dramatically seek to secede. Another coincidence that is remarkable in retrospect is the fact that my colleague, Ntieyong Akpan, who was battling away that day supervising the election in Onitsha North, would eventually become Ojukwu's Chief Secretary in the Biafran administration. N.U. Akpan described the dramatic last days of the regime in his book *The Struggle for Secession 1966–1970*.

All day L.P. Ojukwu sat outside my office with the visiting Chairman of Costains and his wife waiting patiently until the votes had been counted. LP won by a landslide in Onitsha South. Everyone – well, almost everyone – was happy.

My Court work must have improved because later that year I was ordered by the Resident to go to Awgu Division to clear a backlog of cases in the Native Courts that had accumulated whilst the District Officer, Peter Grant, had been sick.

I was now much more confident in Court. I stuck rigidly to a few simple principles. I never worried about how many times I adjourned a case or how long I took to reach a verdict. Secondly, I had decided that in some cases it was quite wrong to believe that everyone in Court except the DO knew what the correct judgment should be. On the contrary, in the absence of registered title, in many land cases no one knew for certain what the truth of the matter was. Despite the assumptions on which the English legal system was based there were cases, I now believed, in which the truth, practically speaking, was unknowable.

The Awgu station was located on a hill that rose sharply from the plain to a distance of some seven hundred feet. At the foot of the hill a road ran arrow-straight across the plain to a little station on the railway line to Port Harcourt called Ndeaboh Halt. Behind the District Office the densely covered hill rose sharply until it flattened out into a plateau of open range land at the crest.

The Court Interpreter in Awgu was a senior and experienced officer named Mr P.O. Onwualu. We soon cleared most of the outstanding cases in Agwu Court. We raced through a number of cases of petty theft. But one land case I adjourned until I could inspect the land. The land in dispute was on the plateau behind the District Office. To reach it took quite a climb through tangled woodland. Monkeys jabbered and screeched in the trees. I insisted on walking round the whole of the area in dispute. Then with the little party of Court officials, judges and litigants I inspected in turn particular landmarks and farms that the two parties regarded as especially relevant to their claims. The inspection took all day.

I returned to Court the following day and finished all the other remaining cases. I said that I would re-inspect the area in dispute in the land case. The case was intriguing because the area in dispute was extensive – probably five miles in circumference – and because neither side seemed to me to have made a wholly compelling case. After the second inspection I said that I would resume the hearing on my return from Achi where there were also cases outstanding.

The visit to Achi, twenty miles north along a red laterite road, was memorable for two reasons. The first concerned Mr Onwualu, who had recently qualified for a government loan. He had bought his first car: a shiny little blue Standard Ten.

On the second morning of the visit I awoke to quite a hullabaloo. A circle of people including a very agitated Mr Onwualu were gesticulating around a clay pit some six or seven feet deep. At the bottom of the pit was the shiny little blue Standard Ten. The only suggestion the onlookers could come up with was that 'cows' must have pushed the car into the pit. I asked Mr Onwualu whether anyone was trying to tell him something. His reply was incoherent. Four youths heaved the little machine out of the pit.

The most interesting case at Achi was described in the court records as 'Bird v Nwankwo'. The case was that a woman called Mercy Nwankwo had alleged that a sacred ju-ju that appeared in the form of an eagle was in fact a human being. For this sacrilege she had been sentenced to six months imprisonment. No woman was allowed to set eyes on the ju-ju and if any did so she would drop dead.

The woman's defence was that whilst her husband was away working on the farm a townsman, Okonkwo, had come to the house demanding to know why her husband had not appeared for community work. She had said that he was working on the farm. When she returned from market a ju-ju mark had been placed upon the house that could only be removed by the priest, who charged two chickens for performing the necessary ceremony. She did not have two chickens and had thus been unable to enter the house and unable to prepare her husband's evening meal.

If there is one thing that drives an Igbo man to fury it is to come home after labouring all day on the farm only to find the grate cold and his evening meal uncooked. When his wife explained what had happened the husband had marched round to Okonkwo and had given the priest a piece of his mind. The priest maintained that this proved that Mercy had called the ju-ju a human being.

I spent ages on the case. Obviously the verdict could not be allowed to stand. But I was also anxious not to undermine the authority of the Native Court, whose members had been unanimous in the judgment. After a long discussion I assured the elders of my support for Native Law and Custom but asked whether they did not agree that it was difficult to apply customary procedures to some of the cases involving the younger generation that seemed to be arising with increasing frequency. It was my opinion that the authority and credibility of the Court might best be maintained by reserving religious sanctions for religious problems. In this case the root of the problem was the failure of the husband Nwankwo to turn up for his share of communal labour on the new road that the village were building as a community development project. The woman was not really involved in the action that had caused the dispute in the first place.

The elders agreed that a majority of them were also members of the new Achi Local Government Council. I explained that the Council had the authority to finance the construction of the road by levying a rate that could be paid either in cash or in kind. If Nwankwo then failed either to pay or to work he could be fined. If he failed to pay the fine he could be sent to prison.

This way the desired result would be achieved without risking disrespect to the ju-ju and without provoking challenge to religious authority. I said that if they agreed I would set aside the present judgement and help them to draft a motion for the next meeting of the Local Council. The elders were very pleased and thanked me at some length for assisting them and above all for explaining how they might put the newfangled system of local government to serve a useful purpose. I ordered Mercy's release but delivered a lecture to the court on the need to respect the authority of the elders and the traditions of the village.

The next morning we awoke again to a hullabaloo in the compound. Where was the shiny blue car? At the bottom of the clay pit, now with a large dent in its side! Mr Onwualu was inconsolable.

When I got back to Awgu, Peter Grant and his wife, Anne, invited me to a very nice dinner. The following day I inspected the disputed land for the third time. The two sides to the dispute could produce evidence to support their claims only to the portions of the land nearest to their villages. They had been farming these nearest portions for two generations. But between the two was an area of land to which each side had only the vaguest of claims. Three generations earlier the area had been subject of sporadic inter-village fighting that they called 'the inter-tribal wars'. The dispute had acquired urgency only with increasing population and increasing pressure on the lands. In effect the courts were being asked to determine what three generations earlier would have been settled by war. I granted to the plaintiff title to a portion of the land claimed in the suit, but only to a portion.

Some weeks later Peter and I met by chance near Oji River. Peter was driving a lorry with a large timber construction on the back. Peter was a keen reader of history. 'What?' demanded Peter, 'was the secret of the success of the Romans?' 'Roads?' I suggested. 'Not roads. Roads aren't a secret,' dismissed Peter. 'The secret that changed history was the discovery of the *arch*,' said my mentor. We had been all wrong in our bridge building. He had met an engineer who had shown him how to build a bridge, Roman style. The result could bear loads thirty per cent greater than the traditional bridge at thirty per cent less cost. The contraption on the back of his lorry was a template for an arch. You positioned the template on the two abutments of the bridge, then filled it with cement mixed with chunks of stone. The stones were the cherries in the cake. When the cement had hardened you dismantled the template and carted it off to the next bridge site. With that burst of evangelical enthusiasm, Peter drove off towards Achi and Awgu.

At the end of the year I succeeded Ian Orchardson as ADO, Resident's Office. There I was taught the elements of office work by the Chief Clerk, Mr A.O. Diribe. Mr Diribe began his first lesson with the words, uttered with the patience born of long suffering, 'This, Kennedy, we call a file.' 'Yes, Mr Diribe.' 'In this square you write the name of the officer to whom the file is being sent.' Of course, I had seen files before. I even thought that I knew how to deal with them, but I had never before seen office work approached with such professional pride. Mr Diribe also taught me how to handle the Resident. At first my drafts would come back from Peter Gunning with half of the text crossed out and new phrases scribbled in. I knew that Peter agreed with the substance of my recommendations but was infuriated to see red ink all over the page. So I studied Peter Gunning's style and pet expressions and tried to write not as I preferred but as I thought that he would prefer. Gradually the red ink diminished and eventually disappeared.

In April, 1955, I finally got away on leave. I left Onitsha at seven in the morning and after various delays reached Kano at eight in the evening. The BOAC DC4 Argonaut was on the tarmac revving its engines prior to departure. I raced up the steps and collapsed into a first class seat. The face of the woman next to me was hidden by the leaves of a huge pineapple that she was clutching to her bosom. 'Just for take-off and landing,' explained a voice through the foliage. I had not eaten since the previous day. After I had wolfed down two biscuits offered with the pre-dinner sherry, the stewardess returned from the galley with a commercial size biscuit tin. 'You seem to need these more than we do,' she said, putting down the tin in front of me. I devoured every last crumb.

I broke my journey home in Rome. There and in Florence I spent a few most agreeable days with brother Jack. One day we had drinks with some of his friends. One of them wanted to know what I was doing in Nigeria. My attempts to explain were brushed aside. No, no. What he wanted to know, he said, was why I and my colleagues thought that we had any right to be in Nigeria in the first place. I explained that we were preparing the country for self-government. 'Yes, yes,' my young friend persisted, 'but why are you there in the first place?' 'Because of John Rushton' did not sound like an answer that would satisfy him.

We expect holidays to be enjoyable. But it is difficult to exaggerate the thrill of a first home leave after twenty months in a humid, tropical climate before the days of air conditioning. The freshness of the air and the quietness were the two things I noticed first. Once, when working in Lagos I won two return air tickets to Switzerland in a raffle. Anne and I flew to Zurich and from there took a train to a tiny village by the Lake. The first night we could not sleep because we could not get used to the silence.

At the end of a glorious English summer and a wonderful leave I asked Anne if she would marry me and to my delight, despite the strange life that she knew I was taking her to, she said yes. I asked Anne's father for his daughter's hand and he gave it in generous terms and welcomed me into the family. He said that he was glad that it was me. I wondered a bit about that. We fixed the wedding for my next leave and I obtained Peter Gunning's permission to have the length of my next tour reduced since the previous one had been extended.

CHAPTER 9

1955: A bridge to last a thousand years

O N RETURN FROM LEAVE I was posted to Awgu as District Officer. I
was delighted to be promoted and given my own division on only
my second tour, even though the promotion brought no increase in pay.
Before going to Awgu, however, I was asked to go to Port Harcourt to
stand in temporarily for the Government Coastal Agent. I reported one
Friday morning to the Resident, Rivers Province, the grand person I had
first met on the MV *Aureol*, Major Godfrey Allen. Godfrey was famous
for his monocle, Rolls Royce and grand piano. He had greeted the arrival
of his latest ADO with the remark: 'Ah, you must be the last, guttering
candle of the Raj!' Still, he invited me to lunch. As I tucked into my
second helping of Manchester Tart, which in those bachelor days was as
near as I got to *haute cuisine*, I stared at a picture behind Godfrey's chair.
'That,' said my host, 'is Switzerland, where the good go to when they die.'
After a pause he added, 'It is where I shall go when I retire.'

I never found out what the Government Coastal Agent was supposed to
do, and after a few days Godfrey transferred me to the Port Harcourt
Planning Authority where I acted as Secretary. It took several increasingly
insistent telegrams from the Resident Onitsha Province before Godfrey
released me and allowed me to go to Awgu, where some minor disturbances
had been taking place following a dispute over land between two villages.

Awgu was a beautiful little division at the base of a spine of hills that
ran through Onitsha Province from Nsukka in the north, through Udi
Division to the border of Okigwe in the south. I was taking over Awgu
Division from my friend and mentor, Peter Grant, who had been
promoted to the post of Community Development Secretary.

When I passed through Enugu, the Regional Capital, on my way to the
new post I received a message from Peter asking if I would drop by his
office. I did so and we talked about this and that and chatted over the
latest gossip. Peter said how much I would enjoy Awgu and how glad he
was that I had been given the division. I could not make out where the
conversation was leading us but after some fidgeting and much rocking
back and forth in his chair Peter suddenly lent forward and said that he
wanted to give me a word of advice. He thought that I would be well
advised to keep away from two particular villages for the next few months.

One was called Obuoffia and one was called Onuoffia. 'Why on earth should I do that?' I asked. 'Well,' said Peter sheepishly, 'You remember the bridges and the Roman arches?' 'Of course, how could I forget them?' 'Well,' continued Peter, 'I built several bridges using the arch templates, including one at Obuoffia and one at Onuoffia.' Then, after a painful pause, 'Unfortunately, they collapsed three months ago. The villagers provided free labour for the construction of the bridges so I imagine that they will not be particularly pleased to see the DO for a while.'

The villages in question were about a mile apart on the same river and located at the foot of the Awgu escarpment, which rose steeply to some 700 feet. After heavy rains, what was normally a gentle stream could become for a few hours a raging torrent rising to a depth of 12 feet or more. Peter bewailed the fact that his engineering friend, who had lavished such praise on the ability of the Roman arch to withstand downward pressure, had neglected to mention lateral pressure. In June of that year in a flash flood, the abutments of each bridge had been pushed aside like skittles and the spans had fallen into the river.

Of course, I ignored Peter's advice and at the first opportunity visited the stricken villages. The villages were situated a short distance from the main road but separated from their farmland by the Offia river. Onuoffia was located about a mile upstream from Obuoffia. To quote Kipling, the two villages were at hating distance from each other. Without the bridges it was impossible to get vehicles to the farms and to transport the produce from the farms to more distant markets. It would have been perfectly possible for one bridge to serve both villages but the villages had been bitter enemies for generations and would on no account agree to share a bridge. Peter's solution had been to build two bridges. For over a year the villagers had collected sand and stone and had then contributed thousands of man hours in free labour to construct the bridges.

I went first to Obuoffia, taking along the District Interpreter and, as a precaution, a Police Constable in case we were run out of town. We left our vehicle on the main road and completed the journey by bicycle. The meeting was held in the Village Square, which had been meticulously swept for the occasion. Under a large tree a chair and table had been placed facing which sat the Chief and village elders in a semi-circle. Behind them stood the young men and behind them the women and children. A huge commotion was caused when a snake fell out of the tree. Everyone scattered in all directions until the snake had been beaten to death. Order was then restored and the meeting resumed.

I began by introducing myself and saying what an honour it was to be DO of such a fine division. I brought the greetings of my predecessor, DO

P.F. Grant. I edged gingerly into the subject of the bridge and the unfortunate calamity that had occurred during the rainy season. DO Grant and I much regretted that the bridge had been unable to withstand the exceptional pressure of the floodwater. I would understand if the Chief and his people never wanted to hear the word 'bridge' mentioned again. But if the people did want to rebuild the bridge and if they were willing to collect the necessary sand and stone and provide the labour, I was there to make a promise to the people of Obuoffia. I would help them to build a bridge of quite different design. It would be very strong. Carried away by my own rhetoric, I added that the new bridge would be strong enough to carry a tank and last for a thousand years. The latter claim seemed to meet with approval but the former made no impression since no one listening had at that time any idea what a tank was. However, I said, there was one condition. There was sufficient money to build only one bridge. Before construction could begin the people of Obuoffia would have to agree to share the new bridge with the people of Onuoffia. The two villages would also have to agree where on the river the new bridge should be built.

The Chief rose to reply. He spoke in terms far more eloquent than any I had been able to muster. He welcomed me to the village and thanked me for my visit. But I seemed to be suffering from a misapprehension that he wished to dispel. There was no need to apologize for the previous bridge. DO Grant was a very good District Officer. He had built an excellent bridge of which the village had been proud. It was true that one night during a violent storm the bridge had been destroyed. But he and the other elders had realized at once that the bridge had been destroyed by a thunderbolt launched by their neighbours and inveterate enemies, the people of Onuoffia. The Chief was pleased to inform me that the ju-ju priests of Obuoffia had been equal to the challenge. They had been summoned in the middle of the night and within less than two hours, by powerful magic had smashed the bridge of the Onuoffias and had cast it into the river. There could be no question, said the Chief, of sharing a bridge with such wicked people.

After repeating my offer and the conditions attached to it, I left the village and proceeded to Onuoffia. In Onuoffia I had a similar meeting, the outcome of which was the same. They would like a new bridge but had no intention of sharing it with Obuoffia.

There matters rested for several months. From time to time I would receive a message from one or other of the villages inviting me to meet them to discuss the possibility of rebuilding the bridge that they so badly needed. Each time I sent the same reply. There could be only one bridge over the River Offia and there was no point in my visiting the village until they had agreed with their neighbours where it should be located.

The station at Awgu was beautifully laid out with flowerbeds and flowering shrubs surrounding both the house and the Office. One morning at 8 o'clock I made my way as usual up the gentle incline from the House through an avenue of franjipanis to the District Office that looked out over the plain towards Ndeaboh. I entered my office to find that the unthinkable had happened. A delegation from the Chiefs of Obuoffia and Onuoffia had arrived to invite me to a *joint* meeting of the two villages. They said that the elders had decided to accept my conditions.

I went along to the village square of Obuoffia, which, as before, had been meticulously swept. On one side of the square were the Chiefs and elders of Obuoffia and on the other those of Onuoffia. Each Chief spoke in turn. The people of the two villages badly needed a bridge so that they could transport produce to neighbouring markets. So after much difficulty they had resolved to accept the DO's terms. They would provide the necessary sand, stone and manual labour for the construction of a new bridge. They had also resolved that the precise location of the new bridge should be left to the DO. I congratulated the Chiefs on their leadership and promised that the new bridge would be one of which they could be proud.

That evening I drove to the home of Major Stan Riggs, who lived a few miles away in the village of Maku. Stan was the Principal of the Community Development Training College in Awgu. He had retired after many years service as a regular officer in the Royal Engineers. He was a specialist in Bailey bridges. I explained the unfortunate experience with Roman arches and said that I had promised the two villages a bridge strong enough to take a tank and to last a thousand years. I needed his expert help to redeem the promise. Stan agreed to help but was taken aback by my promise that the bridge would last a thousand years. I said that so long as the bridge was strong enough to carry a tank and to withstand the floodwaters of the River Offia I did not think that we need worry too much about a few hundred years either side of a thousand. But I rejected Stan's suggestion that we build a Bailey bridge. I had promised what I called a 'proper' bridge, i.e. a permanent structure that would indeed last many generations. We then agreed that Stan would choose the site and specify what materials he needed. It would be my responsibility to obtain those materials.

The preparatory work was soon underway but Stan fretted about the cross-beams that would span the river. These were to be of reinforced concrete and if possible of pre-stressed concrete. Stan worried whether the reinforcing would be strong enough. Eventually he came up with the idea that we should reinforce each of the beams with a railway line. Stan thought that so reinforced, the beams really could last for a thousand years. He knew an engineer in Nigeria Railways who could let us have two discarded rails for next to nothing. My job was to find a way of getting the rails to Awgu, a distance of thirty odd miles from Enugu.

I went to Enugu to see Mike Widdows, a senior engineer in the Public Works Department. Mike had been Provincial Engineer in Onitsha and we knew each other from our time together in that city. Mike believed that all community development work was a well-intentioned but fundamentally misconceived waste of time and that administrative officers should give up their amateurish efforts at engineering and keep to things they knew something about. It was a view that I came increasingly to share but in those days I made the standard rejoinder that when the Public Works Department started to build the roads and bridges that the people needed, we in the Administration would be more than pleased to leave the work to the professionals. In the meantime we would continue to do what we could to help the rural areas to improve their economies and quality of life.

I told Mike that I needed to transport two railway rails to Awgu. 'Oh, no!' groaned Mike, 'You people are surely not still going round playing at building bridges when you have not the slightest idea of the most elementary engineering.' I confirmed that regrettably that was indeed the case. Moreover, I had staked my reputation on building a bridge that would last a thousand years and that Stan Riggs was going to help me to do so.

Mike Widdows proceeded to give me a lecture on elementary engineering in which he demonstrated that adding steel to a structure did not necessarily increase its tensile strength. He ridiculed the idea of the railway lines, which he said would increase the weight (and the cost) but not the strength of the bridge. What we needed to ensure, was that the reinforcing was correctly designed and correctly positioned. Mike then showed me tables of figures from which could be calculated the amount, size and pattern of reinforcing required to support a given weight and breaking strain. Mike knew that I had great respect for his professional knowledge but I explained that I could not build the bridge to the standard promised without some on-the-spot help. The only person in Awgu who could provide such help was Major Stan Riggs, ex Royal Engineers. I was dependent on Stan and the deal was that what Stan wanted I would get. Stan wanted railway lines. Mike said that the only way to get the rails to Awgu would be by low loader. I went round to the

Shell Oil Company and wheedled out of them the loan of such a vehicle. Three weeks later the rails were in Obuoffia.

During the protracted palaver about reinforcing, precious weeks had been slipping by. It was now almost the end of March and the shuttering for the foundations of the abutments was still not in place. If we did not pour the concrete for the foundations before the rains started we would have to abandon the work for a year. Every day Stan and I were at the site of the bridge. Every day the clouds massed ever more menacingly. One Friday a few spots of rain began to fall. I said that this was our last chance. I announced to our small work staff and to the larger force of volunteer labourers that we had to get in the footings that weekend before the rains came. We would therefore work all Saturday and all Sunday from dawn to dusk.

On the Saturday we completed the pouring of concrete in the footing of the eastern abutment. All that remained was the foundation of the western abutment. Once that was in place the rain would not matter.

Sunday was not a good day. I arrived at the site early in the morning to find Stan stomping up and down. Normally the mildest of men, Stan was in a fury. He had brought his wife, Anne, with him to watch the work. No work was taking place. Philip, the foreman mason, had not turned up. I drove off to find the village where I was told Philip lived. Anne Riggs came with me for the ride. I threaded my way through the village until we found the mud and thatch house where Philip lived. He was still in bed. After hammering on the door the reluctant mason appeared. He informed me that his conditions of service did not include work on Sunday. I informed him that if he was not out in five minutes he would no longer be in any service.

Whilst all this was going on a crowd had gathered round Anne Riggs. The children had never before seen a white woman at such close quarters and were gazing at her with rapt curiosity. Anne was a lady of exquisite manners. Suddenly, wide-eyed, she threw back her head and let out a sound, half-scream, half the sort of howl said to be heard only when the moon is full. The circle fell back as a second wild scream came from the lady normally so charming and correct. From the front of her dress, which reached almost to the ground, crawled a little baby of perhaps eighteen months. The baby had crawled through the crowd and under Anne's skirt and then had stood up. It was several minutes before Anne recovered from the shock of feeling what turned out to be a tiny hand in the most intimate of places.

By the time I got back to the site it was almost 10 o'clock but work was finally under way and I reckoned that we had an even chance of finishing the footing before dusk. Then came the next commotion. We were busily engaged on the work on the riverbed when suddenly we heard an angry shout above our heads. Stan and I looked up to see Father McGettrick, Parish Priest of St Mary's Awgu, red hair and white soutane streaming in the breeze, striding the embankment like an avenging angel. 'Ye should be ashamed of yerselves, the both of ye,' he shouted. 'Ye should be in church setting an example and here ye are doing the divil's work on the Sabbath day.' I explained that if we did not get in the foundations before the rain, the work would be stopped for a year. Father was having none of this. He had waited in church but no one had turned up for mass. Then he discovered that the DO had turned out all his parishioners to work on the bridge instead. He was seething.

Normally we and the Holy Ghost Missionary fathers were the best of friends. The Riggses, Father Coleman and I often played bridge or canasta together. But there was no appeasing the parish priest of St Mary's on this occasion. I had not realized until then what good church-going people the Riggses were. In fact after his retirement from the Colonial Service Stan became an Anglican priest and served for many years in the Diocese of Worcester. To my disbelieving ears, Stan suddenly said 'I think that Father is right. We should stop work and keep holy the Sabbath day.'

It was my turn to get angry. I said that on no account would we stop work. We owed it to the people of Obuoffia and Onuoffia to finish the foundations of the bridge before the rains intervened, and that was what we were going to do. As for Father McGettrick, I told him that we tried to render unto God what was God's but this was Caesar's work and he must stop trying to interfere in it. The parish priest stormed off muttering that no good would come of the divil's work. But we finished the bridge and a few months later opened it to great fanfare and rejoicing.

Once each month I drove the 36 miles to Enugu to buy my case of beer, my bottle of whisky and essential stores like soap and salt and Angostura Bitters and to have my car serviced at the SCOA service station. On the way back I often broke my journey in Udi where Norman Perkins was the DO. Norman usually invited me to tea. On one visit Norman's ADO, Emeka Ojukwu, joined us. I had met Ojukwu in London and of course I had met his father during the frenetic Election Day in Nnewi in 1954. Norman said 'Emeka here is talking about joining the Army. He won't listen to me. You talk to him, Frank, he may listen to you.' Norman was a dedicated Administrative Officer. He had served five years in the British Army. It was incomprehensible to him that anyone should consider leaving the Administration for the Army. I told Emeka that my understanding was that there were only four Nigerian officers of senior rank in the Nigerian Army and that of those four only one was from the Eastern Region. I thought that from a career point of view this was just the right time to join the army and I thought that he was making exactly the right choice. That was my only and unfortunate contribution to Nigeria's civil war.

In October of that year the Chief Justice of Eastern Nigeria, Sir John Ainley, came to Awgu to hear a number of appeals to the High Court. Sir John stayed in the Rest House next door and one night I invited him for a meal. After dinner he began to tell me about one of the interesting cases that he had heard that day. The case was a land case that initially had been appealed from the District Officer's court. 'A young ADO' had tried the case. Sir John said with a smile that actually the ADO had gone to considerable pains to try to unravel the facts. I knew of course the 'actually' would be followed by an account of some howler made by the ADO and then it dawned on me that the ADO in question was me! The case was that which had given me so much trouble when I had visited Awgu on loan from Onitsha. I did not 'let on', as we say in Brinscall, and Sir John went on to explain that of course he had had to set aside the ADO's judgment. He conceded that this judgement may well have provided the best solution to a dispute likely to run and run but it was what was called a 'constructive' judgment and there was no provision for that in English law. Solomon may have offered to cut the baby in half but in English law the baby belonged either to one party or the other. At least that is my recollection of Sir John's disquisition. I nodded sagely at the shortcomings of young ADOs and offered another whisky.

In the opinion of many, the Awgu District Community Hospital was the most successful community development project ever completed in the Eastern Region of Nigeria. The project had been conceived and implemented by Dennis Gibbs who had preceded Peter Grant as DO. Denis's wife Erica, who was a doctor, had acted as medical consultant to the project. One village had collected the sand, another the stone and another had contributed manual labour during construction. Denis had worked from morning to night on the project for almost two years. There had been enormous problems to overcome but in 1953 a new cottage hospital with three wards, an operating theatre and running water was opened by the Governor. One of Denis's master strokes was to entrust the operation of the hospital not to the regional or local government but to a voluntary organization, the Sisters of the Holy Rosary, an order of Roman Catholic nuns.

All this happened a long time ago. In the sixties the Biafran war swept through Awgu, which was the centre of some heavy fighting. In the seventies I returned to Nigeria as a British diplomat. When we got the chance Anne and I visited the former Eastern Region. In Awgu we visited first the old house and then the hospital. The Holy Rosary Sisters were long gone and the present matron was an Indian lady. In Nigeria's demanding climate paint peels and colours quickly fade but everything was spick and span. At the entrance to the hospital was the brass plaque, newly polished, that had been unveiled by Sir Clem Pleass in 1955. The matron said that without any orders from her a worker polished the plaque every morning without fail. The plaque gave the date of the opening of the hospital and then read:

> This hospital was built by the people of Awgu Division and their District Officer, D.R.Gibbs.

I took a photograph of the plaque and sent it to Denis Gibbs, then living in Monserrat. Denis had had a stroke but Erica wrote to say how thrilled he was to know that he was so well remembered in Awgu.

Whilst Anne was looking round the hospital I went in search of the bridge. I made my way to the village that had lived in the memory for so many years. Had the bridge that was to last a thousand years survived even ten? At last we rounded a bend in the road above the river Offia. I gazed in disbelief at the sight below. There where my bridge had stood was, of all things, a Bailey bridge! I parked the Range Rover and walked to the middle of the bridge. Upstream some women were washing clothes. Downstream the vegetation on each bank was so thick that you could hardly see the water. In the dry season the river had shrunk to a mere stream. I leaned over the parapet to see what was below but the elephant grass made it impossible to see under the bridge.

At this point a jeep of the Nigerian Army screeched to a halt behind me. Out jumped a Corporal followed by his driver, a Private. 'What you lookin' at?' demanded the Corporal. I said that I was looking for a bridge. As a matter of fact I was looking for a bridge that I had built. 'You no lookin' for bridge. You lookin' for de neked women,' barked the Corporal. The conversation developed into a bad-tempered exchange in which the Corporal insisted that there was no bridge and I replied with equal vehemence that beneath the superfluous structure of the Bailey bridge was a bridge that would last a thousand years. The Corporal assumed the expression of one who knew that all white men were potty but that the one he was dealing with was completely off his trolley. Warming to my theme I said that not only was there a bridge but in the concrete abutment below were engraved the initials of the two men who built it: FK and SR. I ordered the Corporal to follow me.

As we plunged down through the elephant grass the thought did occur that if there was no bridge I was going to be in something of a pickle. I should not have been of such little faith. We pushed back the grass and there, six inches below the Bailey, was THE BRIDGE. For me this was better than the peak in Darien. There still visible in the concrete were the initials: FK and SR. The Corporal could hardly believe *his* eyes. When he had recovered, he became almost friendly. Following the civil war, he said, the Army had maintained a base for armoured vehicles in the area between Obuoffia and Onuoffia. He thought that the Army must have built the Bailey to protect my bridge from damage. I told him with suitable condescension that my bridge had been specifically designed to withstand the weight of a tank. The Corporal climbed back in his Jeep and drove off shaking his head. He had been right all along about white men.

CHAPTER 10

1957: Nether parts

IN MARCH 1957 ANNE AND I were married in the church of St Peter and Paul in the village of Mawdesley. It was a bright day in early spring and never was there a more beautiful bride. By common consent it was a most enjoyable wedding. Anne's sister, Christine, and my sister, Dorothy, and one of Anne's cousins were bridesmaids. My best man was my brother, Michael. Brother Jack, Leo Alston and Herbert McCabe officiated along with the dear old parish priest. Anne's brother, Tom, made a witty speech on his father's behalf. Relatives, friends of the family and from school and university turned up in large numbers to celebrate the occasion.

In April we packed our wedding presents and sailed from Liverpool to Lagos on the Elder Dempster liner, MV *Apapa*. We travelled in luxury and enjoyed the food and the entertainment. On arrival in Lagos we were invited to lunch by the Governor-General, Sir James Robertson. Before lunch the Governor called for a bottle of champagne and everyone drank Anne's health. When Anne told her that we were bound for Ahoada where I was to be District Officer, Lady Robertson commented, 'Oh well, dear, look at it this way; after Ahoada it can only get better!'

Nigeria's railway line followed the contours of a wish-bone. One track travelled north from Lagos through the western part of the country for a distance of several hundred miles to Kaduna Junction. Then a spur travelled all the way south via Kafanchan and Makurdi to Enugu and Port Harcourt. The journey from Lagos to Port Harcourt took over two days.

Anne and I were the only passengers in what was called the first class section of the train. We jogged slowly north through mile after mile of scrub land. During the day time the train was uncomfortably hot. But if you opened the window flakes of soot blew in from the steam locomotive in front. By the second day we had crossed the Benue River and entered the Eastern Region. As the sun began to sink we pulled out of Enugu and began the last stretch of the journey to Port Harcourt.

About thirty minutes out of Enugu the guard came along the corridor and entered our carriage. 'Please, Madam,' he said, pointing to Anne, 'Come.' He made clear that it was Anne who was wanted and not me. Anne followed the guard along the swaying corridor through several carriages until she reached the third class section, crowded with people, their luggage and, in some cases, their animals. On the floor of one of these carriages sat a young woman with legs spread and a baby half delivered. We had been in Africa less than a week.

Anne hastened back to our carriage to explain the crisis. I must do something she said. I made my way to the back of the train. The relatives said that the baby had been stuck for sixteen hours and that the woman was going to die if she did not get help. Unhelpfully, I asked the guard why he had not called for assistance whilst the train was standing in Enugu station. He said that it was only now that he had been made aware of the seriousness of the young woman's situation.

As fortune would have it we were then approaching a part of the country that I knew well. I also knew that although there were no telephones in the area the railway stations along the Lagos-Port Harcourt railway were connected by telegraph. We were about forty minutes from Ndeaboh Halt but the light was already beginning to fade and once it was dark it would be impossible to get a message to the hospital in Awgu. On a scrap of paper I wrote out two messages. The first asked the station master, Ndeaboh, to send the second message to Sister Doctor Awgu from DO Kennedy and to ask the messenger to pedal as fast as he could. The second message told Sister Doctor that we had a medical emergency with a lady in childbirth on the Lagos-Port Harcourt train and that I was going to stop train at the Ndeaboh Halt. I would be grateful if she could send the Kit Car Ambulance to collect the lady.

The Guard stopped the train at the next village and we telegraphed both messages to the station master at Ndeaboh. Back on the train I told the young mother that her baby would soon be delivered in a fine hospital and that one of her relatives would accompany her when she left the train. I told the relative to take enough food for both of them for two days. Then I rejoined Anne in our swaying carriage in first class. We sat with fingers crossed.

It was pitch dark when the train slowed to a clanking halt at Ndeaboh. I could just make out the Ambulance Kit Car by the dimly lit level crossing. In the back were two Holy Rosary Sisters sitting one at each side of a stretcher. A hurricane lamp provided a faint gleam of light. After a hurried exchange of greetings we loaded the lady on to the stretcher and the Kit Car pulled away. The Station Master waved his flag and the train resumed its journey to Port Harcourt.

For a young bride who had been in Africa less than a week the incident was a startling introduction to colonial service life. Today people talk about colonialism as if it were one of the seven deadly sins, but things were not all bad in those distant days. The Guard had taken it for granted that the

DO's bride would help the mother in distress. I had no longer any legal authority in that area and had never before met either of the Station Masters. The Sisters set out in the dark on their errand of mercy because I had asked them to and because that is what they did. The young messenger cycled through the dusk as fast as he could pedal to help a person he would never see at the request of an official he would never meet. Money was never even thought about, let alone mentioned. The young mother in labour would never see us again. A group of individuals, all strangers to each other, just did what they could and went their separate ways. The baby, a little girl, was delivered safely. That girl, if still alive, is today a lady of fifty who may be quite unaware of the drama that surrounded her birth. The system worked because people trusted each other. I do not think that things always work out as well today either in Nigeria or in the United Kingdom.

I had been transferred from the happy hunting grounds of Onitsha Province to Rivers Province, or Port Harcourt Province, as it was soon to become. Compared to Nsukka and Awgu the area of the Niger Delta was a harsher and more demanding environment both climatically and politically. It was a time of rapid change. Shell BP was intensifying its search for oil and had decided to build a permanent base just north of Port Harcourt. One of my first jobs as DO Ahoada was to witness the agreements under which land was transferred from the traditional owners to the oil company. I accompanied the Dutch Surveyor as he marked out the land acquired for an industrial complex near the village of Umubiakani and that for the residential complex near Umukoroshe.

Ahoada was a large division which stretched from a border with Owerri in the north to Port Harcourt in the south and from the Niger in the west to the Imo river in the east. Roads tended to run from north to south. Travel from east to west was much more difficult because of the many rivers that flowed south into the Niger delta. Most of the inhabitants spoke a variant of Igbo called Ikwerre Igbo, though nearer to Owerri and Aba people spoke Igbo proper. In the south west of the division opposite the ancient trading post of Degema Hulk was the kingdom of Abua where the people spoke their own language.

We stayed in Port Harcourt for two days with the acting Resident, 'Syd' Walker and his charming wife. At dinner Anne sat bemused as a column of ants climbed up one leg of the table crossed the surface and marched down the opposite leg without anyone interrupting the meal or the conversation. The following day we collected a new car, a Volkswagen Beetle (which turned out to be much the best car that I have ever driven) and set off for Ahoada.

Anne at rear of DO's house. Ahoada, 1958

The residence in Ahoada was a low bungalow consisting of bedroom, sitting room and dining room. In the dining room was a roughly carpentered table, six wooden chairs and a sideboard. There was no other furniture that I recall. There were wooden shutters at the windows but no curtains. There were no beds and we had to unpack our two camp beds and mosquito nets before we could go to bed.

We were met on arrival by the Chief Clerk, Mr John Gospel Ikiriko and the finance clerk, Mr Uweme. Mr Ikiriko was irrepressibly cheerful however bleak the outlook and on the evening of our arrival the outlook was bleak. He organized the lighting of a pressure Tilley lamp and introduced to us a man who offered to be our cook. Alfred became a valued member of the household but we had to find our own steward and assistant steward.

Gradually Anne fashioned a home in the watery waste land. Through John Gospel Ikiriko we ordered the construction of four armchairs from the village carpenter and cushions to fit from the tailor. Anne bought some cloth and made curtains. From the Prison we ordered a large, square cocoanut matting carpet. It was ten weeks in the making but everyone pronounced the finished article a fine carpet. Each evening Anne set the table with the silver and candelabra that we had received as wedding presents and served delicious meals.

Unless it was pouring with rain, which in the long rainy season it often was, Ahoada's climate was hot and humid. The temperature never varied much, night or day, from the high eighties to the low nineties. The low cloud cover kept humidity high. Shoes would turn green with mould overnight and we used to light lamps in the base of our cupboards to try to keep clothes from rotting in the damp. Instead of rotting I managed by this method to burn my best blue suit.

In the first weeks I travelled round the Division as much as I could, hearing court cases, visiting local government councils and hearing complaints. Until you knew the Division and, even more important, until the Division knew you, you could not hope to do the job of a District Officer. People were prepared to trust their DO but they needed to know that he was there.

Our first tour was to Etche where Alfred surprised Anne by baking two loaves within hours of our arrival using two empty kerosene tins as an oven. We went to Isoba, the headquarters of Ikwerre District Council where one evening we entertained two friends from Port Harcourt, one of whom, Eric Thomas, was to become the Godfather of our eldest daughter. Years later Eric and our other guest, Vic Morandi, used to talk about the beautiful meal that Anne had served that evening by candlelight on the verandah of the Isoba rest house. Two weeks later we stayed in a rest house by Opi Native Court which was only some eleven miles from the centre of Port Harcourt. Anne had to bathe in conditions of minimal privacy. One afternoon she put on a dressing gown and after a second of wide-eyed horror screamed 'Get it off, get it off.' The dressing gown fell open to reveal a lizard on her breast, one little lizard hand clutching a nipple. The beast fell to the ground and scuttled away.

Ahoada probably had in train a greater number of community development projects than any other division in the country. The reason for this was that my predecessor but one was a remarkably energetic Administrative Officer named Stan King who was a committed Community Developer. Unfortunately, without Stan's drive and leadership many of the projects had never reached completion. In some cases the village or community had lost interest; in other cases the projects had turned out to be too ambitious for the resources available. All over the division there were half finished bridges, community halls and feeder roads. I carried out an audit and reckoned there were 34 unfinished projects, the cost of completing which would far exceed our overspent community development budget. My old friend, Peter Grant, now Community Development Secretary and ultimately responsible for that budget, was not amused when I explained the situation. Of the 34 I made a short list of six that I judged needed to be completed urgently. Another six I thought could be completed as and when further funds became available. The rest I allowed to fall into abeyance to be resurrected only if the communities themselves showed a greater interest in completing them.

The first priority I gave to a Bailey bridge project on a road north of Omoku. That we finished, not without difficulty, in three months. Stan Riggs came down from Awgu to launch the bridge. Another town called, if I remember aright, Obelle, gave me endless trouble. This town, which was a few miles from Isiokpu in the centre of the Division had not one but two unfinished community development projects. At one end of the village square was a partially built town hall; at the other end a partially built maternity home. The women favoured the maternity hall over the town hall, the village elders the reverse. There had been no work on either project for a year and a half. After various delegations and correspondence I agreed to attend a mass meeting at five o'clock one evening when all parties would attempt to reach some sort of agreement.

Two or three hundred people turned up for the public meeting. Each party presented its case. I reminded them that the projects were expensive in terms of cement and skilled labour the cost of which government was meeting. Funds were available to resume work on one but not on both of the projects. Once the first project was finished I would do my best to secure funds for the second from a future budget. The public meeting adjourned so that the two groups could negotiate in private.

After forty minutes noisy 'consultation' the senior Chief rose to say that they had had a long and difficult discussion. The town needed both projects but since only one could be completed with the funds immediately available they had decided to make the town hall first priority. This was greeted by vigorous nodding and sounds of assent from the men but by a number of 'Tchah!'s and a rumble of dissent from the women. A tall woman with striking features rose to her feet. She surveyed the crowd, hitched her 'lappa' around her waist and launched into a diatribe delivered with icy disdain. What the town needed was not another talking shop for men but a maternity home. That was what the women needed and insisted upon having. They would never agree to anything else taking priority. They would not be moved from this position by anything that the men might say, the Chief might say or 'DO Kanada' might say. To make sure I had got the point she added with a glance in my direction, 'What de white boy says, I spit on am.' and she spat in the sand. She was not the only one who was spitting. The meeting broke up in disagreement.

We got in the Landrover and drove off. I was seething. 'White boy' indeed! 'Who was that woman?' I asked Mr Ikiriko. The woman's name, he said, was Clara Jack.

In Ahoada I continued the practice of having 'petition time' every day at 11 o'clock. One Saturday, at quarter to twelve, Mr Ikiriko said 'Petitions finished, Sir. Can close office.' The office was a low building with wooden louvres. I pointed through the open window to a women dressed in tattered clothing. She was sitting under a tree with a baby playing by her side. 'Don't mind her, Sir, she is crazy woman.' But I insisted on going to speak to her. Mr Ikiriko and Mr Iheanacho accompanied me. Every Saturday the woman walked seven miles to Ahoada with her baby, waited patiently through the morning and then walked seven miles home. Mr Ikiriko said that the woman had been crazy since the delivery of her child and was suffering from some sort of post parturition depression. I asked the woman what she wanted. She said that her child was ill but would be cured if she could see the Queen. (Eze nwanye, woman king as the Igbos translated the title.) I explained that although the Queen was Queen of Nigeria her palace was in London many thousands of miles across the sea. It was not possible for me to arrange for her to see the Queen. The woman repeated that she needed to see the Queen so that her baby would be cured. Once the Queen saw her she would understand.

Each week the woman came and sat under the tree and each week I said that it was impossible for her to see the Queen. I begged her to stop making the long weekly journeys but she simply repeated that she knew that the Queen would help her.

I remembered that some weeks earlier I had received a letter from a man in Isiokpa complaining that an enemy in the village was making bad mischief against him. The enemy, he said, had stolen a photograph of him from his trunk and at night behind closed doors was holding the photograph over the flame of a paraffin lamp. This man, said the writer, 'is oxidizing my nether parts.' If the magic did not stop he would surely die. I gave orders that the next time a police constable was in the area he should get the two men together and warn both against the use of violence, physical or psychic.

I wondered whether the doll and pins technique might be put to benign as well as malign use. One Saturday I took a photograph of the lady and her baby. When she came the following week and took up her usual position under the tree I showed her the photograph. She was astonished. Although it was too far for her to travel over the seas to Buckingham Palace I said that I was going to send her picture to the Queen. When she saw her picture the Queen would know at once what was in her mind and what her baby needed. I gave one copy of the photograph for the lady to keep. The second copy I said that I would send to the Queen. The woman nodded with the air of one who never ceases to wonder at the time it takes for the penny to drop with men. 'Ah hah!' she said. 'That is good. I thank you, DO.' She picked up her child and started the long walk home. I never saw her again.

At the beginning of February 1958 our old friend, William Hoole, and his wife came to stay with us for the weekend. On Sunday morning we played a rubber of bridge. Looking over my shoulder through the open door Bill said, 'I think that there are some people to see you.' I said that they would be on their way home from church. After a while Bill said, 'There are some more people. They seem to be looking for you.' I went to the gate to speak to them. That was how the riots began in Ahoada.

The period 1955 to 1957 had been difficult. As Independence approached relations between the regions and between the Eastern Region and the Federal Authority and between the colonial government and some of Nigeria's political parties had come under increasing strain. There were fears that the centrifugal forces might split the country apart.[1] To accommodate some of the forces Britain decided to grant internal self government to the Western and Eastern Regions in advance of that to the Northern Region.

There was intense competition between the NCNC party in the east led by Dr Nnamdi Azikiwe and the Action Group party in the west led by Chief Obafemi Awolowo. The wealthier Western Region had introduced free primary education and in the recent election campaign Nnamdi Azikiwe's had pledged that he would do the same in the Eastern Region. UPE, Universal Primary Education, had been the main slogan of the election campaign. The government's financial advisers warned that the government of the Eastern Region would not have the resources to implement the pledge. The warnings were ignored and some in the Colonial Office with whom Dr Azikiwe had only recently emerged from a bruising dispute over his personal finances and the African Continental Bank might not have been unduly distressed to see this difficult politician come a cropper.

As the year 1957 progressed it became clear that the cost of providing free primary education would far exceed forecasts. Once fees were abolished the number of children registering for the first class rocketed. The budget deficit soared. By the end of the year the administration faced bankruptcy. They had no choice but to reintroduce fees for the school year beginning January 1958. They did so for all classes except the first. A wave of anger swept through the Region.

Even today the gap between the demand for education and the financial resources to meet that demand is the most intractable problem faced by

---

[1] viz 'The Eastern Crisis of 1955–57' by Martin Lynn, *Journal of Imperial and Commonwealth History*.

the governments of many developing countries. Nowhere was the demand for education stronger than in Eastern Nigeria. In the nineteen fifties the burden of paying school fees had fallen in many cases to the mother of the family. It was the women who would suffer most from the reintroduction of fees. They believed that they had been betrayed by politicians who were feathering their own nests and who had broken the one election promise that was important to women. Igbo women were often the leaders in public protest. They had led the tax riots of 1929 and they led the education riots of 1958.

My first concern on that Sunday morning in 1958 was for the staff and Councillors of Etche District Council. By the roundabout route we were forced to travel Etche was some 90 miles away. A round trip took the best part of five hours. Bill Hoole and his wife packed up to return to Onitsha and I set off for Etche. Anne was four months pregnant and I was very anxious not to leave her alone in Ahoada, which was bound to be at the centre of the coming demonstrations. Although she was very reluctant to leave I persuaded her to stay for a few days with the young Californian doctor and his wife at the Seventh Day Adventist Hospital a few miles down the road. With the doctor's permission I parked our Volkswagen beetle at his hospital. I was afraid that the DO's car would be too tempting a target for a demonstrator to resist.

Although the effective strength of the police unit in Ahoada was less than 20 constables at the time I took with me to Etche one lance corporal and three constables. I told the lance corporal that his job was to protect first the staff and their families and then the property of the District Council but that he and his men would have to do so by persuasion. They should on no account try to use force. I told the Secretary of the Council that I would come back the following morning but that after that they would be on their own for several days.

Two weeks earlier two Nigerian ADO cadets had joined my staff. It was my job to train them. One, Akkio Abbey, was a former teacher, newly arrived from Ibadan University College. The other, T. Achi Kanu, had just graduated from Fourah Bay College in Sierra Leone. The next few weeks were for them an abrupt and at times frightening introduction to their new career. I put Akkio Abbey in charge of office security. In particular I instructed him to keep a detailed record of what happened in the coming days. I knew how fallible memories could be and wanted to have a reliable chronicle of events in case we were required to appear before public inquiries or courts of law. Achi Kanu was to help me with visits to outlying parts of the division.

A State of Emergency was declared in the divisions of the Eastern Region. By the beginning of March the Emergency measures had been lifted in all divisions except Ahoada. Under the decrees democratic processes were suspended and the divisions in effect returned to direct rule. Exceptional powers were vested in the Divisional Officer, including the power to requisition transport and impose curfews. The DO was responsible directly to the Governor for the period of the emergency. I made frequent use of some of the powers.

Late on Sunday half a riot unit of police, twenty five men, under the command of Assistant Superintendent Hyacinth Ohanu, arrived from Port Harcourt on temporary posting to Ahoada. The unit was accommodated in the barracks. For ASP Ohanu we put up a camp bed on the verandah of our dining room. It was a pleasure to work with Hyacinth Ohanu and we soon developed a perfect understanding. Without ASP Ohanu things might have turned out very differently in Ahoada in February 1958.

Early Monday morning I set off for Etche with Hyacinth Ohanu whilst Achi Kanu made for Isoba, the headquarters of Ikwerre District Council. The Lance Corporal I had left in Etche turned out to be a natural comedian entertaining crowds of women as they came to demonstrate and joining in their ceremonial dances. He apologized for not being in uniform when I arrived. I assured him that whatever he was doing was right by me and that he should continue in the same way. The Council staff and their families in this isolated outpost were full of thanks for the support that we had given them.

We had arrived in Etche just in time to intercept a crowd of 200 or more women on their way to the Council headquarters. Our vehicle practically blocked the narrow road with thick bush on each side. I climbed on the bonnet of the Landrover and Hyacinth interpreted. The exchange that followed was to be repeated many times in the coming days. The women denounced the politicians for their greed and false promises. I explained that the full implementation of UPE had been postponed but not abandoned. Any child who had started school the previous year would still receive education free of charge. The women told me to stop trying to protect the scoundrels who were their politicians. They had no quarrel with the DO. 'No,' cried a section of the crowd, 'tell the Queen we want to return to colonial rule.' I said that I understood their disappointment but I was their DO and was there to tell them that they must not break the law or damage Council property. The women said that each quarter of the village had given their word that they would demonstrate against their politicians. We reached a compromise. I would allow them to proceed with the demonstration and they gave me their assurance that they would do no damage. That is what happened.

We got back to Ahoada by mid afternoon and an hour or so later an agitated Achi Kanu and party arrived back from Isoba. I asked Achi how things had gone. 'Danger and doom, Sir,' Achi intoned. 'Nothing but danger and doom.' Despite the best efforts of Achi and his little band of policemen a crowd of women had ransacked the offices of Ikwerre District Council and dragged the furniture into the compound. They had then danced round a bonfire of the piled desks and chairs jeering at the local councillors. At that moment, said Achi, I felt a tug and saw my government-issue pocket diary snatched from my pocket and flung onto the blaze. I said at once: 'Theft of government property, criminal offence section 42, paragraph 33, Laws of Nigeria.'

As I struggled to contain the disturbances in Ahoada division my first thought was to determine how they were organized. Was there a central planning committee? Were directions passed through the political parties or the unions or the cultural associations? Or were the demonstrations erupting more or less spontaneously as the women of one community followed the example of their neighbours? I never did find out. Each night I sent a situation report to the Acting Governor with copies to the Provincial Police Commissioner and the Provincial Secretary. The Acting Governor sent me a note expressing appreciation for the reports but I never received any intelligence in return. If Special Branch had briefed the regional government on how the protest was organized the information was not passed on to the administrative officers in the field.

My second thought was that if I was to get a handle on things in a division as large as Ahoada I would have to establish some sort of control over the division's transportation network. This was not an easy proposition. Ahoada was an administrative hub on the Ahoada River. Roads entered the town from the four points of the compass. On the outskirts of the town the District Office and the Council Offices lay on one side of the road to Abua. On the other side of the road were the Residence, the staff houses, the Police quarters and the Prison.

When night fell on the Monday evening I sent out police patrols to reconnoitre the roads entering the town and discourage movement along them. Lorry drivers were doing a brisk trade transporting large numbers of women in preparation for demonstrations in Ahoada the following day. We worked through the night, the police keeping watch in shifts. Our cook, Alfred, brought me a thermos flask of soup which he replenished from time to time.

By 7.00 a.m. on Tuesday morning sizeable crowds of women were drifting into the township. I talked to the crowds and tried with varying success to persuade them that they had made their protest and should now go home. I ventured as far as Elele, 11 miles away and Elele Alimini, 5 miles away but dare not expose Ahoada township by going further afield. Among the crowd at Elele and two hours later in the crowd at Elele Alimini I noticed a familiar face, that of Clara Jack.

During the morning I began to receive written messages from Chief Jackson Mpi, Chairman of Ikwerre District Council, a prominent churchman and leading citizen. Chief Jackson had recently finished building an impressive new house in Isiokpu. The messages begged me to come at once and rescue him from a threatening crowd. Each time I replied that I would come shortly and that in the meantime he should not attempt to resist by force. I also received plaintive little notes from a timber merchant in Isiokpu named Sid Kennedy. The notes said that he was receiving large numbers of unwelcome visitors and that the sight of a friendly face would be most welcome. I replied that I would certainly come and that in the meantime he should keep talking to his visitors. By noon Chief Mpi's messages had become frantic. One said that he was sitting on the first floor of his house with a shot gun across his knee which he would certainly fire if the crowd attempted to force their way in. I was still facing large crowds and dare not leave the station. I sent a police corporal and two constables in a Landrover to rescue Chief Mpi. I ordered the corporal to drag him out by force if necessary. An hour later a grumpy but shaken Chief arrived in Ahoada and Mrs Akkio Abbey kindly agreed to put him up for the night.

By 4.00 p.m. the situation in Ahoada had quietened down. Crowds of women were still drifting around but the crowds were smaller and as the sun declined people were beginning to think of the preparation of the evening meal. I decided that it was safe enough to risk an expedition to Isiokpu, 25 miles away. ASP Ohanu loaded his men into the five ton lorry and we and a sergeant climbed into a Landrover. The sergeant brought along five canisters of tear gas. We drove straight to Chief Jackson Mpi's house, which was located some hundred yards up a narrow, earth road off the main Owerri–Port Harcourt road.

We came on an extraordinary scene. Hundreds of women were swarming all over the house and the compound outside. Every bit of moveable furniture and fixtures had been dragged out of the house and flung on to a pile. Women were excitedly plundering every room on every floor of the house. Some were even hacking away with matchets at the corners of the house in an attempt to fell the building completely. Who was standing on top of the pile of furniture, eyes flashing and waving a bottle of kerosene, but Clara Jack? The women were so engrossed in what they were doing that they did not notice our arrival. I threaded my way through the mob and into the house and standing at the foot of the stairs yelled, 'Out, out, everybody out'. The crowd stopped in mid air as it were. They could hardly believe how I came to be there. After a second's pause they started to clatter down the stairs and within a few minutes we had completely cleared the house and the compound and closed the large iron gates.

It was at that point that everything started to go wrong. As we formed up in the narrow road in front of the house a large number of the women faced us from the direction of the main road and the rest from the little side road. We had in effect divided the mob into two groups. Hyacinth Ohanu's men cleared the road for a distance of some twenty yards. When he turned to push back the other group the first lot edged back to their original position. All the time the women were becoming bolder. They had overcome their terror at the shock of our arrival and the volume of abuse from such as Clara Jack was rising. Hyacinth tried a baton charge in each direction having first thrown a tear gas canister. They did not work. We faced two problems. When we charged in the direction of the main road the women fell back but eventually regrouped because their homes lay in the opposite direction up the side road. When we charged in the direction of the side road the women fell back but would not disperse and abandon their 'sisters'. As luck would have it a strong breeze was blowing from the direction of the side road. When we threw a tear gas canister we charged into our own tear gas and as far as I could see were its only casualties. When we threw a second canister one woman ran forward and threw it back at us. The situation threatened to spin out of control. If we cut and ran the mob would resume their demolition of the building and of our authority. If we stayed we were not going to hold the mob much longer. I told Hyacinth to have the lorry and the Landrover turned round and reversed quietly up the side road as near to us as they could reach. We divided the police into two. Twelve constables formed a line facing the crowd at the side road. The other twelve I formed into a snatch squad. I drilled six pairs of constables so that each pair identified one of the leaders of the group backing on to the main road. I told the constables that they must concentrate on that particular person and no other. I made one more futile appeal to the women to go home and then in the noise and clamour we made a last charge in the direction of the side road whilst the snatch squad charged towards the main road picking up the six targets as they went and bundling them into the back of the lorry. We managed to get all the police into the lorry and the lorry on its way before the crowd quite knew what was happening. Finally, Hyacinth and I and the sergeant raced for the Landrover and drove off. The lorry went straight to Ahoada whilst

I directed the landrover to Sid Kennedy's establishment a few miles further down the road. We found Sid gently swinging in a hammock and sipping Johnny Walker Black Label. He had survived repeated visits by chatting to the demonstrators and distributing five pound notes to their leaders. After sharing a whisky each we set off on our return journey. At the junction of the main road an angry crowd of young men armed with staves was waiting for us. With much yelling I persuaded the driver of the Landrover to steer straight at the crowd and accelerate through a hail of staves and other projectiles.

When we got back to Ahoada I was surprised to discover that news of the incident at Isiokpu had preceded us. I had known that the reaction would be strong. I had not expected it to be so swift. A small group of women had marched on the prison and demanded the release of their sisters from Isiokpu. Achi Kanu had barred their way with a small contingent of eleven policemen and had managed finally to persuade the women to go home. Achi was alarmed, as he had every right to be. 'Attack on Her Majesty's prison,' he had told the women, 'High treason. Laws of Nigeria Chapter 42, article 18.' I told Achi that he had done very, very well.

It was by now completely dark. I asked Mr Ikiriko to hire a lorry as discreetly as he could from a reliable source in the town. I did not want to use our lorry with the official logo on the sides. I asked the Chief Warder to prepare the necessary documentation for the transfer to Port Harcourt prison of our six women prisoners. The lorry edged out of the compound at nine o' clock and I followed with Hyacinth Ohanu in the Landrover. We drove forty four miles to our Provincial headquarters and saw the prisoners safely behind the thick walls of Port Harcourt prison. Then Hyacinth and I drove to the house of Jock Rollo, Senior Superintendent of Police in charge of Port Harcourt Province. We knew that staying with him was Mr Leslie Brown, Deputy Commissioner of Police, Eastern Nigeria. Les had come from Enugu with a force of 300 police to assist Jock. We needed some of those policemen. Hyacinth and I discussed how we were going to tackle the two senior officers. It was decided that I should make the pitch.

Jock's wife, Anne, explained that the Deputy Commissioner and her husband were taking their baths. She offered us each a beer. We almost snatched the bottles from her hands. It was now after ten at night and we had had nothing to eat since morning and nothing to drink except Sid Kennedy's whisky. We were tucking into our Star beers when Les appeared in a dressing gown. He had not got half way down the stairs before he called out, 'If you have come to ask for reinforcements, there

With Senior Superintendent of Police, Jock Rollo, in Port Harcourt, 1959

aren't any.' He asked how many canisters of tear gas we had used that day. Four, I replied. Les said that in Diobu that day on the outskirts of Port Harcourt he had used over 130 canisters. Hyacinth and I exchanged glances but made no comment. Les went on to say that his instructions were to hold the towns and major centres of population. If he had to let the rural areas go, so be it.

I told the Deputy Commissioner that that was fine by me but I wanted it on record that I had warned what consequences were likely to flow from the decision. In Isiokpu we had taken six prisoners. There was certain to be a major reaction. The next day women would come in unprecedented numbers to force the release of their comrades. With only half a unit of 25 men I might be unable to prevent the District Headquarters from being overrun. I also said that if the prison came under attack I would have no option but arm the police. I would be tied down with no room for manoeuvre. I pointed out that if I had had a second half unit that day I would have been able to get to Isiokpu much earlier and we would not be in the difficult situation in which we found ourselves. Les observed drily that we should not have used our resources in dribs and drabs and I should not have left a contingent in Etche.

We climbed into the Landrover and before starting the engine stared for a moment into the dark. Addressing the windscreen Hyacinth remarked what a bloody successful meeting *that* had been. I asked him whether everybody in his service was as bloody-minded as his Deputy Commissioner.

It was well after midnight when we got back to Ahoada. Even at that time crowds were moving into the township. Patrols reported that lorries were still ferrying people into the town. I was particularly angry with the traffic on the Abua road where lorry drivers had ignored repeated warnings. I wanted to secure that area because it led to the rear of the station. I told the police patrol to give the drivers one last warning and if they still continued to ferry people to bring them in and to remove the distributor heads from their vehicles. Two hours later the patrol arrived with a driver. I told the driver that his vehicle was requisitioned and locked the distributor head in the safe. A little while later a second driver was brought in and his vehicle disabled. Hyacinth Ohanu doubted whether I would get away with the ploy but I was ready to take my chance in any tussle with the lawyers.

Around three o'clock in the morning I called off the patrols so that all the police could snatch a few hours sleep before the beginning of what was going to be a long and very hot day.

By 7.00 a.m. hundreds of women had already gathered in the vicinity of the District Office. By mid morning the number had grown to over 1,000 and by early afternoon I reckoned the crowd exceeded 2,000.

Around 8 o'clock as Hyacinth and I were discussing our tactics for the day we heard a squealing of brakes and shouting of orders. We went outside to see half a unit of police tumbling out of two lorries. A police Inspector saluted and reported for duty. Les Brown was possibly not such a bad sort after all.

In handling the riots in Ahoada I had several pieces of good fortune. The first was Assistant Superintendent of Police Hyacinth Ohanu. I had never met him before and we worked together for only six days but we hit it off immediately and for those six days worked as a perfect team. In all the din and confusion we never had a misunderstanding, each anticipating instinctively what the other would do and would need. I could not have had better support. The second stroke of luck was the battery operated loud hailer that the Inland Revenue, with quite other purposes in mind, had sent to me only the week before. The device was indispensable in controlling huge crowds. Our third great asset was the sun. In the area of the Niger Delta the dry season is brief but we were in the middle of it. All day from seven in the morning to five in the evening the sun beat down pitilessly. I made sure that the demonstrators stood in that sun hour after hour.

From the beginning I had trouble with the newly arrived Inspector of Police. We had lined up his men along the verge of the Abua road. Some

Assistant Superintendent of Police, Hyacinth Ohanu. Ahoada 1958

of the women were jeering and taunting the police constables. The Inspector announced that he was going to order a baton charge. This was the last thing that I needed. For one thing a charge would drive the women through the compound of my house in the direction of the prison. Secondly, I could hear ringing in my ears the words of Ian Jackson at Nnewi three years earlier, 'Sent in police 9.00 a.m. By 9.30, spent force.' It was just nine o'clock. I said that there would be no baton charge. The Inspector declared that if any woman touched his men he would 'strike them down' and he brought his swagger stick crashing through the air with a great swish.

All morning I repeatedly talked to the women, deploying the usual arguments. They argued back and demanded the release of their sisters. From time to time I pushed through the crowd and met demonstrators at the cross-roads at the entrance to the town and tried to dissuade them from joining their comrades. It was unbearably hot and some women grew weary and began the long trek home, but they were a minority. Most stayed and the crowd got larger and larger and more restive and bad-tempered. In the early afternoon as I was making one of the interminable appeals I noticed a car edging along the periphery of the crowd. I wondered who the bloody fool might be to risk his vehicle, which I noticed was a VW just like mine. A moment later I said with a start 'My God, it *is* mine!' There was Anne nosing through the crowd and waving at the women as though she were the Queen Mother on a State Visit. I rushed over to be told that she absolutely could not stay at the Seventh Adventist mission a moment longer. She was just dying for a cigarette. I implored her to lock the car away in the garage before it sustained any damage. I was told not to be so melodramatic.

By now the crowd were running out of patience and the leaders were stirring them up for direct action. I was determined to keep them in the sun at least until 5.00 p.m. but I was forced to play my last card. I said that there were no women from Isiokpu in the prison. This brought angry jeers and a roar of denial but I went on arguing the point. Finally I offered to prove the fact by taking their leader into the prison to see with her own eyes the truth of what I was saying if they could agree on who that leader should be. I told them to consult and chose a leader. This led to protracted wrangling. Eventually I said that I would take four delegates into the prison provided that I had a firm guarantee that the report of the delegates would be accepted. There was more arguing but in the end four representatives were nominated and agreed. Several times I repeated the question: would they accept the report of these delegates. They would. It was now approaching four o'clock and the crowd were a little quieter, clearly puzzled by the unexpected turn of events. I took the chosen four into the prison and had the Chief Warder escort them first round the men's section and then round the women's section of the prison. They soon came back and said that they were satisfied that their sisters were not there. I invited them to go anywhere they wished inside the prison and insisted that they make a second inspection of the women's department.

There was great excitement as we emerged from the prison. I refused anyone permission to speak until we had rejoined the main body of the crowd. Some of the women ran alongside us as we walked the short distance from the prison to the District Office. One or two of these women broke away and took a short cut running through the garden of my house where Anne was serving tea to two nervous Catholic missionaries who had turned up seeking reassurance. Anne said that when the women suddenly appeared running through the garden Father O'Brian had immediately dived under the dining room table expecting an onslaught that fortunately never materialized.

I invited the four representatives to speak in turn. They said their sisters were 'No der.' The announcement was met with blank incredulity. The crowd genuinely could not believe what they were being told. It must be some sort of trick, some of the crowd shouted. I reminded them of the terms on which the representatives had been allowed into the prison.

There was shouting and disagreement between one section and another but the prevailing opinion was that they should not move until their sisters had been released. It was now after five o'clock and I calculated that the police would be able to last the one and a half hours of daylight remaining. Most of the women were exhausted. All were hungry.

The government offices formed a sort of horseshoe. At the bend of the horseshoe I stationed the Landrover and climbed on the bonnet. We had tried all day to keep the women away from the offices. Now I encouraged them to come ever closer until they were packed like sardines against the office walls and filled every square inch of the space between the buildings.

I called for someone to interpret for me into Ikwerre Igbo since a majority of the crowd did not understand standard Igbo. No one moved. Even my own staff on the edge of the crowd looked at their feet but did not move. Eventually a man stepped forward. 'I will interpret for you, DO,' he said. It was Tom Ikweme, the County Council Treasurer. I had spent the last nine months fighting Tom who at the time was on bail awaiting trial on charges of embezzling £11,000 from the Council Treasury. He was a brave and brilliant interpreter.

For the last time I went through the set address. Their disappointment was appreciated. Their grievances would be redressed. Free primary education would be restored as soon as practicable. But now they had to go home. I pointed out how patient I had been but warned that if they did not disperse as soon as I had read a message from the Queen they would be dispersed forcibly. I then read the Riot Act, which Tom translated in great style into the Ikwerre language. Hyacinth had moved four of his men into designated positions in the crowd. I gave one last warning and at an agreed signal the four police quietly released four canisters of tear gas in the very centre of the crowd whilst the two units of police moved forward on the signal of the Inspector's whistle. The surprise was total. The crowd exploded in panic and struggled one with another to get away from the gas. At each signal of the whistle the police advanced fifty yards and halted. Within half an hour the whole area was clear. The last rays of light were disappearing. There was not a soul on the streets of Ahoada and not a sound to be heard. The women had crammed themselves into the houses of friends and strangers alike. No one had cooked or eaten. I patrolled the streets for a further half an hour until it was pitch dark then cancelled all patrols and stood down the rest of the police.

After eating the supper that Anne had prepared I collapsed in bed for the first time in three days and slept for a straight eleven hours.

The Commissioner of Police in Lagos reported each day to the Governor General on the situation in the East. On that day he wrote:

4 February. Ahoada: Women demonstrated but no violence.'[2]

That was not the end of the riots in Ahoada but it was the end of attempts to attack the divisional and county headquarters. I knew that from then on the initiative was ours. I could go in search of the demonstrators and tackle them on grounds of my choosing.

In the next few days we dispersed scores of crowds in any number of locations. We kept to the routine that had been successful in Ahoada township. I addressed the crowds. If they refused to move I read the Riot Act and at the pre-arranged signal Hyacinth's men rolled in the tear gas. At one gathering when I got to the end of the Riot Act and in the name of the Queen commanded the assembly to disperse peaceably to their homes the crowd, to our great surprise, did as they were bid and dispersed peaceably.

I was still puzzled by the ability of the demonstrators to mobilize huge crowds at short notice. The roads were now virtually clear of motorized transport. The carburettor head ploy had proved very effective. Even so, police patrols would report that the roads were clear to a distance of thirty miles and thirty minutes later I would be told that a crowd several hundred strong was gathering fifteen miles away. Finally the penny dropped. The demonstrators were not playing by my book. We were moving along the metalled roads but they were moving from one village to another by ancient paths that long preceded the modern roads. It was as though we were moving along the rim of a giant bicycle wheel but the demonstrators were moving up and down the spokes. We were on the periphery. They were at the hub. The women were being ferried on bicycles by scores of young men. When they intercepted such groups I instructed the police to remove the rubber valves from the bicycle tyres and throw them into the bush. Knowing how difficult it is to find a golf ball in the rough I reckoned that the owners would not find many of the valves.

At noon on the Friday the Inspector of police reported that for the first time since Sunday all roads were clear. He asked, 'What do we do now, Sir?' 'Now, Inspector,' I replied, 'you and I get Clara Jack.' After five days of non-stop mischief it was a fair bet that Clara was catching her breath at home. We drove to the deserted village and tracked down her house. I hammered on the door telling the Inspector to go round the back. He was too slow and when I heard a noise raced round the back to see Clara crashing through a plantation of maize. After a short chase I brought her down with a tackle and bundled her into the Landrover. We handed her over to the care of the Chief Warder of Ahoada Prison.

---

[2] Colonial Office Archives CO 554/1955. Disturbances in Eastern Nigeria.(CO 554/1955).

On Saturday morning after a brief skirmish on the Omoku road we visited Mr Ashirim Unosi who lived in a densely planted compound about four miles from Ahoada. Ashirim was the Chairman of the County Council. There had been several rumours that morning that he was to receive an unfriendly visitation. We arrived just as Ashirim's domestic servants were threading their way through the bush with armchairs and other items of furniture on their heads. I told them to turn round and take them back. Ashirim and I had not always been on good terms. We had spent much time at loggerheads over the administration of the County Council and in particular over the award of contracts. But all that was forgotten. I do not believe that anyone before or since has been as glad to see me as Ashirim Unosi was that Saturday morning. He did not actually kiss me but it was a close run thing. His relief knew no bounds. We celebrated the attack that did not happen by downing two cold beers.

Things did not always go our way. At first I had to go practically on bended knees to get extra police. But after two weeks when I no longer needed them they came unasked and in abundance. One day a whole riot unit of special service police turned up under the command of a young British Police officer. He and his men had been flown in by chartered aircraft from Lagos. To give him something to do I sent the unit on a patrol of an area of the division which until then I had not had time to visit. What exactly happened I never found out. After passing through the town of Omoku on the way up the young officer and his unit found themselves ambushed in the centre of the town on the way back. They had to fight a pitched battle to extricate themselves from the town square. After firing off a score of tear gas canisters and grenades the unit ran a gauntlet of 200 yards through a hail of missiles. In his report the Superintendent reported that 'so steadfast under fire' (i.e. *his*) fire were the crowd of demonstrators that he thought that there might have been men among them in disguise. In fact groups of young men did join in the fighting. The Superintendent swore to me that he and his men had done nothing to provoke the people of Omoku to this violence but I could never persuade myself that he was telling me the whole truth.

The other event that I remember of that day was of going to the house for a cup of tea with Anne and tuning in to listen to the five o'clock news on the BBC's overseas service. The third item on the headlines was a report of a riot that had occurred in the southern Nigeria town of Omoku earlier that afternoon. I was astonished. I could not even telephone Port Harcourt. The young officer had reported by radio to his boss in Lagos and someone in police or government headquarters had passed on the information to the BBC stringer. Two days later at my insistence we went back to Omoku with two hundred police in a show of strength.

In another unsatisfactory incident a British ADO who had volunteered to help me, found himself separated from his police and given some rough treatment in a free-for-all in a village some twenty miles away. It was a Saturday afternoon and I had sent him on what I thought was a quiet reconnaissance patrol with twenty five police and a newly arrived Inspector. I had met the Inspector only that morning but had had no reports of trouble from the village to be visited. I did stress to the ADO that the two things of crucial importance were for him to keep close to the Inspector and for them both to keep the police together as a unit. Around four o'clock a dishevelled and agitated ADO was back at my house saying that he must see me immediately. He was covered in dust, shirt in tatters, stockings around his ankles and stripped of wallet and watch. He had signed a note promising to get hospital treatment for someone allegedly injured by the police. He was most anxious that I should honour this pledge. I assured him that that was something that I was going to do without a moment's delay.

I mustered all the force that we had available and shortly after six set off for the village with fifty police in four lorries. It was pitch dark when we thundered into the village square. I lined up the four trucks and ordered the drivers to direct their headlights onto the mud walls of the village. For half an hour I had the Inspector in charge bawling out orders and the police unit marching and counter marching. The idea was to make the villagers think that a rather nasty regiment several times our size had arrived in the village. The trick seemed to work. When I ploughed into the middle of the village the young Chief appeared. He was profuse in his apologies. I said that I wanted three things: the cash, the watch and the ransom note that the ADO had been forced to sign. I was also going to collect the woman who had allegedly been injured.

The young Chief at once produced the note and the purse containing twelve shillings and sixpence. He made an abject apology for the fact that half of the strap of the wrist watch was missing. In the dark they had been unable to find it. I made a great to do of the missing bit of useless leather. This would not do at all, I said. I said that I would return the following morning with even more police and that I would give the village until then to produce the other half of the strap. I also insisted in carting off to hospital, much against her will, the old lady who had a swelling on her neck that she had obviously had for some time. But, I told the Chief, the crowd had said that the lady had been injured by police. They had demanded hospital treatment and that was what she was going to get. We drove back to Ahoada where I deposited the old lady at the Seventh Day Adventist Hospital and asked my friend Harold the Doctor as a favour to me to keep the lady in for seven days treatment.

The following morning just as I was about to leave Ahoada with three trucks and 50 police to continue the charade who should turn up but John Craig, the Acting Provincial Secretary, Port Harcourt. It was John who had asked me to let the ADO join me for a week even though I said that I did not need any additional help. John had obviously been alarmed by what the ADO had reported to him and had come to see the damage for himself. I invited him to join us on the morning expedition.

When we arrived in the village the Chief and elders were waiting in the square. I lined up the Police in three ranks and had the Inspector go through some parade drills. I then introduced John Craig. So serious had been the offence committed the previous afternoon, I said, that the Provincial Secretary had come in person to see the village for himself. I could see that John was beginning rather to enjoy it all and piled on the melodrama. With vague memories of the War of Jenkins Ear and, I hope, no trace of humour, I demanded the return of the missing half of the watch strap. This brought a slightly incredulous glance from my boss. The young Chief made his way forward through the crowd and with profuse and abject apology tendered, with arm outstretched, the scuffed bit of leather. John was most impressed. I was astonished.

My worst experience occurred when I visited a village a few miles from Elele Alimini. I took twenty five men in a lorry and a sergeant and four other men in the Landrover. Purely as a precaution I asked the sergeant to bring four canisters of tear gas.

The village could be reached only by a narrow earth road through thick bush. A few hundred yards from the village we were forced to halt. One of the timber cross pieces on a small wooden bridge was broken. There was no other way forward. The bridge would certainly not bear the weight of the lorry but we dismounted and managed to ease the Landrover across. I instructed the driver to turn round the lorry and reverse it as close as possible to the bridge so that it would be ready for a quick get-away on our return. With the sergeant and four constables we continued in the Landrover on our patrol.

The events of that morning seem in retrospect unreal. Even as they were happening I felt as though I had somehow become involved in the bizarre happenings of a Mack Sennet comedy. As luck would have it we emerged from the bush and entered the village square at the very moment and at the very spot that a crowd of some fifty or sixty youths were assembling to do battle – against us! With traditional markings on their cheeks and war garlands around their heads they were ready to fight. They were brandishing staves and chanting war cries. The sight of our little vehicle seemed to throw them into a fury. They seemed incensed and insulted to be confronted by a force as small as ours. With me frantically yelling in his ear and missiles hitting the cab from every direction the terrified driver drove through the middle of the crowd and into the centre of the empty square. Unfortunately there was no other exit. At the end of the clearing we made a screeching u-turn and came back in the direction that we had come. Again we ran the gauntlet through a hail of projectiles and screams of abuse. We got out of the square and headed down the little forest track with the youths in hot pursuit.

We squealed round the last bend before the bridge. There blocking our path was the lorry at the end of the bridge! Still facing in the wrong direction! Not a policeman in sight! Jumping out of the Landrover I shouted to the sergeant to bring the tear gas. 'Sorry, Sir,' said the sergeant. He had left the tear gas canisters in the lorry! I could already hear the beat of our approaching warriors. I did not know whether to throttle the sergeant, to weep or be sick.

I sent off the Landrover driver in search of the missing unit and lined up the four constables and the sergeant in line abreast across the narrow road with batons drawn. I issued stage directions for the comic performance to come. The advance party of the youths came jogging round the corner and ground to an uncertain halt at the sight of a white man and a line of five policemen with drawn batons. My one thought was that if we turned our backs we were done for. I went into a charade of parade ground drill. I bawled out the order 'Quick march!' The valiant coppers pretended to march but following my previous instructions advanced only inches. 'Halt!' The front line of the youths actually wavered. 'Quick march!' I repeated and so on. But luck was running out. More and more young men were arriving and shouting to those at the front the Igbo equivalent of 'Get on with it.' The youths looked in puzzlement from Landrover to lorry and from white man to batons of the thin blue line. Were they missing something or was this as ridiculous as it looked? Just as they prepared to make the charge that would finish us off there came at last the sweet sound of approaching cavalry. Our missing policemen came racing round the corner and I never saw a sight more welcome than that of those little blue grey uniforms. I just waved them on and they went on running in best Keystone Cops style past the truck, past the Landrover and past the brave little band of their brothers straight at the warrior youths, who turned and fled.

★   ★   ★

The 1958 riots were a major crisis in the governance of Nigeria's emerging democracy. In his despatch of 23 April to the Governor General and the Secretary of State for the Colonies, the Governor of the Eastern Region of Nigeria, Sir Robert Stapledon wrote:

> I think that we had to have an emergency sometime and we were lucky to have it sooner than later. While we narrowly escaped it getting out of hand we are healthier for having had it.

That was with the benefit of hindsight. Sir Robert and his colleagues in Lagos and in the Colonial Office in London had been less confident in the first nervous days of February when as one official observed, 'Ministers were quite hard to find, even in Enugu.'

Senior officials had been well aware by the end of 1957 that the train was heading for the buffers. They knew that the Regional government would be forced either to reintroduce school fees or scale back on expenditure on education. Nor had they forgotten that the imposition of a thirty shillings education rate had led to the Aba women's riots of 1929 when the rioters had forced the cancellation of the rate. Officials in Lagos and in London grumbled that the Federal authorities – the Police – were going to have to deal with the mess created by the incompetence of the newly independent Regional government. They supposed that the Police *would* succeed sooner or later in restoring order but did not know how far the disorder would spread or how long it would last.

The crisis of 1958 bit at several levels. It tested the relationship between federal and regional authority and that between a Nigerian government on the threshold of Independence and the Colonial Power. 'Bring back the Queen' was a frequent cry of the rioters. The crisis was also a test of the confidence of elected Nigerian politicians in their British officials and of the loyalty of those officials to a government in whose service they had enrolled only a few years before when they had transferred from Federal to Regional Government employment.

The circumstances of 1958 were exceptional since the riots occurred in that brief period between the grant of internal self government to the Western and Eastern Regions in 1957 and full Independence in 1960. The rioters were protesting against the policies of regional and local governments but challenging the Federal authority responsible for the maintenance of law and order. One of the principal instruments used in the management of the crisis was the declaration of a State of Emergency by the Federal Government but the agents who exercised the special powers under the emergency decrees were officers of the Regional administration.

Dr Nnamdi Azikiwe, Premier of the Eastern Region of Nigeria, visiting Ahoada in 1958

Another element in the crisis was the personality and position of the Premier of the Eastern Region and leader of the NCNC party, Dr Nnamdi Azikiwe. Though his power base was his Igbo homeland his ambition was always to lead an independent Nigeria and, to an extent that was not the case with all his rivals, his vision did embrace the whole nation. Some would say that Azikiwe's vision and ambition stemmed from the fact that he was himself a member of what would be called today the Igbo diaspora. He had been born in Zunguru in the Northern Region and his father was a railwayman from Onitsha. That was precisely what frightened many in the Northern Region. That Region's leaders were determined not to be dominated by the Igbos, a sizeable number of whom lived in the principal towns of their region.

Zik was one of the greatest of the first generation of the political leaders of independent African countries. A trained journalist, he was arguably the most accomplished speaker in a nation of orators. A man of great charisma he could also be vain, erratic, careless of detail and vindictive. A politician of outstanding promise, he never quite delivered the leadership that his country cried out for either in the crises of the fifties or the much greater calamities of the sixties.

Since 1955 Zik had been involved in running battles with his most senior British officials. The regional budget for that year had deliberately omitted provision for expatriate allowances for a number of senior administrative posts whose incumbents Zik wanted replaced. The Governor, Sir Clem Pleass, was forced to exercise his reserve powers to pass supplementary estimates.

More recently Zik had been the centre of a major row over his involvement in the Africa Confidential Bank, whose directors included several members of his family. The bank was said to be virtually insolvent and had been refused a licence in 1953 because it had failed to meet the requirements of the 1952 Banking Ordinance. At the direction of Dr Azikiwe's government, the Eastern Marketing Board transferred £2million to the ER Finance Corporation to enable it to purchase a majority of the shares of the bank and to deposit large sums, which not only rescued the bank from insolvency but, it was said, also helped to finance the NCNC's election campaign in Western Nigeria.

In response to a motion tabled by the Opposition in the Eastern House of Assembly the Governor appointed a Commission of Inquiry to look into the matter. Zik was hauled before the Forster Sutton Tribunal.

The findings of the Forster Sutton Tribunal must have come as a disappointment to some in the Colonial Office. Although the Governor, Sir Clem Pleass, and the Governor General, Sir James Robertson, were anxious to avoid making a martyr of Zik there were others in London who thought that the time was ripe for the troublesome politician to get his come-uppance. It did not happen. Although Zik had obviously been guilty of serious misconduct he was not found to be in breach of any specific law. He was not, it seemed, disqualified from holding office. As for the battle for public opinion in the East, Zik won that hands down. Addressing the Tribunal he said:

'Being black people does not mean that we are impervious to justice and decency. Being white people does not make colonial Governors paragons of perfection.'

The Tribunal censured the Premier, though in the understated terms beloved of the British. 'Dr Azikiwe's conduct with regard to the African Continental Bank,' said the Tribunal, 'had fallen short of the expectations of honest, reasonable people'. This was meat and drink to Zik. 'The Report of the Tribunal,' he riposted, 'had fallen short of the expectations of honest, reasonable people.' Now that he had been dragged by Colonial officials through an ordeal by fire, he said in a radio broadcast to the nation, the people would speak. He dissolved the House and in the election that followed won a thumping majority. Sir Clem Pleass went on leave never to return and a distinguished career came to a sad and bitter end.

These Olympian battles took place far above the heads of the officers serving in the field administration. Closer to home were the battles between Premier and Governor over the structure of the administration itself. Zik had insisted upon the abolition of the post of Resident, which he saw as a focus of Colonial power, even though with the approach of Independence the exodus of many of the most senior British administrative officers had already begun.[3] To weaken the structure further just as it was assuming the burdens of transitional government made no sense from an administrative view point but the government pushed through the reorganization despite the opposition of the Governor.'[4]

In 1957, after his re-election, the Premier proposed a further reorganization of the Provincial administration. The Governor was aghast at the prospect of yet another reorganization but the Colonial Office pointed out that since the Region was now self-governing there was no action the governor could take to block the proposed reform. 'This,' mused an official, 'is presumably what Regional Self Government means.'[5]

Under the new proposals the administration was to be concentrated into ten Provincial teams each under a Local Government Commissioner. Each team was to consist of a Provincial Commissioner who was an elected politician and a Provincial Secretary who was an administrative officer. The two were to be in a similar relationship to that of Minister and Permanent Secretary. In practice the Provincial Secretary exercised most of the functions previously exercised by the Resident and provided the essential link between the Divisional Officer and the Regional Government.

The Provincial Administration and the Police took the strain of the 1958 riots. The widespread breakdown of law and order that had been feared did not occur. The District Officers never lost control of their divisions. Relations between the Regional and Federal Governments emerged in better shape. The loyalty of British Officers in the field to their new political masters was demonstrated in dramatic fashion in the early weeks of 1958. From then on many elected politicians saw their Divisional Officers in a new light. There was some anecdotal evidence that even Zik was beginning to have second thoughts about the wisdom of abolishing the post of Resident.

---

[3] For an account of the staffing crisis in Nigeria caused by the exodus see Anthony Kirk-Greene's *On Crown Service*, pp 63 et seq.
[4] Colonial Office Archive CO554/1655 Self Government for the Eastern Region of Nigeria 1957–59.
[5] Colonial Office Archive CO 554/ 2129 Political Situation in the Eastern Region of Nigeria.

Chief Jackson Mpi's rebuilt house. Isiokpu, 1959

During six weeks of rioting in the Eastern Region four civilians were reported killed and four others seriously injured. The Police sustained seven casualties, including one shot in the stomach. Some six hundred people were eventually brought to trial. One Police estimate put damage to property at £20,000. The actual cost must have been much greater.

In Ahoada the emergency lasted longer than in any other division in the Region. 93 cases of damage to property were reported. Firearms were not used in any of the disturbances. There were no fatalities and, so far as I could ascertain, no serious injuries.

Clara Jack and the six ladies of Isiokpu were sentenced to three months imprisonment. Chief Jackson Mpi's house was rebuilt and reopened in a grand ceremony over which a bishop presided. It is still there, now surrounded by a ten feet high wall but essentially unchanged and still owned by the Mpi family.

For work in the riots Assistant Superintendent Hyacinth Ohanu received the Queens Police Medal and I was made an MBE. The Ikwerre District Council passed a vote of confidence in their District Officer.

My greatest reward was the look on Ashirim Unosi's face when I walked into his compound that Saturday morning. Not only delighted, he was astonished that the DO with whom he had spent so much time

Invested with insignia of MBE by Sir Robert Stapledon. Enugu, 1958

squabbling should have come to his rescue. He realized at last that we were
on the same side. Thereafter we worked happily and closely together but
it seemed a pity that it had taken a riot to bring this about.

When the crunch came, despite any doubts in Enugu and Lagos, the
District Officers kept the peace with negligible force and little bloodshed.
They were able to do so because of the trust placed in them by ordinary
citizens, including those who had rioted. That trust had been earned over
many decades by decent people who worked in relative obscurity for little
reward other than the respect of the community they served and the
satisfaction of doing a job they believed to be worthwhile.

In a meeting with the Governor General, Sir James Robertson in July
1958, Dr Azikiwe said that he thought that feelings in the Region had

improved since the 'outburst' and that it had helped the party and the government. He had had a wonderful demonstration of loyalty during his recent tour in which he had visited 30 Divisions.

The Acting Chief Secretary of the Regional Government, Hugh Elliott, sent a message inviting me to stay overnight at his house in Enugu. He said that the Premier, Dr Azikiwe, had returned from his tour impressed by the co-operative relationships that existed between several of the British Divisional Officers and local politicians. He had singled out Ahoada as a conspicuous example. Being Zik, the Premier could not refrain from adding that he only wished that his newly appointed Nigerian administrative officers were working so effectively with their political counterparts. Whenever I met Nnamdi Azikiwe in later years whether as Premier or as Governor-General or as President I never heard him refer to the events of 1958 but he always went out of his way to treat me with exceptional courtesy and friendship.

For the next fifty years, Omoku Peter who drove the Landrover during those six memorable weeks in Ahoada sent Christmas greetings to me and the family. 'Dear Sir, what of madam?' he would write, 'and of Sarah and the children?' At the end of the civil war Omoku apologized for his silence during a conflict in which two members of his family had been killed.

It seems that Sir Robert Stapledon had been right. The emergency had been a close run thing but we were healthier for having had it.

At eleven o'clock one Saturday morning in July Anne walked the few yards to the District Office and sat on the ledge of the open window as I was finishing off the petitions. 'Do you want me to come?' I asked. No, Anne replied, it could wait. After lunch we went for a siesta. Some minutes later Anne said that the apple pie that we had just eaten had not agreed with her. Moments after that I was scrambling for my watch, sitting on the edge of the bed and timing what must be the contractions. The baby had decided to make an early appearance. We dived into the Beetle and set off on the 44 miles journey to Port Harcourt. We paused at the Seventh Day Adventist hospital where Hal glanced at Anne and waved us on: 'Keep on going,' he grinned. When I accelerated over the corrugated surface Anne said 'Slow down.' When I slowed down Anne said 'Faster'. The VW in those days had no petrol gauge. I was in a silent panic because I had already switched over to the reserve fuel tank. There was only one filling 'station' between Elele and Port Harcourt – at mile fifteen. This consisted of one 44 gallon drum of petrol with a pump operated by a fifteen year old boy. I told him to put in a gallon of petrol, 'Quick, quick.' Instead the boy shouted to his pals in Igbo: 'Come, see de white woman.

She go deliver.' We managed to get away without coming to blows – just! What a relief to drive at last through the gates of the Braithwaite Nursing Home! The relief was short-lived. Being Saturday afternoon half the staff were off duty. Leaving Anne with a nurse I dashed round to the residence of the acting Provincial Secretary, Tony Saville. Using Tony's phone I tried to track down the Doctor in charge, John Holgate. He was judging a baby show somewhere in Aggrey Road! I did track down another doctor and friend, John Elbert. John agreed to go to Anne's assistance until his colleague arrived. In the meantime Anne had received some assistance from Dr James Henshaw of Calabar who, fortuitously, was in the hospital because his own wife, Caroline, had delivered a baby there a few hours earlier. By a coincidence Anne had known one of James Henshaw's relatives at the Domestic Science College in Manchester.

By the time that I got back to the hospital Sarah had arrived. There she was, still in the delivery room, lying on a green-sheeted table. She was smiling peacefully and was quite the most beautiful baby you could imagine.

Later that evening, still in my shorts, I returned to Ahoada, leaving Anne in the unfamiliar hospital in a city where she knew hardly a soul. Being a District Officer was easy. Being a District Officer's wife was a different matter altogether. James Brooke, the White Rajah of Sarawak, in order, as he said, to ensure the happiness of his people, banned from the kingdom missionaries, lawyers and wives of administrative officers. It is a fact that memsahibs have not always escaped criticism during periods of British imperial and colonial rule. But the wives that I knew in Eastern Nigeria seemed to me heroines all. They kept husbands happy, raised children and ran households on a shoestring. My one serious criticism of the Colonial Office regime was that a District Officer's pay was far short of the minimum needed to bring up a family and educate children. In our case the problem was solved by the rapid promotion that followed the exodus at Independence of more senior officers. Eventually, of course, members of HMOCS were granted terms comparable to those of Foreign Office Staff in respect of leave and educational allowances. But by then the horse had bolted.

In his memoir of service in Eastern Nigeria Frank Bex describes how he was forced to resign from the Colonial Service because he was unable to bring up his family of three small children on his existing pay.[6] By such managerial lunacy did the country lose when most it needed them the services of an outstanding and dedicated officer.

---

[6] Bex, Frank: *Lucky Me, Memoirs of a former District Officer in Nigeria*. Privately published. For copies contact fbex@Waitrose.com.

Sarah, Anne and I returned in triumph to Ahoada the following Saturday. In the kerosene heated fridge I had left a bottle of champagne to celebrate the baby's arrival – to us a luxury almost unheard of. I opened the door of the fridge to find the bottle half empty. Jonathan, our steward, a young boy whom Anne had trained from scratch, had a knack of getting half a step ahead of the game. He explained that he had opened the bottle to let the contents 'breathe.' Anne calmed me down pointing out quietly that it really did not matter. Just to prove her right, at that very moment Sid Kennedy and his partner, Rob White, marched in carrying a bottle of cold champagne.

Everybody in the town of Ahoada welcomed the new arrival. Every morning gangs of prisoners came to bring water for our domestic tanks, to cut grass in the garden and to sweep the drives. Down went the buckets and the brooms and the matchets and prisoners and warders crowded round the pram to see the baby. When Anne went for a stroll, children squabbled as to whose turn it was to push the pram. Everybody in the Station and in the town took a proprietary interest in the new baby. We were told that because she was our first born, female child, we should call her by the Igbo name, Adha. In fact she was baptized Sarah by Bishop Whelan of Owerri. Father Horrigan and Father O'Brian officiated and

Anne, Father O'Brian and Bishop Whelan (holding the baby) after Sarah's baptism. Ahoada, 1958

Tony Saville, Mrs Abbey and Eric Thomas were godparents. With Sarah's arrival we were at last regarded as a proper family and accepted as full members of the Ahoada community.

In the late nineteen eighties I was serving as Minister in the British High Commission in Lagos and had been asked to visit an industrial plant in Port Harcourt. When I reached the airport for the return journey to Lagos I was told that my flight would be subject to a delay of two hours. The new international airport was much further north than the old airport and I realized that it was quite near to the town of Isiokpu. I told the driver of the hired car that I wanted to see if I could find an old friend. I soon found the village. The first person I asked had never heard of Clara Jack. Some distance further I approached a group of youths sheltering from the rain on a corner. 'Over there,' said a sixteen year old.

It was appalling weather, pouring with rain and, for the Delta, miserably cold. The front of the house was barred and shuttered. I hammered on the door but there was no response. I went round the back. The three out-houses were deserted. I went back to the group on the corner. 'She's in there,' insisted the youth. I went again to the back of the house. The buildings had mud walls and corrugated zinc roofs. The door of one of them was ajar. A wooden shutter creaked back and forth against its frame. The rain beat down on the pan roof and fell in rivulets into the open drains.

I pushed at the half open door and peered into the dim, half light. Against the wall was a narrow iron bedstead. On the bare slats of the bed was a piece of straw matting. On the mat was curled what at first glance was just a bag of wrinkled, skin and bone. Her only covering was a piece of grey cloth round the waist. There was nothing else in the room: no furniture, no mats on the floor, no pictures on the wall. Not even a coat of whitewash on the mud walls. I called her name but the figure did not move. Using my few remaining words of Igbo I shouted that I was Kanada, the DO. We had known ourselves many years ago. We had had palaver many years ago. I was the white boy, Kanada. Slowly, she swung her thin legs over the side of the bed and sat with head down facing the floor. Finally, she seemed to remember and to recognize. 'Kanada!' she cried, 'Le kwe'm'. 'Look at me.' She turned up her face and stared sightlessly with eyes like milk-white marbles. I could not imagine anything sadder or more desolate. I stuffed into her hands what money I had with me and ran back to the car to get a sleeveless pullover. I told her that I had to go but would come again. She should wear the pullover. It would prove that I had been.

Some weeks later I arranged for Clara Jack to be taken by car to Port Harcourt and examined by a visiting Ophthalmic Surgeon. He said that ten years earlier he would have been able to save her sight but the blindness was now irreversible.

It was Clara's misfortune that she had no children of her own and no blood relatives to whom to turn for help. She was living with the son of her husband by another wife. He was a teacher at the local primary school. His wife was a nurse. They both went out each day to work leaving Clara alone in the tiny out house. The wife provided Clara with food but their joint incomes left nothing over for anything else. The step-son said that Clara's eyes had begun to fail during the Biafran war. Her husband, Jack, had also been sick. There had been sufficient money to buy medicine only for one of them. This does not explain why Clara Jack was left all day totally alone without care or companionship. It was not the Igbo way to leave a relative in such solitary distress.

Our daughter, Sarah, married an oil service engineer and by a strange coincidence they were posted in the early nineties to Port Harcourt. From time to time I had sent Clara Jack money and Sarah visited her on several occasions. Her circumstances were still wretched. One summer Anne and I spent a week in Port Harcourt with our daughter, her husband and two little grandchildren. We sent word to Clara Jack that we were going to call on her: Anne, myself, Sarah and little Emma and Kate.

A crowd of neighbours and friends gathered outside the house for the special occasion. Clara sat in the sunshine wearing her finest cloth; revelling in what she regarded as her proper place: the centre of attention. We all made speeches and handed over gifts and my son-in-law's driver translated. Before we left, Clara turned to her neighbour, snapped her knuckles and cackled: 'Ayee! Look at it! When de white boy be DO I spit at him feet. Now he bring his piccin see me and his piccin's piccin!'

CHAPTER 11

1959: Without fear or favour

WE ARRIVED IN ENGLAND in June 1959 after a tour of twenty six months and stayed until November. Brother Jack met us in Liverpool and for the first time lifted his little niece on to his shoulder. The summer never seemed to end and I spent much of it working for Anne's father on the family farm. I returned to Nigeria by air in November, a few weeks ahead of Anne and Sarah. We were posted to Degema in the Niger Delta but I was asked first to assist John Smith with the Federal elections in Port Harcourt. So far as I remember, the elections in Port Harcourt city went off without incident. Anne then flew out with Sarah to join me. We left our car in the care of the Public Works Department and made the rest of the journey to Degema by launch.

Degema Division belonged to a different world both in time and in space. It was an island accessible only by water. The division was bounded on the west by the Niger and on the east by the New Calabar and Bonny Rivers. The great rivers of the Santa Barbara, the San Bartholomeo, and the Sambreiro, interconnected by innumerable creeks, flowed through the division from north to south. The rivers had been named by the Portuguese explorers who had arrived several centuries earlier. The endless mangrove swamps of the Niger Delta and the sand bar that separated the Delta from the Atlantic Ocean had always blocked access from the sea. It was only in the middle of the nineteenth century that James Lander had finally determined where the great Niger river flows into the sea. The old towns of Bonny, Opobo, Abonnema and Brass had for centuries controlled international trade with the interior, whether the trade was in slaves or palm oil or mixed goods. On occasion these towns had defended their commercial monopolies by force of arms and merchants in Liverpool and London had backed their respective partners in the conflicts.

Port Harcourt was a railway town built during World War I to ship coal from the mines at Enugu to Lagos and beyond. With the coming of the railway and the spread of motorable roads the towns of the Delta were increasingly by-passed and their commercial dominance broken. Merchants from other parts of Nigeria and from overseas could trade directly with the great markets of Onitsha and Aba.

On one side, the little island of Degema looked across towards the town of Abonnema and on the other, to Abua in Ahoada Division. As well as the District Officer, the island housed the Government Medical Officer, the local manager of GB Olivant, and two or three other commercial representatives. There was a tiny waterside where the launches were moored, two tennis courts and a club, called the Admiral Benbow. New members of the club had to do obeisance to an effigy of the Admiral Benbow that had been taken from the prow of an ancient sailing ship.

It was possible in those days to travel mile after mile through the mangrove swamps without seeing a soul. Occasionally one might pass a fisherman slowly paddling against the current. He might fish all day before dragging his canoe on a mud bank to spend the night in a tiny wooden hut hardly bigger than a dog's kennel.

In the lonely waterways you sensed the presence of ghosts of former days. It was said that the great harbour at Ikassa had been able to accommodate the Grand Fleet at anchor in 1914. On one side of this beautiful, vast, empty stretch of water stood the bare walls of an hotel abandoned before it had been half-built. In the cemetery in nearby Brass lay the graves of several members of the expedition to the interior led by the great nineteenth century German explorer, Barthes. Also there were the graves of young British sailors who had been slaughtered in their beds in the Nembe raid of 1912.

Bonny was a lovely little town. Just round the point of the estuary hippos played on beaches washed each day by the ocean and uninhabited, save for occasional fishing settlements, for hundreds of miles. You could hear Wordsworth's 'mighty waters, rolling evermore.'[1] Near the water's edge was the Bonny Government School. The school had been built in 1905 before the colonial government had established a presence in the interior of the country. The entrance hall of the school was paved with stone flags brought in ballast by sea from England. On one wall was a fading picture of King Edward VII. Facing it was sepia print of Piccadilly Circus in 1907 with horse drawn trams locked in an early version of the traffic jam usual in that spot.

There was a civility and dignity about members of the old families of Abonnema, Abua and Bonny not always found in their more excitable neighbours to the north. One of my less glorious exploits was a trip to Bonny when I was to carry the cash needed for the monthly wages of the staff of the District Council and Maternity Home. When the launch was ready to cast off I went to collect the cash from the Treasury to be told

---

[1] Ode on Intimations of Immortality.

that the Chief of Bonny had called earlier in the day and had taken it with him. I was aghast. The Chief was chairman of the District Council whose cash balances I was to check! If any cash was missing who now would be responsible? The Finance Clerk patiently explained that I might have to anchor overnight and that in any case the Chief would certainly reach Bonny before me. I was not reassured.

We sailed non-stop as fast as the launch would go and arrived in Bonny at dusk. Even though it was almost dark I insisted in going round to the Chief's house. He greeted me with great courtesy. I went straight to the point and wanted to collect the money. The Chief invited me to a drink. The brasher my questions, the more gracious were his replies. He asked about the royal family and the weather in England. He asked whether a certain gin was still sold in London. (I discovered later that its production had ceased before the First World War.) The Chief insisted that I stay for dinner and, in that small town on the edge of the Atlantic Ocean, served wine in what looked like Venetian crystal that may have been in the family's possession for hundreds of years. Finally, the Chief said, 'Ah, yes, the money.' He beckoned to a servant who rolled back a carpet and removed a stone flag beneath which was a safe. He unlocked the safe and took out the bags of cash from the Degema Treasury, seals unbroken. I mumbled my thanks and stumbled out to search for a hole to crawl into.

Degema was a place of much beauty and historical interest but it was a very lonely posting for Anne when I was away visiting the more distant parts of the division. It never occurred to us that we might be witnessing the last days of this silent, empty world of creek and swamp and water where hardly a bird flew and the only sound was the flip flap of crabs scuttling in the mud of the mangroves. It all changed with brutal suddenness; like the opening scene of Coppola's film *Apocalypse Now* when the camera pans along a line of palm trees under low cloud in another delta. A sound of throbbing engines grows louder and then in a searing flash the palms are gone, leaving a line of smoking, burnt out trunks.

Not long after we left Degema, Shell-BP confirmed that they had discovered oil in commercial quantities at Yenagoa, just a few miles from Nembe in Brass division. An off-shore oil terminal was built in Bonny and, years later, a multi-billion dollar natural gas liquefaction plant.

The civil war divided some of the tribes of the Delta from their mainland neighbours. Port Harcourt was a divided city. At the beginning of the war the property of many Rivers families was sacked by their Igbo neighbours. When federal troops retook the city it was the turn of the Igbos to flee and suffer the awful retaliation that war engenders. War and the ongoing dispute over the distribution of revenue from oil have left a legacy of violence which has continued up to the present day. In 2004 government helicopter gun ships swept the creeks in an attempt to suppress the murderous activities of rival gangs. Great motorways are under construction both east-west across the Delta and north-south linking the mainland to the coast at Bonny.

But we have wandered into the future. On those Saturday mornings in Degema in early 1960, Anne would walk with Sarah to the little office where I worked. Sarah had just started to walk. I would sit her on the desk whilst I locked up the files. Then we would walk together down to the little quay and watch the boats going to and fro across the water to Abonnema as we waited for the launch from Port Harcourt. The launch brought the mail and the Chief Clerk would leaf through the pile to see if there were any personal letters for us. One Saturday there was such a letter. It was from the Chief Secretary. I was to be transferred to Enugu to take up the post of Principal Assistant Secretary to the Premier. Anne and I walked across to the Admiral Benbow Club to celebrate. So, after just a few months we left the beautiful but desolate post of Degema Division in Rivers Province.

In 1960 the administrative capital of the Eastern Region was an attractive town. The word Enugu means On the Hill and its gentle elevation gave the town a pleasing climate. Enugu was a mining town and a railway town as well as the seat of regional government. From beneath the hill was mined the coal that the railway to Port Harcourt had been built to carry.

There was a buzz about Enugu in 1960. Independence was just a few months away and we all, Nigerian and British, politicians and business-men, public servants and professionals were caught up in the excitement of the momentous change. Many of those British Colonial Officers most disappointed at the pace of political development had already left on premature retirement. We who remained tended to be younger, more optimistic and, one must concede, more naive and inexperienced.

In the Federal election in the previous year Dr Azikiwe and his NCNC party had failed to win the largest share of the popular vote and his hopes of becoming the independent country's first Premier had been dashed. He had also failed to reach agreement with Obafemi Owolowo's Yoruba-base Action Group party in the Western Nigeria Instead, Dr Azikiwe had settled for a position as junior partner in an alliance with the NPC party of the north. Together they formed the Federal Government and Dr Azikiwe resigned his post as Premier of the Eastern Region to move to Lagos. He was succeeded as Premier of the Eastern Region by Dr Michael Okpara.

My immediate boss was the Chief Secretary of the Region, Jerome Oputa Udoji. Unusually for a Nigerian, Oputa Udoji after graduating from King's College Cambridge and being called to the Bar, had opted for a career in public service rather than in the law. His first postings had been in the Western Region and he had returned to the Eastern Region with the approach of independence. Udoji identified completely with the aims and ideals of the administrative service established by his British predecessors. Although appointed by Dr Azikiwe when he was Premier his relations with the great man were always subject to a certain strain. No wonder. Udoji had been blamed publicly in the House of Assembly for the failure to submit the annual budget on time. This was a contemptible way to treat a civil servant who had no right of reply, when the fault, as Zik well knew, had been entirely that of his own ministers.

In those days Nigeria still operated a constitution based largely on the British model. As well as Cabinet Secretary the Chief Secretary was also head of the civil service. Although Permanent Secretaries were responsible for their own departmental staff the Premier's Office was responsible for the posting and promotion of Administrative Officers both in the government departments and in the field. A second Permanent Secretary in the Premier's Office, Albert Osakwe, was responsible for submitting recommendations for promotion and for personnel issues such as conditions of employment. I reported directly to the Chief Secretary on a wide range of other issues.

Some of my time was spent preparing answers to Parliamentary Questions addressed to the Premier and checking draft Ministerial speeches to see that they conformed to what the Premier maintained was Government policy. But by far the worst part of the job and the most time-consuming concerned the allocation of Personal Assistants and of residential accommodation. The frequency and length of leave of senior officers made planning of leave cover very difficult. With the sudden departure on premature retirement of large numbers of the most senior staff it became almost impossible

Trained Personal Assistants and Secretary Typists were in short supply. We still had a handful of expatriate ladies in this category and their services were the subject of intense competition. Each Permanent Secretary demanded as of absolute right the services of one of these ladies. When I pointed out that since there were far fewer of the ladies than there were Permanent Secretaries such rights could not be upheld, I would be treated to a stream of invective laced with reminders of the seniority of the speaker and the insignificance of the spoken-to. People who for years had been personal friends suddenly became snarling opponents. At first I would try patiently to reason with them but as the weeks went by I adopted the tactic of listening patiently for twenty minutes to a Permanent Secretary's rant before telling him that if he did not like my decision he had two options; one, he could go running to the Chief Secretary or, two, he could lump it. The tactic did not improve things but it made me feel better.

The allocation of living quarters for senior staff in Enugu was far and away the worst job that I have done. There has been nothing since to compare with it. It was part of their conditions of service that expatriate officers should be provided with accommodation. With the promotion of increasing numbers of Nigerian officers to senior post they also became eligible for senior staff accommodation. To ease the shortage, blocks of flats were built. Everybody wanted to live in a house and not in a flat. I allocated the units of property according to seniority and date of occupation. It was not practicable to keep a house or flat empty beyond a certain length of time for a particular occupant and it was not practicable to shunt all staff to new quarters each time a senior officer returned from leave or other assignment. This meant that occasionally an officer would be offered a quarter seen as less desirable than some other quarter currently occupied by a more junior officer.

It was a revelation to me to discover how emotional people would get over the matter of accommodation. Senior officers would come stamping into my officer in a frenzy of indignation. A frequent opening salvo was that they had 'never been so insulted in their lives' to be expected to live in such and such a quarter. Many had been worked over by their wives. Some wives marched in on Monday morning with husbands trailing sheepishly behind. It would be obvious as soon as they crossed the threshold that the couple had been rowing all weekend over the house question. They would be staying temporarily in the government rest house. The wife would have told the husband that she was going back on the next plane if she were not given such and such a house. The demand was usually accompanied by invidious comparisons with the people who were living in the coveted property.

Sometimes I would make a recommendation to the Chief Secretary about the allocation of a particular house. Udoji would come bouncing into my office. 'Why am I being bothered with this nonsense?' he would want to know. 'Because,' I would answer, 'when I do not bother you, you come bouncing into my office demanding to know why such and such a chap has been poorly treated.' He would eventually grin and shrug 'OK'. but little by little I did persuade him that the only way to save ourselves untold grief was for him to refuse to intervene and to stand by my decision whether that decision was good, bad or indifferent. After a few months the tantrums gradually diminished and the disgruntled, with the occasional exceptional blow-up, ceased to rattle their cages.

We did have one memorable blow-up over the allocation not of houses but of Administrative Officers. Oputa Udoji was going on leave and Albert Osakwe was to act as Chief Secretary in his absence. Albert was Permanent Secretary (Establishment) in the Premier's Office. He had lost out to Udoji in the competition to be the first Nigerian Chief Secretary to the Premier. This had left a certain tension between the two, though Albert always took a relaxed view of things. He was an excellent cricketer and perhaps the best batsman in the Region. He approached work rather as he approached the wicket – with a certain laid-back elegance. (His critics would say that he was 'too damned laid back for words'.) He would frequently ask me, speaking about our boss, 'Why does he get so *excited*?'

On the Friday evening before Udoji's departure Albert and I were summoned to the magisterial presence and given a lecture on how to conduct ourselves in our master's absence. The Chief Secretary did not want to return to find that he had the usual mess to clean up. We were suitably shocked at the imputation. I did manage to slip in a question on the tricky matter of posting the most senior Administrative Officers, some decisions on which were expected in the coming weeks. Did he wish these to await his return? He did not. With weary exasperation Udoji reiterated that officers should be posted to Divisions strictly in the order that they returned to duty and the posts became vacant. The policy was to be carried out without fear or favour and without exception. In earlier days officers had been posted to Provinces and the Residents had posted officers within the Provinces. Given the differences in language and culture between many of the provinces this well-tried system had worked very well. With the abolition of Residents and the retirement of many senior officers it was no longer practicable.

Udoji had not been gone long when a nasty dilemma arose over a vacancy in the division from which I had been transferred earlier in the year: Degema Division. No one wanted to go to Degema Division, where there were no roads and you travelled only by water. The first officer to become available was a very senior District Officer named Charles Croasdale. Charlie had just returned from a long leave in England. Charles Croasdale was in fact the most senior District Officer in the Region. He was top of the long grade list, as we used to say, and although he had never been promoted he had lived and worked happily in Eastern Nigeria for over thirty five years.

Not only had Charlie arrived in Nigeria before I was born, he himself came from Pleasington, a beautiful little village less than five miles from my beloved Brinscall. Indeed Charlie may have been the only other officer in the British Colonial Service who had even heard of either village. Charlie was not married and always drove a Morgan motor car. When he went on UK leave he would load up the Morgan with his luggage, his steward and his cook and drive out of the compound. He would cross the Niger at Onitsha and drive along the coast of West Africa, through the Sahara Desert and across the straits of Gibraltar and continue until he came to Pleasington.

Charlie had spent several tours in a Division called Orlu. He regarded Orlu as home and as his fiefdom. He had been made a Chief of one of its communities – a matter of questionable propriety for an administrative officer, I thought. But Charlie had been absent on extended leave and another officer now occupied the post in Orlu.

Albert and I struggled with the problem for some time. Albert would drop into my office and ask 'What are we going to do?' This would be followed by 'What is Udoji going to say?' To the latter I would reply that whatever we did was going to be wrong. Eventually, we recalled that we had been instructed to post staff on a strict first come, first served basis. 'Without fear or favour,' Albert recalled. We posted Charlie to Degema.

The smelly stuff ascended to the ceiling with remarkable speed. First, Charlie refused point-blank to go to Degema. When persuasion failed Albert and I began to raise the ante. We pointed out that absence from duty might attract penalties of a serious kind. Pension rights might be affected. Suddenly, we sensed a breakthrough. Charlie moved to Degema. But hopes were no sooner raised than dashed. When Charlie arrived in Degema he took one look at the place and jumped back in the launch, which he ordered to make full speed for Port Harcourt. Back in Port Harcourt he booked himself into the Government Hospital and announced that he was suffering from high blood pressure.

He was not the only one. Michael Okpara, the Premier, who knew nothing of what his office had been up to, out of the blue received a letter from Zik demanding an explanation of what was happening to an officer named Croasdale. Charlie had written a personal letter to the great man in Lagos. After expressing undying admiration for Zik's life-long fight against colonialism Charlie had complained that he too was suffering persecution at the hands of colonialists in the Premier's office. In fact, he was being 'tossed from pillar to post like a cricket ball'. Albert did not seem to mind the accusations of colonialism but, as an Oxford Blue, he took exception to the sporting metaphor.

It was unfortunate that Udoji should choose this precise moment to return from leave. He was, as they say, incandescent. If there was one thing that Michael Okpara could not stand it was the interfering letters that arrived with insufferable frequency from his predecessor in office and Party leader. If there was one thing that Udoji could not stand it was to be carpeted by the Premier for the alleged shortcomings of his office. Albert and I were marched once more into the office of the Chief Secretary. We received what was described in the Navy as a right rollicking.

I had drafted a reply to Charlie's letter to Zik. The draft was tweaked and chopped around and passed from hand to hand but eventually the letter was posted and it was signed not by Zik or by Michael Okpara or even by Udoji. The letter was signed by Albert, the cricketing colonialist.[2] As soon as Charlie received it he resigned. He was less than a year away from final retirement in any case. On his way home Charlie passed through Enugu and I gave a farewell lunch in his honour. Anne cooked a marvellous fish curry to which Charlie did full justice. No one would have guessed what a row had gone on between us.

The great event of 1960 of course was the long anticipated Independence Day. On 1 October Britain's largest colony became a sovereign state, a member of the United Nations and of the British Commonwealth. The Queen was represented by Princess Alexandra at the celebrations.

Every officer in the Regional government headquarters was called in to help with the Independence Day celebrations. In charge of the organization was my good friend Tony Saville, former Provincial Secretary Port Harcourt and currently in charge of the Enugu Township. When we reported for duty I was miffed to be told that my job would be to welcome VIPs from overseas and take charge of their luggage! I said that instead of seeing the ceremonies I would be hunting for suitcases that had gone astray. Tony remarked that in that case I had better see that they did not go astray, hadn't I?

The midnight ceremony, when the Union flag was hauled down for the last time and Nigeria's new flag raised for the first, was a moving and beautiful experience which none of us present, whether Nigerian or British, have forgotten. Meeting and greeting the VIPs turned out to be quite interesting. The Sardauna of Sokoto, splendid in his colourful robes, was a striking figure. Obafemi Owolowo and the Prime Minister, Tafewa Balewa, were equally impressive. Nnamdi Azikiwe had invited from the US a number of distinguished black American academics who were prominent in the civil rights movement. Some of them were obviously

---

[2] Albert Osakwe later had a distinguished career in the Nigerian Diplomatic Service and served as Ambassador in Zaire. After retirement he returned to live in Onitsha. He suffered a tragic death when he was murdered in his own home.

puzzled at being met at the airport and taken to their quarters in a shiny white open top car by a British civil servant. But then this was Nigeria's Independence. Alabama, Mississippi and Georgia were still segregated.

On 2 October a series of celebrations were held in the Stadium. Anne was eight months pregnant with our second child but she did not want to miss this event. We took our places along with ten thousand others and listened to a series of excellent speeches by the nation's political leaders. Abubakar Tafewa Balewa was especially gracious in his address. The climax of the programme was a demonstration by the Fourth Battalion of the Nigerian Army. We were sitting in a place that was on the opposite side of the stadium to the car park and I became increasingly anxious as a breeze began to blow from the north. I suggested that we should begin to edge towards the exit but Anne was enjoying the spectacle. A few minutes later the sky began not to darken but to redden. The atmosphere was eerie. I had never experienced anything quite like it, certainly not so early in a dry season. Tiny particles of sand were being blown south from the Sahara desert, something you would normally expect months later when the Harmattan was at its height. I shepherded Anne to the exit and down the wooden staircase.

We had moved less than fifty yards when the heavens opened. With the downpour of rain came out of the stadium a tidal wave of people, all rushing for shelter towards the outer gates of the stadium and the road to the town. The situation was scary because in the rush for cover no one had a thought for anything else. I was very afraid for Anne whom I thought might be knocked down at any moment in the crowd of swirling, yelling, people. Suddenly a youth not more than eighteen years of age noticed Anne's condition. 'Hiyye,' he screamed above the turmoil, 'see de woman get piccin'. Immediately a group of young men formed a circle round Anne, pushing back the crowd and screaming at anyone who came within arm's length. They escorted Anne through the gate and all the way to the car. When we reached the car I tried to give the boys money. They waved me away and scampered off towards the town. I looked back towards the Stadium. The rain had stopped. Leading back to the amphitheatre was a river of discarded flip-flops, stuck in the mud that had separated them from their owners. I wondered how well we would have fared if we had been caught in similar circumstances outside Old Trafford or Stamford Bridge or Highbury.

The celebrations went on for a week. Overseas countries contributed to the entertainment. There was competition, especially between the USA and the USSR, as to who would lay on the best show. The British provided plays by Shakespeare. The US were far more ambitious. They announced that they were going to stage *Rose Marie* on Ice! They were going to make an ice rink in a vast marquee on the cricket field. I was hugely impressed. Every day I would drive past the cricket field to see how the freezing was coming along. The poor old US of A. They experienced problem after problem with the compressors and never did succeed in getting the water to freeze. The Soviets laid on a variety show in a school. Despite the awful stage and poor lighting they brought the house down with an unbelievably brilliant conjuring act. The Nigerian audience talked about the show for weeks afterwards. The Americans tried to recover the position on the Saturday evening with a concert by Louis Armstrong and his All Stars. But the great man was out of sorts. He rushed through his act as fast as he could go and refused to entertain requests for encores. He would obviously have preferred to be in Philadelphia or any other US city and was going to get back there as fast as he could.

On the Sunday evening we played bridge with our close friends, Joe and Alison Widdell. After the first rubber Anne called me into the bedroom and said that she thought the baby was on its way.

Unlike in Ahoada when we had had to make the hair-raising journey of 47 miles to Port Harcourt, we were less than a mile away from the hospital in Enugu. But it was still a close run thing and Mark, like Sarah, chose a weekend in which to make his appearance. Ten o'clock on Sunday evening was not the best time to turn up at a small hospital in Enugu.

The nurse on duty was a young Nigerian girl who did not look a day older than nineteen. The doctor was off duty and out of town. The nurse asked me to go and fetch Matron from the Nurses' Quarters whilst she prepared Anne for the Labour Room. As I was going out of the door she called me back and said that there was no time to go looking for Matron. I was to stay where I was in case she needed me. Twenty minutes later the young nurse reappeared to say that I was the father of a little boy. We were delighted and deeply indebted to the young girl who had proved such a calm and professional midwife when Anne most needed her. The following morning Dr Savage said how pleased he was that everything had gone well. A few weeks later Mark was baptized by Bishop John Anyaogu. Norah Beck, Joe Widdell and Oputa Udoji were godparents.

One of the problems facing Nigeria at Independence was the shortage of Nigerian staff of sufficient ability and experience to replace the departing British in the most senior posts. It is a contentious issue. The British often argue that in the rush for independence sound administration was sacrificed for immediate political ends. The counter argument is that responsibility for training senior staff in sufficient numbers and over an appropriate time-scale lay with the British, and if Nigerian leaders had waited until these goals had been achieved the country might be waiting still for independence. My view is that there is truth in both contentions. From the late forties onwards much greater priority should have been given to the selection and training of Nigerian staff for senior appointments in the Administration, the Police and the Armed Forces. The contrast at Independence between the number of Nigerians practising law and the number in the senior ranks of the civil and military services was striking. On the other hand the development of an efficient and incorrupt civil service takes time. Its members have to be offered prospects of a reasonable career in a stable environment free from political interference. They also need to be paid what Macaulay called 'a decent competence'. In the years since Independence successive Nigerian governments have devalued and demoralized the country's public services – with devastating results.

When Artie Shaw died he asked that his epitaph should read: 'He did the best he could with the material available.' That is what we in the Premier's Office tried to do in 1960. Graduates were recruited in unprecedented numbers into the Administration and other senior services. Despite provincial reorganization and the haemorrhaging of its most senior staff the field administration managed just about to continue doing its job. Senior officers tried to initiate new recruits into the craft of the trade and the traditions of the service. I remember one gathering of the newly recruited administrative cadets. At one of the seminars, one of the cadets suggested that ADOs ought to have a working, as well as a ceremonial uniform. Udoji dismissed the idea out of hand. The question showed, he said, a failure to understand the very concept of a *civil* service. No doubt he was right but I had sympathy for the young man's question. It seemed to me that the British Administrative Officers in the field, with their white skin and khaki shorts, had always worn uniform.

One Saturday morning in November, 1960, I was working alone in the Premier's Office when the telephone rang. The call was from a young man called Crescent Ugwu in Onitsha. He was a newly appointed ADO cadet and I remembered him because he came from Aka near Ukehe, which was the village in Nsukka Division that John Nwodo and my old lorry driver, Sylvanus Eze, came from. The young man called me Frank and was very apologetic for ringing me. It was obvious that he was very worried and I sensed immediately that he was right to be so. He said that he was asking for my advice. He had been instructed to accompany a detachment of police who were going to serve eviction notices in a town south of Onitsha the following Monday morning. I asked him why he had not appealed to his senior officer, Norman Perkins. He said that he had not been able to speak to Mr Perkins because he was busy with an enquiry into the affairs of Onitsha market.

Obosi is a town a few miles south of Onitsha. It is the home town, amongst other famous sons, of Emeka Anyaoku who served with such distinction in the post of Secretary General of the Commonwealth. For generations Onitsha and Obosi had been in dispute over the ownership of a tract of land. Vast sums had been spent in litigation. Twice the case had gone on appeal to the House of Lords. In the present instance the courts had awarded title of a parcel of the land to Onitsha and had ordered the removal of some houses belonging to 'trespassers' from Obosi. The execution of the order was certain to encounter resistance which I thought might well result in violence and rioting.

I rang the District Officer, Ben Okagbue, and asked why the young man had been given such a dangerous mission. Anyway, where was the SDO, Norman Perkins? Ben said that Norman was conducting an Enquiry into corruption in the allocation of stalls in Onitsha Market. He, Ben, had relieved him of all other divisional duties.

I tracked down Norman Perkins at home. He was writing his report on corruption in Onitsha Market. Norman was a senior officer of many years experience. I knew that he would not take kindly to any back seat driving from me. Nevertheless I pleaded with him to interrupt his report-writing for just a few hours on the coming Monday morning and supervise the Obosi exercise in person. He declined. His orders were to put aside all other work until the report had been completed. He maintained that Ben Okagbue was in charge and perfectly capable of handling the matter. I argued that neither Ben nor the cadet had sufficient experience for a mission of this kind. Ben was a friend of mine but until recently had been an Education Officer. I also understood that Ben came from the Onitsha area and this might be a further complication. I had spoken to Ben and sensed that he agreed with my arguments although out of loyalty to his boss, could not say so. I failed to budge Norman.

After speaking to Uzo, his wife, and many telephone calls I eventually tracked down the Chief Secretary, Oputa Udoji, and told him the story. He was not thrilled to have his weekend interrupted. He said that Norman Perkins was very experienced and that we should leave the matter to him. I went over the arguments again. I said that there were always enquiries into corruption in Onitsha Market. Surely, Norman Perkins could leave his report-writing for three hours? I begged Udoji to give Perkins a direct order that he must personally supervise the execution of the eviction notices. Udoji refused. He believed that once you put a man in a job you must back him to carry it out. That was a sacrosanct principle of administration. I was no more successful with Udoji than I had been with Perkins.

It was afternoon by the time that I got back to Ben. I asked him the name of the Police officer who was to lead the contingent on Monday morning. He did not know. I said that both the SDO and the Chief Secretary were confident that he and the Police would carry out the operation successfully and peacefully. I said that all would be well if he worked closely with the Police. He should find out immediately – this Saturday afternoon – the name of the Police officer who was to be in charge of the operation and make himself known to him. I stressed that it was vital that he should keep the young ADO at his side throughout the operation. They and the Police must stick together at all costs. I asked Ben more than once whether he understood what I was saying. He did.

Finally I got back to the cadet and told him that the Chief Secretary and the Senior District Officer were confident that the operation could be completed without trouble and had every confidence in his and Ben Okagbue's ability to carry it out. I told him that he must stick to Ben like glue and that both of them must stay close to the officer in charge of the Police at all times. It was absolutely critical that they and the Police should work closely together and in no circumstance must they allow themselves to be separated. I said that provided they did that there was nothing to worry about. With an assurance that I did not feel I said that I was sure that everything would be OK. Crescent Ugwu said that he was very grateful for my help. He would do just as I said.

Shortly before noon on the Monday morning the telephone rang. On a bad line from somewhere near Obosi came the strangled voice of Ben Okagbue. 'Where is the ADO?' I interrupted. 'There has been some trouble,' said Ben through the crackling atmospherics. 'Ben, where is Crescent Ugwu?' I repeated. It had been very difficult, said Ben, in a voice cracking with emotion. There had been resistance. When the staff of the Land Office had attempted to serve the notices the crowd had attacked the Police. Then the Police had charged. He himself had got separated from the Senior Inspector and could not see what had happened to the ADO. The Police were searching for him now. Perhaps he had taken shelter in one of the dwellings.

At around four o'clock on that Monday afternoon in 1961 the phone rang again. It was Ben in great distress telephoning from his home in Onitsha. The Police had recovered the body of the murdered ADO.

Things can go wrong regardless of intentions and plans. I have been involved in other failed operations and some of them resulted in the loss of innocent lives. But none was more tragic or avoidable than that which resulted in the death of Crescent Ugwu, the young man from Ukehe, the first son of his village ever to be educated overseas. He was setting out at the very beginning of a career in the Administrative Service of which he was so proud. He had appealed for the protection that he knew in his bones that he needed and we his superiors had failed to provide it. I still hear that telephone ringing in the Premier's office on the morning of Saturday, 12 November, 1960.

There were other, happier Saturdays. We enjoyed our life as a young family in Enugu. We lived in a pleasant little house in a street off Abakaliki road and got on well with our neighbours the Mackenzies. In the mornings Anne ran a little nursery school. Among her pupils were children of the ministers of the first post-Independence government. Mark grew into a little boy and pedalled endlessly round and round the veranda on a tricycle with a bottle of Ribena dangling from his mouth. Later in 1961 I was promoted out of the long grade and our salary doubled. For the first time in our wedded life we did not feel that we were living on the bread line.

Sometimes on Saturday mornings before lunch, as in Degema, Anne would come with the children to collect me from the office before going on to the Enugu Club for a pre-lunch drink and swim for the children. On one such morning I introduced Sarah to Oputa Udoji. I explained that Chief Udoji was my boss and that if I was naughty he might smack my bottom. After that if I displeased Sarah she threatened to tell Chief Udoji and tell him to smack my bottom. Udoji liked that story.

Sadly, the happy time in Enugu came to an end prematurely when we received a letter from home saying that my father was seriously ill with cancer. We hastened back to spend a last leave with him.

Now in his nineties, Jerome Udoji is living out his old age in Ozubulu by the banks of the great river. He still writes from time to time to enquire about his godson, Mark. He invariably asks whether Sarah is satisfied with her father's conduct and whether she needs him to take any corrective action.

CHAPTER 12

1962: Konijus and Tubonijus

O N RETURN FROM LEAVE I was posted to Port Harcourt as Provincial Secretary. This meant that my links with Onitsha Province had finally been severed. Although I would miss the familiar landscapes and our many friends in what is now Anambra State I was glad to be going to the Region's most important commercial and industrial centre. Nigeria was now producing oil in significant quantities and Port Harcourt was the epicentre of the new economy. Port Harcourt, I thought, was the place to be.

Shell-BP had moved its headquarters from Owerri to Port Harcourt and had surrendered an extensive Oil Prospecting Lease for a smaller Mining Lease. The company had finally admitted that oil was being produced in what were called 'commercial quantities'. Other international companies were bidding for rights to explore the areas surrendered by Shell-BP and the off-shore areas where drilling was expected to go to greater depths than had yet been attempted in West Africa. Just outside the city of Port Harcourt construction of the country's first oil refinery had begun.

In 1961 Port Harcourt Province consisted of Ahoada Division, the city of Port Harcourt itself and Ogoni Division, the 'Ogoniland' later made famous by Ken Saro-Wiwa in his campaigns against the oil companies and the Federal Government. The post of Provincial Commissioner was filled by a young politician named Michael Ogon. The Provincial Secretary, a government official, and the Provincial Commissioner, a political appointee, were supposed to work together in the same way as a Minister and his Permanent Secretary. The analogy did not really hold because the Provincial Commissioner, unlike a Minister, had virtually no executive power and was accountable to no legislative chamber, though as an elected politician he was a member of the regional legislative chamber. In the course of time – and at considerable cost to the taxpayer – the Provinces evolved into States, each with its own legislature and Governor.

Mike Ogon had a reputation as a left-wing 'firebrand'. He had been a member of the NCNC Youth wing and belonged to a group of self proclaimed Socialists of whom my friend Basil Okwu from Awgu Division was also a member. Mike hailed from Ikom in the hilly north east not far from the border with the Cameroons. He had been a teacher in a Catholic mission school and had been involved in all manner of scrapes. On one occasion, desperate for cash to finance an election campaign Mike had talked a naïve parish priest into making him a loan of over a thousand pounds 'just until the end of the month'. The end of the month came but no sign of Mike. This precipitated a major row because the cash was needed to pay the salaries of the teachers. Every teacher in the diocese was up in arms. Mike was hauled in by the Ministry of Education. The priest was hauled before his bishop.

Mike took the view that life was intended to be fun and he and I soon became friends. He never interfered in administrative matters nor did he involve me in any constituency problems. He did ask for occasional help with speeches. I remember him once attending a gathering of international socialists. Among those attending were a group of Maoists from China. This was the first time that I had heard the term 'Maoist'. I pointed out that political speeches were outside my remit and anyway I was not a socialist. Mike's reply was: 'Yeah, yeah, yeah, just let's get the d____d speech done, shall we, Frank?' In the speech I quoted a remark attributed to Lenin (or perhaps it was Trotsky) that the trouble with fellow travellers was that you never knew when they were going to get off the train. Since Basil Okwu had recently been accused of being a fellow traveller this, I was told later, brought the house down. Mike returned in high glee. Thereafter when we had to work up one of his speeches he would call over his shoulder as he left my office: 'And, Frank, put in a bit of that Lenin stuff.' I once asked Mike *why* he was a socialist. 'Isn't everyone?' he said.

On a rare visit to Enugu I bumped into the Chief Secretary. What was going on in Port Harcourt, he wanted to know. A raised eyebrow indicated puzzled innocence. 'You know,' he said, 'that you are supposed to be managing Mike Ogon. From what I hear you are making him worse.' 'Oh,' I replied, 'I thought that the Provincial Secretary was to work to the Commissioner, not the other way round.' 'Very funny,' said Udoji, un-amused. 'You know of course that Mike Ogon is a rascal?' 'Yes,' I said, 'but a likeable one.' I thought that I detected perhaps the merest hint of a smile. So I climbed in the car and drove off.

At the end of 1961 we faced elections to the Regional House of Assembly. I toured Ahoada Division and Ogoni Division. Registration appeared to have proceeded smoothly for a poll to be held before the end of the year. Then I had a call from the Chief Secretary. He had received complaints about the political situation in Okrika in Degema Division. Udoji asked me to visit the place and appraise the situation. Specifically I was to determine whether there was a reasonable prospect of holding an election in Okrika that would be seen as free and fair.

Okrika is an island in the Delta some fifteen miles east of Port Harcourt but administratively it belonged to Degema which at that time was part of another Province.

For generations the inhabitants of Okrika had been divided into two feuding groups that called themselves Koniju and Tuboniju. Originally the Koniju had been farmers and the Tuboniju fishermen. The Koniju were concentrated in the township on the northern side of the island nearest to the Ogoni shore. The Tuboniju were more dispersed, living on the south and west of the island and in a number of tiny little off-shore islands on that side of the main island.

A dispute had been raging over the right of succession to the Chieftaincy of the island of Okrika. Each party had a candidate. The DO Degema was conducting a public enquiry in an attempt to resolve the dispute. For five consecutive days I sat in on the enquiry and listened to witnesses from one side and the other droning on in mind-numbing detail. There was not a scintilla of common ground. It was not obvious that the enquiry would ever end. Indeed, an endless enquiry seemed preferable to most of the alternatives. The quarrel had nothing to do with party politics and did not originate with the Chieftaincy dispute. Each side had wished to field a candidate under the NCNC banner but as only one could do so the Tuboniju candidate was campaigning as an independent. For both sides the election was merely a battlefield on which to fight the ancient enemy.

It was clear from a cursory examination that the election registers were packed with false names, names of deceased relatives and duplicate or triplicate registrations. On polling day there would be widespread attempts at multiple voting. Each voter was to have a thumb marked with indelible dye but the polling clerks had all been recruited locally and would be subject to intimidation and intolerable pressure to turn a blind eye to irregularities. There might also be attempts to tamper with the ballot boxes at the end of the poll. I was particularly disturbed by an incident that had taken place at a registration centre just in front of Saint Peter's Cathedral Church. Towards the end of registration an argument had developed into a fracas in which a man had been killed. The man was a Tuboniju. It was alleged by the Tuboniju that in the crowd that day in civilian clothes had been a prominent Koniju figure who was a serving officer in the Nigerian Police. In response to my enquiries the Police confirmed that on the day in question the officer had indeed been on leave from his post in Northern Nigeria.

I reported to the Chief Secretary that the electoral rolls contained many fraudulent entries and that on polling day there would be widespread attempts at multiple voting. The likelihood of violence was high. In my judgment to guarantee a free and fair election in Okrika would require a presence of 300 police. I knew that such a request was out of the question. A few days later the Regional Government published the equivalent of an Order in Council authorizing the poll in all constituencies in the Region except Okrika in Degema Division. The election in Okrika would be held in January the following year. F. Kennedy was designated Electoral Officer for the constituency of Okrika.

In the following weeks I made several visits to Okrika. I met all the polling clerks but made no changes either to the physical arrangements or to the staff appointments. However, away from the island I made quite different dispositions. As far west of Port Harcourt as Okrika is east, near the old creek town of Buguma, there was a long established boarding school named Kalabari National College. Having made sure that none of them came from Okrika I recruited thirty of the most senior boys to be polling clerks in an election at an undisclosed venue and appointed the Head Master as Assistant Electoral Officer. I left behind two members of my staff to train our new polling clerks.

Before dawn on polling day the official government launch collected the Head Master and his team and brought them by river to Okrika where I was waiting with a substantial body of Police: not three hundred but well over one hundred. Shortly before polling began I visited each Centre and paid off the previously appointed staff, replacing them with the new recruits from KNC. The Okrika staff were astonished but also relieved to be extricated from what would have been a dangerous and well nigh impossible job. At each polling station I posted two police constables and kept a strategic reserve of 50 police near the centre of the island.

The poll went off without incident. The observers had been taken by surprise. They wanted to object but were not sure on what grounds they should do so. At the conclusion of the poll we loaded the sealed ballot boxes onto trucks that were waiting at the nearest point on the Ogoni shore. The boxes were then taken under Police escort to Port Harcourt. The Head Master and his happy warriors climbed aboard their launch and sailed off to Kalabari, pleased with their pay and satisfied with a piece of work well done. The votes were counted in the Port Harcourt Municipal Hall by specially recruited electoral staff. The defeated candidate and his supporters objected to the result in impassioned terms and vowed to lodge an appeal, but in the event never did.

In 1962 Port Harcourt was entering a period of huge social and economic change. The city had been built as a railway terminus during World War I on a peninsula surrounded by creeks of the Niger Delta. The engineers of the Nigeria Railways had done a good job. Built to a simple grid system the roads were surfaced and well drained and the residential plots adequate. The inhabitants were proud of their city. Port Harcourt claimed the proud title of Garden City and was admired throughout the country. To its disbelieving citizens today, the title seems a cynical joke.

A major preoccupation of the Provincial Secretary, Port Harcourt, was the Port Harcourt Planning Authority of which he was Secretary. The members of the Authority were appointed by the Minister of Health and Town Planning and exercised authority under specific legislation. A young American PhD student used to follow me around asking how it all worked. I was not too sure myself. The Authority had a small staff of some thirty people, who were employed on very modest wages. With an increasing population and rising prosperity land values soared. The Planning Authority sought to provide sites for commercial and industrial use as well as for residential purposes. As in other administrative centres the areas of government-owned land inherited from the Colonial regime were rapidly developed. Because of their favoured locations many of these areas of Crown Land were extremely valuable. A plot in a high class residential area in Port Harcourt or Lagos was usually far more valuable than a government pension. Banks were willing to finance the development of the plots which could be let for several years rent in advance to executives of incoming international companies. For a retired civil servant ownership of a plot could be the difference between wealth and penury. Ministers, judges, bishops, citizens of influence as well as senior civil servants all pressed for the allocation of plots in the choice locations of Port Harcourt.

At the other end of the spectrum penniless farmers and their families flooded into the slums that were expanding on the periphery of the city. The Planning Authority lacked the resources, the experience and the power to exercise anything approaching effective control over the economic forces surging through the city. The situation was aggravated by the fact that until 1961 the city boundary ended at mile two along the road to Owerri. Beyond that boundary people were free to build as they liked without the hindrance of the limited control exercised by the Port Harcourt Planning Authority. And they did. A festering slum developed outside the city proper that soon became known as Mile 2 Diobu. The deteriorating situation had been obvious since at least 1958 and it was a scandal that the Regional Government took until 1961 to extend the boundary to Mile 5 and bring the Diobu slum under the remit of the Port Harcourt Planning Authority.

Whilst we were reasonably successful in developing sites for industrial and high class residential use we failed abysmally to provide a decent environment for the poorest sectors of society. The problem was deeply frustrating. I had frequent arguments with government architects and technical advisers. They made great efforts to design suitable low cost housing and drew on examples from developing countries elsewhere. The resulting housing units were invariably outside the purchasing power of the people we were trying to house. I argued that the technical experts should start with a sum of money that a slum dweller was known to afford and then offer the best design that such a sum could purchase. We would still be left with a slum but with a marginally more salubrious slum than the present. The experts rejected the argument on the grounds that such a design would not meet minimum health and hygiene standards and professional integrity would not allow them to be associated with such developments.

The alternative solution, of course, was to provide subsidized housing. I wrote several times to the Ministry of Health arguing that only by the injection of serious money by the government was the deteriorating situation in Port Harcourt going to be brought under some sort of control. The answer was always that the funds needed did not exist and in any case the situation in Port Harcourt was not significantly different from that in other large centres of population in Nigeria. It is easy to be wise after the event but it still seems sad that more of the rapidly growing revenue from the newly discovered oil was not devoted to strengthening the public environment of centres such as Port Harcourt so that they were better able to stand the shocks that the new oil wealth created.

Life in Port Harcourt was not all work by any means. Anne and I had a hectic social life. A wide circle of friends included Stan Gray, the manager of Shell and his wife, Mary; Hedley Sheldrake of BP whose firm was building the new oil refinery; John Elbert a doctor, formerly in government now in private practice, and Franco Osagie and Mike Ogon. We would hold dinner parties at each others' houses and after dinner there would be dancing. Around Christmas time we often played charades. On one memorable occasion a lawyer friend, Nabo Graham Douglas, was given the task of performing 'Macbeth'. Nabo, whose nephew Anne taught in her nursery school, was over six foot three and weighed around fifteen stone. Nabo was beside himself with rage whilst we, his wife Christine included, rolled around in paroxysms of laughter at what turned out to be a mime of someone giving birth. Nabo never could understand why we failed to recognize the 'Macbirth' performance.

We also spent many Saturday evenings and sometimes other evenings as well at two newly opened night clubs. One was in the Cedar Palace Hotel. The other, our favourite, was a tiny box built on the outskirts of the city and named Scooby Doo. For several weeks after its opening the only music played in the club was from two records. One was Scooby Doo and the other was Mac the Knife sung by Bobby Darren. They were played over and over again, all night long. After two or three months the French lady who managed the club flew to Paris and after careful research returned with two more 45 rpm discs. That doubled the Club's musical repertoire. One evening in the Scooby Doo, Franco Osagie asked John Elbert which drink was least damaging to health. John said champagne. 'Drink nothing but good champagne, Franco, and you will never be ill.' Whether Franco was ever ill I do not know but twenty years later Anne and I spent a weekend at his home in Benin. Franco took me upstairs and proudly showed me two of the bedrooms. They were stacked floor to ceiling with cases of Dom Perignon 1971 vintage champagne. Franco warned 'But always carry a swizzle stick. You must take out the bubbles!'

During our stay in Port Harcourt the British Council organized a visit by the Royal Shakespeare Company. John Neville led a strong cast which included a very young Judi Dench. One of the plays was *Macbeth* (which prompted our charade title). I gave a post theatre reception for the cast and a group of thirty or forty friends. It was memorable for two events. The first was that during our party we noticed from the veranda that a robbery was taking place at a store nearby and the thieves were making their way by the bottom of the garden. As Jock Rollo, the Senior Superintendent of Police, was in the party some of our guests felt that the least they could do was to give chase to the robbers.

At the time the party took place South Africa's position in the Commonwealth was a subject of much discussion and Britain was under pressure from the black nations of the Commonwealth to support the country's expulsion. The Nigerian press was vociferous in its attacks on Britain. A number of my Nigerian guests had gathered round Judi Dench and she asked them why their newspapers were being so horrid to her country. The Nigerians loved the directness and sincerity of the lovely young actress and soon the whole party had gathered in a circle round her. She won all hearts.

By 1962 I was thirty six years old and the time seemed ripe for a career change. Whilst I enjoyed working for Nigerian ministers and fully understood the reasons for the policy, I did not wish to remain in a structure where promotion to the most senior positions was blocked. Many British administrative officers had transferred to other colonies but with the possible exception of Hong Kong this had little appeal for me. Nigeria had been Britain's largest colony. I did not wish to move to a smaller, less developed country and repeat the process of preparing for Independence all over again.

Some colleagues had retrained for other professions, such as law or accountancy. This I seriously considered but by this time Anne and I had two children and I felt that I could not afford to be out of work for an extended period. Another possibility was a career in business or industry and I received a number of offers that were very tempting. I sometimes wonder whether I made the right choice but the possibility of seeing more countries of the world as an officer in the British Foreign Service persuaded me to enter a competition for appointment to the Administrative Class of the British Civil Service and Commonwealth Service. I sat the final parts of the examination in London and when told that I had been successful I was required to return to Nigeria to serve a year's notice in residence.

My friend Oputa Udoji, the Chief Secretary of the Eastern Region, kindly invited me to choose whichever job I wished for my last tour. He wanted me to take the post of Deputy Permanent Secretary, Ministry of Local Government, where I would be Permanent Secretary in all but name. Local Government was one of the busiest departments in the government, but in those early post Independence years many of the County and District Councils had still little idea of how the business of local government should be done. Many of the politicians refused to vote for reductions in expenditure that were necessary for the annual budget to balance. The Councils would send the unbalanced budgets to the Ministry of Local Government for approval. The Ministry then had to spend countless hours reworking income and expenditure estimates and in effect imposing the rewritten budgets on the miscreant councils. This seemed to me a thankless chore in an idiotic situation. With Udoji's permission I returned to Port Harcourt to spend my last tour as Provincial Secretary there.

The big task facing the Administration in the closing weeks of 1962 was the national census. Earlier censuses had been the subject of bitter disputes between the Regions. The results were of enormous importance because the size and shape of electoral constituencies were based on them. Politicians in the West and East Regions were extremely sceptical of the census returns, which showed the North as the most populous region. This time the census was to be carried out in accordance with rules laid down by the United Nations whose agents were to supervise the operation.

The first task facing the Administrators was to divide their area of responsibility into 'enumeration areas', that is to say, areas small enough to count in a single eight-hour day. On the day of the count, movement was to be forbidden and all citizens required to stay in their homes. Preparations seemed to be proceeding satisfactorily in the Province. I visited my old division of Ahoada. Everything seemed under control. I visited Ogoni. The District Officer said that everything was under control. I called up the District Officer, Port Harcourt. Everything, he said, was under control. 'Er, that is everything except a minor difficulty in Diobu.' 'Which part of Diobu?' I asked. 'Mile 2', replied the District Officer.

The Mile 2 Diobu slum was a rabbit warren and a census officer's nightmare. In the worst section there were no streets. Houses and flats crowded in on each other in one huge, crooked, jumble. They had been given numbers in the order in which they had been erected. Your house might be number 7. Your next door neighbour's might be number 132. Demarcating numeration areas in such a jungle was no easy task. A few days later I called on the DO again. The problem was still unresolved but he had now switched his best ADO to Mile 2 Diobu. A week later with a solution as far away as ever I instructed the DO to take personal responsibility for Diobu and get the area demarcated, but it was clear that the task was beyond the capability of the relatively inexperienced DO and his team.

I had read in *Time Magazine* of the plans of the new American President, John F. Kennedy, to bring a fresh energy and determination to solving the problems of the world. In particular he was establishing a Peace Corps of young volunteers to work in developing countries. I knew that some of the first of the Peace Corps had just arrived in Lagos. From the old lags they met the usual scepticism. I remembered my first breakfast in the Ikoyi Club and the greeting of the Superintendent of Customs. I wrote to Udoji in Enugu and said that I would like the services of an American Peace Corps graduate for four weeks.

Udoji was quickly on the phone. 'What is all this Peace Corps business? If you need another assistant why does he have to be American?' For Udoji, of course, the only university worth talking about was Cambridge. 'Look, Oputa,' I replied, 'If we send a young British graduate into this mess in Diobu he'll come back with a dissertation explaining why the job is impossible. We have no time. I don't want an academic. I want a practical, "Can Do" person. That is what these Americans claim to be.' 'Oh, have it your way,' said Udoji, unconvinced, but too busy to waste time on the latest eccentricity.

The Head of the Peace Corps in West Africa was delighted to discover that he had a customer. Ten days later Russ McGovern, graduate of Michigan State University and member of the United States Peace Corps strode into my office. He was the all-American boy from the Mid-West, just as I had imagined he would be: twenty two years of age, six foot three in his socks, freckled face. He was even wearing a baseball cap – which he removed with a flourish. 'Russ McGovern reporting for duty, Sir.'

I took the young man over to a map on the wall and explained that we had to divide the Province into areas of population small enough for one person to count in a single day. Most of the work was complete but there was a congested area in a suburb called Diobu. I wanted him to demarcate Mile 2 Diobu into enumeration areas. Any assistance he needed I would try to provide. Russ looked at me for some seconds. Had he come all the way from Michigan for this? 'Is that all?' he asked. 'That's all,' I said. Russ climbed into the Chevrolet kit-car and roared off towards Diobu.

The following morning Russ called into my office. The work was going well. He expected to be finished by Friday. Wonderful, I said. On Friday Russ again dropped by. The work was going well but it was going to take a little while longer. Great, I said. Some days later Russ called again. He wanted to explain that inside Mile 2 Diobu between the barber's shop on the west and the decrepit Mbonu flats to the north there was a jumble of property without streets or drains or sanitary lanes. It was difficult to demarcate what was a virtual maze. 'Now, Russ,' I said, 'you are getting warm. This is why you are here.' 'How much longer do we have?' asked Russ. 'Two weeks maximum,' I told him.

From then on Russ worked in Mile 2 Diobu every day from 6 in the morning until dusk without a break. I noticed that he now went off armed with compasses and all the gear a surveyor carried. He was becoming known to everyone who lived in Diobu and many of the local youth were volunteering to help the engaging young visitor with his strange obsession. But Russ had still not cracked the problem.

Time was running out when Russ came into my office with his last request. Could I let him have £20? No problem, I said. In Port Harcourt Club Russ had met a man who owned a two-seater Piper aircraft. The man was willing to fly him over Mile 2 Diobu if he would pay for the petrol. Russ had a box camera and was going to try to photograph the problem area if I would pay for petrol, films and development of the films. I told him that if he took the photographs I would do the rest.

Russ spent two hours flying back and forth over Mile 2 Diobu, leaning over the side of the cockpit and taking photographs with his little camera. He came back with half a dozen reels of negatives. I drove to Umubiakani and asked Shell's geologists if they could develop the films and blow them up to a size that would show every house, flat, hut and hovel. Two days later across the wall of the District Office some twenty feet by six stretched an arial photograph of Mile 2 Diobu. We marked off suitably sized enumeration areas and then Russ matched the pictures with written descriptions and identification points. The census in Diobu was completed without further hitch. I wrote to the Head of the Peace Corps (with a copy of course to my Chief Secretary) to say that Russ McGovern had shown all the flair and persistence we could have hoped for in solving to a difficult practical problem. He had performed a valuable service to Eastern Nigeria and could not have been a better ambassador for his country.

I thought that I had heard the last of Okrika but one Friday before Christmas the phone rang. It was Ron, the new Senior Superintendent of Police who had recently taken over from Jock Rollo. He said that there was trouble in Okrika. He had despatched half a unit of 25 police to the island by road. He was following with another 50 police by river and would arrive later in the afternoon. I explained that Okrika was nothing to do with me. A year earlier I had been appointed Electoral Officer for the specific purpose of conducting the election on the island but that was all. Okrika was in Degema Division and outside my jurisdiction. The SSP said that the DO, Degema, was aware of the position but he would not be able to get to Okrika in time. The SSP hoped that I might talk to the parties that were squaring up to each other and perhaps keep the lid on things until he arrived with the second contingent of police. Why the SSP was coming with the second and not the first contingent of police was never made clear. I presumed that we were talking about our old friends the Koniju and Tuboniju and very much doubted whether anything could be done at this late stage. Nevertheless, provided that Enugu agreed, I said that I would drive over to the island and see if I could keep the two sides talking until the SSP arrived with his men.

The Okrika disturbances were an administrative shambles and I take no pleasure in recalling them. Although it never occurred to me at the time, they probably exemplified the weakening grip exerted by the administration as the country began its slide into instability and civil war. Five years earlier the administration had managed, by the skin of its teeth, to contain the backlash against the reintroduction of primary school fees in Eastern Region of Nigeria. Now we seemed unable to manage the threat of communal violence in an island whose population probably did not exceed twenty or thirty thousand. But in 1958 in Ahoada we worked in close harmony as a single management team. In 1963 in Okrika we were anything but that. A newly appointed Nigerian District Officer was unfamiliar with his Division and unknown to its people. The Officer in charge of the Police had arrived recently from a departmental job in Lagos.

The Senior Administrative Officer – me – was from a different province and had no authority over the DO or the SSP and indeed had no locus standing in the matter at all.

I drove myself to Okrika in the early afternoon and parked my VW beetle under the usual palm tree before being ferried across the creek in a canoe. As I approached the centre of the island I came across the three policemen peering nervously round the corner of a house towards the main street. In what I thought was my best Dixon of Dock Green style I told them to follow me. The main street might have been the set for one of Clint Eastwood's Western movies. Separated by some fifty or sixty yards two large barricades had been erected blocking the street from one side to another. From behind the barricades young men were shouting abuse and throwing occasional missiles at each other. Two ju-ju priests were doing little jigs and, I presumed, calling down maledictions on their respective enemies. A good deal of effort had obviously gone into the preparation of this set-piece confrontation. The Koniju and Tuboniju had been cheated of their battle at the time of the election. They did not intend to be side-tracked this time. It was clear that the curtain was going to be raised very shortly.

I soon ran into difficulty. I had failed to bring a loudspeaker with me. When I stood in the centre of the road between the two sides I found that I could not make myself heard. I was forced to move from one side to another. Whilst I was talking to one group I could hear an increasingly restive group behind my back. The surprise at the sudden appearance of an uninvited white man soon began to wear off. My general tactic was to urge the groups to identify their leader so that I could engage him in talk that would lead towards negotiation. I claimed that large forces of law and order were on the way and that their best bet was to talk to me. They did not really buy this line but at least the clock was ticking away. An hour or more had passed when one of my policemen came to urge me to come to another part of the town where fighting had broken out. I had no option but to relinquish my position at the barricades.

The first contingent of police under the command of a Superintendent of Police had now arrived. We were led to a row of houses said to be occupied by Tuboniju. The Koniju said that the occupants were trespassers. As we watched a number of youths climbed on to the roofs of the houses and began to set fire to the thatch. I told the Superintendent that if we did not put an immediate stop to this the riot would spread all over the island. He said that we should await the arrival of the SSP and the larger force. After an exchange of views we did clear the youths from the roofs. I then insisted that we charge the group and make one or two arrests. The SP made clear his reluctance to do this but did not actually refuse. I led a half-hearted charge with the SP lumbering slowly by my side. I grabbed one of the youths and looked round to find that the SP and his men were falling behind, I believed, deliberately. I released my prisoner and asked the SP what he wanted to do now. He said: wait for his boss. I said: 'OK, now you have got your riot. Get on with it.' The Superintendent led his men to a nearby school where they sat and smoked whilst the mayhem developed around them.

A short time later the SSP arrived with his fifty men. I told him that we had only been able to delay things for an hour or so and had failed to clamp down on the first attempts at arson. In my opinion this was now a straightforward police action. I asked him whether there was anything else he wanted from me. He said no. So I walked back to the waterside and got one of the Koniju to ferry me across the creek. In retrospect I always felt that I was wrong to leave when I did. The SSP was asking in everything but words for moral support. If I had stayed a major bust-up between me and his Superintendent would have been a certainty and one between me and the SSP was a possibility. But they would have been preferable to what followed.

That night Anne and I played bridge with Chief Chanrai, the manager of the Port Harcourt branch of the Chanrai chain of retail shops and one of his branch managers. The Chief broke the seal on two brand new packs of cards and after a thorough shuffle dealt to Anne and me the most extraordinary hands we ever played. In the first two rubbers I made two small slams and one grand slam. The Chief presented me with the packs and said that however long I lived I would never again have such good cards. He was right.

About 11 o'clock the phone rang. It was the SSP phoning from Okrika. He said that the situation was OK. There had been some firing of Dane guns but the shots were only *feux de joie*. Some young people had been letting off steam at the beginning of the holiday season. I asked whether he wanted me to join him on the island. He said that it was not necessary. So I said OK.

On Okrika there was a little sub-Post Office run by a young Assistant Postal Agent whom I had met during the election. The Post Office was situated in the middle of the island, roughly on the fault line between Koniju and Tuboniju territory. At 7.15 a.m. the next morning my telephone rang. It was my young friend, the Postal Agent in Okrika. He was sheltering under the counter of the Office. Fighting had been going on all through the night. Several people had been killed and a number injured. The young Postal Agent in Okrika became my 'deep throat'.

Every day the Police would report that the situation was generally calm. Every morning for five consecutive days the Postal Agent would ring me at 7.15 a.m. and tell me how many people had been killed during the night and how many he thought had been injured.

On the Saturday afternoon the Koniju and Tuboniju fought a pitched battle from their canoes in the middle of the main creek. Five people were said to have died of gunshot wounds. I was incensed at what I thought was turning into a farcical defiance of law and order. Originally my sympathies had inclined towards the Tuboniju but as the week went on the disturbances took on a different pattern. During the day the streets would be relatively calm. Each night the Tuboniju would send raiding parties in canoes to attack the Koniju section of the town. The Koniju could not easily retaliate since the Tuboniju were living in a scatter of small islands that faced across the creek towards the main island in a rough crescent. They had at their command many more canoes than the Koniju. Our old friend, Louis Allen from Durham University, was staying with us at the time. I took him to visit the island. The streets were almost empty but some small buildings were still burning from the fighting of the night before.

The disturbances culminated in a night battle round the residence of Chief Samson Adoki of the Koniju. Four of his grown up sons had returned to defend the house. It was alleged that the Tuboniju were fighting to recover the body of one of their dead. The fighting raged all night long. Chief Samson's sons defended their property with Dane guns and shotguns and four old cannon. When my Postal Agent rang at 7.15 I told him to pack his bags and get off the island until I judged it safe to return.

A few days later the SSP and I were summoned to meet Mr Nolan Millet in Okrika. Mr Millet was the Inspector General of Police, the senior officer in charge of Police in the Federation of Nigeria. He had stopped over in Port Harcourt in a flight from the Cameroons to Lagos. It was clear from his opening words that the Inspector General was a man whose patience had finally been exhausted. The Inspector General wanted to know what should be done. The SSP said that he was tempted to suggest that the two sides should be left to fight it out. It was hardly worth risking the life of a constable in such a senseless quarrel. I said that it was a scandal that after ten days of bloodshed the disturbances were still dragging on. The Inspector General indicated that he was asking for a plan of action, not a sermon. He wanted to know what should be *done*.

I maintained that *what* we did was less important than that we did *something*. At present we were dancing to the tune of the Koniju and

Tuboniju – the latter more than the former. We had to recapture the initiative. As a start I would suggest three things. First, I would seize every Tuboniju canoe I could find, tow them out to the main channel and sink them in the deepest water I could reach. 'You can't do that!' interrupted the SSP, 'It would be illegal.' I said that I was telling the Inspector General what *I* would do. I would 'requisition' the canoes, sink them and leave the owners to fight us in court. The Tubonijus were making fools of us. We had to stop their nightly attacks over the water. The Inspector General said: 'OK, do it. Next?'

I said that secondly I would bind over Chief Samson Adoki and the Chief of the Tubonijus to keep the peace. They were supposed to be fighting over the succession to the chieftaincy but neither had shown any sign whatever of chiefly responsibility. I said that we should read the riot act to them and warn them that any more violence and they would both be thrown into jail. The two Police Officers were quick to accept this suggestion.

My third proposal was that we should land at night with a force of police on the off-shore islands. This was the last thing that the Tubonijus would expect. 'Can't be done,' said the SSP. 'Haven't got the landing craft. Anyway, it's against the law to make arrests at night.' The Inspector General looked at me. I said that I would find the boats. It would take me forty eight hours to get them to the island. We could make the landings on the Wednesday night, beginning say at 10 p.m. In the meantime we ought to be able to persuade a magistrate to issue the necessary warrants. The Inspector General said: 'Do it.' That was the end of the meeting.

I borrowed two aluminium-skinned boats from Shell's marine department and had them towed out to Okrika in the early evening of Wednesday. Each was powered by an outboard engine and at a pinch could carry up to 16 people. When darkness fell we landed first on the main island to patrol the old town where the Konijus lived. I told the SSP that it was essential first to secure our rear and make sure that we were not caught between two fronts. The Koniju old town was deserted. The occupants had fled before the raiding Tubonijus. The night was pitch dark but the Police carried powerful torches and we made our way through the old wooden houses, some of which had been built in Victoria's reign. I felt badly about invading the privacy of the absent owners. One house had a library. Books, some very old, and pages from a tattered bible lay scattered on the floor of the ransacked property. We left behind a dozen police to patrol the town.

It was midnight by the time we were making our way across the creek to the Tuboniju islands. We went as quietly as the outboard engine would allow. A moon had begun to rise. Because we were constantly wading to and from the boats I was wearing gym shoes and shorts. I was bitten incessantly by mosquitoes. We landed three or four men on each of the five largest islands. I instructed them to make no move until they heard a whistled signal. The SSP and I went with the last three men to the largest island. As we approached the shore the SSP said 'Do you think this is wise? We have no idea what is waiting for us.' I said: 'Don't worry. The people in the houses know even less. They are much more afraid than we are.'

We landed on the little island and marched up to the first hut as whistles sounded faintly on the other islands. We hammered on the door. There were obviously people inside but no one responded. We repeated the exercise on several other houses with similar results. I told the SSP that that was it and suggested that he leave the Sergeant and two constables on the island to keep the inhabitants inside their houses until daylight. When we got back to the main island the SSP asked whether I would be coming back in the morning to make sure that all was well. I said that the riots were over. I would not be coming back to Okrika ever again.

Two weeks later I went down to a fierce attack of malaria.

In fact I did go back to Okrika. A few months later the SSP and I were invited to witness an ancient ceremony. The Koniju and Tuboniju had finally made peace. The ju-ju priests conducted an ancient ritual that lasted all day. So rarely had the ceremonies been performed that the priests had to stop a number of times to consult the oldest men as to what they should do next. The ceremonies ended with a number of sacrificial animals being towed out to the middle of the creek in a canoe. There the canoe slowly sank and with it the bitterness and conflict of a generation.

Thanks to the courtesy of the Governor of Rivers State I managed to make a flying visit to Okrika in 2004. The island is now joined to the mainland by a bridge. Much of course has changed. But Chief Samson Adoki's house still stands. St Peter's Cathedral Church looks much as it did forty years ago. The spirits of the Koniju and Tuboniju still seem to be sleeping peacefully in the ancient waters.

Okrika was not the only thing that kept us busy at that time. Shell was drilling for oil just north of Port Harcourt. During the early hours of New Year's Day when changing the bit on a drill, whether by mistake or by accident, there was a blow-out. A column of flame shot up hundreds of feet into the air. The noise could be heard seven miles away in Port Harcourt. It sounded to me like a dozen steam locomotives charging together down a railway tunnel. We evacuated a nearby village and later agreed the compensation to be paid by Shell for the damage to livestock and property suffered by the villagers. It was surprising how many goats and sheep each person in that particular village turned out to own. But those costs were trivial compared with the cost of putting out the fire.

To extinguish the blaze, Shell called on the services of the great Red Adair. He arrived within forty eight hours, flying in his own plane from Argentina. I was greatly impressed by the flamboyant Mr Adair. So fierce was the heat that it seemed impossible that anyone could get close enough to get the well under control. Adair first had pipes laid to secure an ample supply of water. Then having built great shields of corrugated metal on which huge jets of water played continuously he cleared the site of all debris, including the twisted metal of the previous well-head. Finally – two or three weeks later – he extinguished the blaze by an explosive charge and corked the well.

We must have been fit in those days. Anne ran her nursery school each morning and I worked during the day. But as well as the hectic social life at weekends and several week nights too, spent with friends at the Scooby Doo or Cedar Palace or in each others' houses, we somehow managed to fit in large amounts of tennis, cricket and bridge as well.

Towards the end of the year came the terrible event of John F. Kennedy's assassination. Anne had taken the children swimming in Port Harcourt Club. As I went to collect them I stopped at the table of a group of American oil drillers from Texas. I told them that the President had been murdered. 'Good', said one. 'Couldn't stand the bastard.' Back home I listened on the short wave radio to reactions to the news from around Africa. The tyres of a red sports car screeched to a halt on the gravel by the front porch. In burst John Elbert. 'Thank God, thank God', cried John, arms up-stretched. He had heard the news and thought that it was I who had been killed.

The following week the Catholic bishop of Port Harcourt, Bishop Okoye, sent his parish priest to ask me to deliver a panegyric on John F. Kennedy at a memorial service he was to conduct in the cathedral church. I said that I did not think it appropriate for me to give the address since I was neither American nor Nigerian. The arguments were brushed aside. I had one undeniable attribute for the job: my name was Kennedy. So I gave the address. It was the first time that I had ever spoken from a pulpit. The church was packed. The Vice Consul from the US Embassy had flown from Lagos to be present. There was no mistaking the depth and sincerity of the feeling of those present that evening. I noticed a man on the third row. As I spoke, a tear rolled slowly down his cheek.

By 1963 Port Harcourt was booming. The number of rigs drilling for oil, on and off-shore, rose month by month. A pipeline had been laid to

Bonny where large, ocean-going tankers could now load oil without coming into the narrow channel. The construction of the oil refinery at Eleme had been completed and was supplying refined product to the domestic market. Alcan and Michelin were the latest industries to move to sites in Port Harcourt's new Industrial Estate. A mission from the Federation of British Industries visited the country to assess investment opportunities. They asked me what were the chances of the Federation avoiding a clash between the largely Hausa Northern Region and the largely Igbo East. 'No better than fifty-fifty,' I told them, 'but this is a market that you cannot afford not to be in. If the UK fails to invest, other countries certainly will. The risks are factored into the rewards.'

In the meantime at the Planning Authority we continued to struggle with the consequences of this explosive growth on Port Harcourt's social and economic development. A young American PhD student was writing a thesis on local government in West Africa. He would follow me around with his clip-board dutifully writing down the answers to his earnest questions.

It was then that I had an idea that might be called in today's graceless jargon, a 'no-brainer.' The Planning Authority, the majority of whose board members were also Members of the Municipal Council, had been generous in their expressions of appreciation of my efforts. I told them that I would like to ask as a favour a farewell gift. 'Anything. Just name it,' beamed the Chairman.

We had completed plans for a new residential area at Mile 4 Diobu. It was a very simple, middle-income layout which would permit the construction of two or three hundred houses on little plots arranged in a grid system. The Authority would construct the roads and the drains and was about to put this work out to tender.

I reminded the board of the problems facing the Authority and of the failure to which the slums at Mile 2 were depressing testimony. We were trying to build new residential areas but within a short time the roads that we built were pot-holed and the drains blocked. We did not have the money to build to the standards required by the conditions. Yet it was widely believed that whenever a contract was put out to tender money changed hands between the contractor and members of the board. The atmosphere was getting less friendly by the minute but I ploughed on. Every pound paid in bribes from a contractor, I said, was a pound taken from the pockets of the people.

I told the board that I would be leaving Nigeria shortly on retirement. The Diobu Mile 4 Development was the last with which I would be associated. The favour I wanted to ask was this: Would the board agree to execute this one project without demanding or accepting a bribe from contractors. The sums involved were not large but it would be a marvellous thing if I could leave in the knowledge that despite all the charges of corruption we in the Port Harcourt Planning Authority knew that we had carried out at least one completely clean project.

After an embarrassed silence there was much shuffling of feet, clearing of throats and assumptions of injured innocence. The Chairman did not understand how the Secretary had managed to get such ideas. It went without saying that the Mile 4 Diobu contracts would be placed and executed without any irregular payments. I thanked the Chairman and the Board for that promise.

Normally tenders were opened and processed in the offices of the Planning Authority. It was at this stage that the unofficial auctions took place and bribes changed hands. On this occasion I had specified that bids should be addressed to the Provincial Secretary's Office. As each tender came in my Secretary recorded its number and the address on the envelope. He then handed the envelope to me and I locked it unopened in a safe to which I had the only key. I carried the key with me at all times.

I had decided that only three people would be involved in processing the tenders. My Secretary and I would handle the administration but I needed the help of one other person if the award of the contract was not to be challenged on technical grounds. I mulled over this problem for several days. Eventually I thought of the man in the third row of the cathedral church at the night of the service for John F. Kennedy and the tear that had rolled slowly down his cheek. He was the Government Engineer in Port Harcourt and had no involvement in the Planning Authority. I went to see him.

I reminded him of Nigeria's reputation for corruption. This extended, I believed, to the Planning Authority. We were robbing the people we were supposed to be serving. I was working on one last project before retiring from Nigeria and had promised the board of the Planning Authority that on this one occasion the contracts would be placed without any bribes being paid or accepted. I could not make good my promise without the professional help of one other person. I had to trust one other person. I wanted to know whether he would be that person. I stressed that he should feel under no obligation to accept. This was a purely voluntary arrangement outside normal duty. If he declined I should understand perfectly. But if he said yes he had to commit completely to what we were trying to do. The Engineer said that he would be delighted to help and he would regard it as an honour to do so. We shook hands. I was very relieved to have help from such a source. I explained that the tenders would remain in my safe unopened until the day on which the Planning

Authority was to meet. Only three people would be involved in scrutinizing the bids: him, my secretary and I.

The meeting of the Authority was due to start at 10.a.m. My secretary and I arrived at my office at 4.30 a.m. The Chief Engineer arrived at 5.00 a.m. We proceeded to open the safe and list the tenders alphabetically. I then handed the tenders to the Chief Engineer and asked him to examine them for technical competence and relevant experience and give an overall evaluation of each bid taking into account the price. Of the 20 or so tenders I asked him to produce a short list of not less than three and not more than five contractors that in his judgement had submitted reasonable bids.

By 9.30 the Chief Engineer had completed his task and at 9.45 we walked the few hundred yards from my office to the Council Chamber where the Planning Authority was to meet. We had rigged up a large blackboard on which my secretary wrote the names of the contractors and the details of their bid. Below the third name he drew a line in chalk. I invited the Chief Engineer to give a brief review of the tenders and explain why some for one reason or another were defective. I invited questions. There were none. I explained that the first three had been judged by the Chief Engineer to have submitted reasonable tenders. Any one of them would be acceptable to me.

To my surprise the Chairman said that there was no need for further debate. We could proceed straight to the award. There was no need for a secret ballot. We could decide the matter by a show of hands. No one demurred. No one offered a comment. I said that the board would be invited to vote on each tender in turn. My secretary would record the votes. I called for a vote on the first tender. No one moved. The second tender was from a firm called Southern Construction Company. I called for a vote on Southern Construction Company. Every hand in the room shot up. I could not believe it. 'No need to go further,' said the Chairman. 'The board has chosen.' I sat in my chair in baffled silence. After some moments I rose and adjourned the meeting until later in the day. My secretary gathered up the tenders and we walked out.

In my office I continued to sit in stunned silence. I gazed at the ceiling and asked what could possibly have gone wrong with my 'foolproof' system. Shortly after 2.00 p.m the door was flung open. In charged Alex Onyeadu. He had driven all the way from Owerri where he worked in Shell's Land and Legal Department. 'What the hell are you doing?' he wanted to know. 'How could you award a contract to a gang like the Southern Construction Company?' he asked. Six months earlier, he maintained, I had said publicly that the company was unfit to work on a government contract and would never again be awarded a contract as long as I was Secretary of the Port Harcourt Planning Authority. I said that I had never heard of the company. 'Well of course you haven't,' said Alex. 'They changed their name three months ago, didn't they?' Banging the table Alex went on to say – if I remember the figures correctly – that the company had paid a bribe of one hundred pounds to the Chairman and half that to each member of the board. I asked was he sure. He was absolutely sure. The money had been paid the previous evening. I said that I did not see how it was possible. The tenders had been unopened until the morning of the bid. The only person involved in the technical evaluation had been the Provincial Engineer. He was the one man I had chosen to trust and he had pledged to protect that trust. 'Where do think that these people at Southern Construction come from?' Alex asked. 'No idea', I confessed. Alex named a town I had never heard of in a Division some two hundred miles away. 'And where do you think,' asked Alex, 'your friend, the Provincial Engineer comes from?'

I do not think that I had ever experienced anything more dispiriting. I studied the terms of the instrument which had established the Planning Authority. It seemed that to execute a contract legally it must be signed by the Secretary of the Authority. I marched back across to the Council Chamber where the Authority was still in session. I announced that I was not going to sign the contract with Southern Construction Company because (a) the company, which had traded previously under another name, had an appalling record and (b) I had been reliably informed that bribes had been paid to secure the award of the contract to this company. The Authority would reconvene in a few days time in an Extraordinary Meeting and would reconsider the tenders.

Reactions were not slow to arrive. I received a letter from Ray Coatswith, whom the reader last met on the veranda of the Nnewi Community Centre during the Federal Elections of 1954. Ray was now Permanent Secretary to the Minister of Health and Town and Country Planning and the most senior remaining British Permanent Secretary in Enugu. The Minister was concerned, wrote Ray, at reports that I had refused to sign a contract awarded by the Port Harcourt Planning Authority to the Southern Construction Company. He hoped that I would sign and execute the contract without further delay. I replied by telegram saying that I had refused to sign the contract because I was reliably informed that the Southern Construction Company had paid bribes of £100 to the Chairman and £50 to each member of the board of the Port Harcourt Planning Authority. If the Minister were so to instruct I would comply immediately but I would not sign a contract with the Southern Construction Company in the absence of an explicit instruction from the Minister.

Within minutes an agitated Permanent Secretary was on the phone. What was I playing at, Ray wanted to know, sending such a telegram *en clair*? Was I trying to embarrass his Minister or what? I knew perfectly well that following my telegram his Minister could not possibly instruct me to sign. 'Well, then,' I replied, 'in that case I am not going to sign the contract.' I heard no more from the Minister but that was far from the end of the matter.

At the Extraordinary Meeting of the Planning Authority I said that the board could choose to award the contract to any of the first four firms in the evaluation list but if they continued to press for the award to Southern Construction I would not execute the contract and would turn over the papers to the Police to investigate the charges of corruption against each member of the board. Without grace but without further obstruction the board agreed on the award to one of the other four companies.

The directors of the Southern Construction Company were by no means finished. The following morning I opened the newspaper to read a banner headline in the *Nigerian Spokesman*: 'Kennedy accused of accepting a bribe of £9,600.' A few hours later I was served with a writ commanding me to attend a meeting of the magistrate's court to face a charge of accepting a bribe of £9,600 to block the award of a contract to the Southern Construction Company. I was charged with acting *ultra vires* and misusing my office for malicious and personal reasons. The sum in question was equal to approximately five times my annual salary at the time.

The Southern Construction Company had engaged the services of one of the city's top legal law firms. After some delay a nice young man arrived from the Atttorney General's office in Enugu. He said that he had come to represent me. He had been in the job three months. The French mail boat began to seem more and more remote.

Whether the directors of Southern Construction had any influence with the magistrate I never knew but the hearings followed a curious pattern. The Court would be called to order. My Counsel's representations would be brushed aside and the case would be adjourned. Three times I went to court and three times the case was adjourned. It seemed that I would be run out of time as my departure date got nearer and nearer. The case was reported in lurid terms in the daily press. It was not every day that a senior British Administrative Officer faced such charges in court.

On 23 December I was sitting outside Court No 3 waiting to be called for the fourth time. Hurrying from another court, wig and gown flying and a huge pile of briefs under one arm passed Nabo Graham Douglas. Nabo was probably the top lawyer in Port Harcourt at the time. Nabo stopped in mid-flight. 'What on earth are you doing here, Frank?' enquired our friend of the Macbeth charade. I explained. 'Just hang on,' said Nabo, 'I will be back as soon as I can make a presentation in Court No 1.'

Our case was finally called and the magistrate took his seat just as Nabo came bustling in. Nabo asked permission to speak. Granted, said the magistrate. 'Your worship,' said, Nabo, 'with the Court's permission I have been appointed by the defendant as Assistant Legal Counsel.' 'Granted,' said the magistrate. My young Crown Counsel smiled. 'Permission to speak, Your Worship', said Nabo. 'Granted,' said the magistrate. 'My client,' said Nabo, 'after ten years distinguished service as an Administrative Officer, is due to leave the country on retirement on a ship which sails on 4 January. It would greatly inconvenience my client and his family if they were prevented from leaving on that date. I therefore wish to stand personal surety for any amount that the court may award against my client in this case.' 'That will not be necessary, Mr Graham Douglas,' said the magistrate. 'The plaintiff's case is without merit as may be seen from several precedent cases. Case dismissed.'

It was all over in minutes. Nabo dismissed my thanks with a smile.

On one morning during the last few days in Port Harcourt I bumped into the Government Engineer. 'How could you?' I asked. 'You were the one man I had to trust and you gave me your word.' 'You do not understand,'he said. 'My family have to live in that community.' But his head hung down. He would not meet my eyes.

When I returned to Nigeria as a British diplomat in 1978 the first person to call on us in Bourdillon Road was Nabo Graham Douglas. After a terrible civil war Nabo had risen to be Attorney General and Federal Minister of Justice. At one period Nabo had been imprisoned but after the war his wife became pregnant and delivered the child they had wanted for years. Nabo and Christine rejoiced in what they were convinced was a miracle and a blessing from God.

We sailed for Marseilles on the French ship, *Jean Mermoz*. Sarah was five and Mark three. Each day the children would play in the little swimming pool on the upper deck. Sarah would climb the steps of the diving board, rise on her toes and execute a perfect little dive and the ladies round the pool would murmur, '*Ah, la petite Anglaise.*' The news bulletin issued each day from the bridge said that '*le beatlemanie*' was sweeping America. I asked several people what was this '*beatlemanie*'. They did not know either.

CHAPTER 13

1964: Not one of us

Anne and I were back in England for the first time in our married life and the first task was to find somewhere to live. We looked first in Blackheath where our friends Ian and Mary Orchardson had been living since their return from Nigeria a few years earlier. When we had no luck in Blackheath we turned to the nearby town of Beckenham where a new development of thirty houses was under construction. The site backed on to Beckenham Park. The broker who arranged our mortgage urged me to buy instead a house in a wonderful location on Chislehurst Common. The house was more expensive but a better property in every way. I declined to take the advice and have regretted it ever since.

But we were very happy in Foxgrove Road Beckenham. The twenty nine other families turned out to be congenial neighbours with similar jobs and similar interests as ourselves. Most had young families and the children all became firm friends. Although over time we moved out to other parts of the city or the country many of our Beckenham friendships have survived to this day. Michael and Anne Richardson were wonderfully kind guardians to Sarah and Mark when they went to boarding school and Monty and Jill Freedman were equally kind to our daughter Ruth. Michael and Helga Nelson have always kept in touch and we visit each other frequently in this country and in France. Michael Nelson retired as a main board director of Reuters. Monty built a very successful business as a franchisee of automatic car wash machines. Michael Richardson became a senior Scientific Officer in Whitehall. Our other neighbour, Tony Toller, made a career in advertising.

When I returned to the United Kingdom the Foreign Office and the Commonwealth Office were still separate departments with separate overseas services, although the latter were shortly to be merged into a single Diplomatic Service. I had assumed that I would be posted to the Commonwealth Service. To my surprise and irritation the Civil Service Commissioners posted me to the Ministry of Labour. When I protested they replied that after careful consideration they had decided that I had the qualities needed in the Ministry of Labour and they would stand by their earlier decision. This was not what I had had in mind at all when I had opted for a public service job but I had no option but to report nonetheless for duty at the headquarters of the Ministry of Labour in St James's Square. My office was in Cleveland House on the corner of King Street and St James's Square. The Minister's office was in a building on the opposite corner of Duke Street and St James's Square and several times a week I would make the short journey across the Square from one office to the other. By a coincidence I returned to the very same location twenty years later when I joined British Airways. My office was in Enserch House, the building in which the Minister of Labour had had his office. Equally remarkable was the fact that the Chairman of BA, Lord King, who was also chairman of Babcock, had his office in Cleveland House. So several times a week and sometimes several times a day I would make the very same journey but in the opposite direction that I used to make twenty years earlier. I point out this extraordinary coincidence to anyone willing to listen but have yet to find anyone who thinks it nearly as interesting as I do.

The people in the Ministry of Labour, especially my boss, Norman Singleton, the Under Secretary, were very kind to me and I am sure that a career in that department would have been full of interest, not least during the great battles with the trade unions under Barbara Castle and later Norman Tebbit and Margaret Thatcher. But I wanted to return to an overseas job and after a few months persuaded the Civil Service Commissioners to allow me to transfer to what became the Foreign and Commonwealth Office.

I found it exciting to be at the centre of Whitehall after my years 'in the bush'. In those days security posed few problems. We walked to work in Downing Street and entered the Foreign and Commonwealth Offices by a little door opposite No 10. I could not get over the fact that in those days we still had coal fires in Whitehall. Although of course the buildings were centrally heated each office would have a coal fire laid and ready to light. I always lit mine – much to the annoyance of those who had to clean out the grate the following morning.

It was a far cry from Itchi Native Court. Intellectually the work was more challenging than that in the Colonial Service and we worked long hours. Telegrams would pour in from the embassies or High Commissions in the client countries and everyone worked until his or her desk was clear of traffic each evening. How do you know, I asked, when to reply to a question off your own bat and when to seek approval from higher authority? You'll know, I was told. And so it was.

Preparing answers to Parliamentary Questions was always interesting. The normal procedure was to prepare an answer to the question tabled by the MP and then to offer draft answers to three or four supplementary answers that you guessed that the MP might ask. When Harold Wilson was Prime Minister he dispensed with the draft supplementaries and demanded only a background note setting out the facts. He did not need civil servants, he said, to tell him what to say.

Alec Douglas Home, the fourteenth Earl of Home, as Harold Wilson liked to tease him, was a different kettle of fish. When he was taking Prime Minister's questions he would follow slavishly the answers to supplementary questions that we had prepared for him. On one memorable occasion we had prepared four possible supplementaries and the MP put his follow up question in precisely the terms that we had predicted. I could hardly believe my ears when Alec instead of delivering the reply that we had prepared for that question proceeded to read out the answer to one of the three questions that the MP had not asked. Even more bizarre, none of the listening MPs seemed to notice that anything was wrong. Alec gave a little grin and sat down. The next morning he sent round a note thanking us for our work on the PQs.

For a time George Thomas, who went on to become a much loved Speaker of the House, was Minister of State in the Commonwealth Office. He would often summon me to his office, sometimes to discuss a Parliamentary Question and sometimes, in the early days, just for a chat. 'Now, Frank,' he would say in his lilting Welsh brogue, 'you must make the answer to this question a particularly good one. You see, Harold will be in the Chamber by the time we get to this and we must make a good impression, mustn't we?' On George's mantelpiece were photographs of Keir Hardie, his mother and his local preacher. One day the Minister asked, 'Now Frank, what do you think of Scott-James?' Since the Under Secretary in question was my boss I hurried to confirm his excellent qualities. 'Yes, but he is not one of *us*, is he?' pressed the Minister. I admitted that Scott James might not see our relationship in just those terms but I was not sure where the conversation was leading. 'Look, Frank,' said George, 'I think you and I are the only grammar school boys in this place. The rest, you know, they're all public school. You and I need to stick together. I bet *they* all stick together, those public school people.' I assured him that Scott James was not a bit like that. George did not seem convinced.

I was assigned to the department that dealt with economic issues in East Africa. Towards the end of 1964 it was decided that a new department should be created to deal with the administration of overseas aid. A number of us were asked to move, with our files, to a building at the other end of Victoria Street to help with the establishment of the new Overseas

Aid Department. (Today the much more important DFID, Department for International Development.) Promotion prospects were brighter in the new department and some of those on temporary loan opted for permanent transfer, but I was anxious to return to the department that I had so recently joined.

The Minister was Barbara Castle. From my little experience she was easy to work with: quick to assimilate a brief and always appreciative of the work of her civil servants. She was fastidious about her appearance – her famous red hair always beautifully arranged – and, like Margaret Thatcher, she was never reluctant to exercise her charm on members of the opposite sex. And of course, in George Thomas's terms, she was 'one of us'. I liked her homely Northern touches. When a meeting was running late into the afternoon she leaned across to her Private Secretary and said: 'Ring Tom (her long time partner) and ask him what time we are going to the pictures.'

One of many commissions of enquiry into the future of the Britain's overseas services was led by Sir Val Duncan, the chairman of RTZ. I was impressed by the Duncan Report and took its recommendations seriously. The thrust of the report was to recommend that in Britain's changed circumstances following the end of empire much greater priority should be given to commercial work in our overseas services. I decided that I would opt for commercial work in future postings and so I did, though not always wisely. Before my first overseas posting I was sent on a Commercial Training Course in the City of London. As preparation we were asked to read the Report of the Committee on the Working of the Monetary System which had been presented to Parliament by the Chancellor of the Exchequer in 1959. The Report was a wonderfully lucid, brilliantly written exposition of a complex process. I should not have been surprised. The Chairman of the Committee was none other than Lord Ratcliffe of Werneth, whose Reith Lectures of 1951 I had so admired. But for the lucidity and elegance of the writing we should give credit also to the Secretary to the Committee, a young Robert Armstrong of the Treasury.

The most important event in 1965 was the arrival of our lovely daughter, Ruth, and the Kennedy family became complete eighteen months later with the arrival of our youngest son, Jonathan. Both were born in Beckenham's Maternity Hospital. All parents love their children but we have been blessed with four wonderful children who have not only tolerated the endless peregrinations of their parents but insist that they have enjoyed the diversity of an overseas life that has ranged from the comforts of suburban Atlanta to the rigours of life under a Marxist regime in Angola.

My first diplomatic posting was to Dar-es-Salaam in Tanzania as First Secretary, Commercial and Economic. We lived in Oyster Bay and spent our weekends swimming and snorkling among the coral reefs that bordered the lovely harbour and neighbouring islands.

One of my tasks was to negotiate the terms of a grant of £7 million in aid – a large sum in those days, particularly for the UK government. Tanzania was already something of a darling among the aid donors, who positively competed for the privilege of supplying aid. I remember the disappointment of Barbara Castle and her Permanent Secretary when it was announced that the Chinese were to be allowed to build a railroad from Dar-es-Salaam to Zambia, even though it was far from clear that the project would be economically viable.

One Sunday afternoon we were driving through the empty streets of Dar-es-Salaam to buy the children ice cream when suddenly Sarah screamed 'Daddy, daddy, stop the car!' I stopped the car and ran to the rear seat. I thought that the child must be ill. Sarah clambered out of the car. 'Quick, Daddy,' she said standing to attention, 'our President is coming.' I looked up and sure enough a cavalcade of black limousines was approaching at a stately pace. The first car flew the President's flag. I also stood to attention as 'our' President passed.

Everyone loved Julius Nyerere. He was a wonderful speaker, adored by all his countrymen and admired everywhere for his integrity. Full of homely wisdom he made no claim to knowledge of economic issues of any complexity. He was much influenced at the time by the writing and advice of a French agronomist who had written a book entitled *False Starts in Africa*. There were many such.

Late in 1965 President Nyerere's government concluded a conference on the country's economic policy with a document that it termed 'The Arusha Declaration'. This was a socialist manifesto pledging the country to the revival of agriculture by small-scale farming and voluntary labour. The country's major companies, most foreign-owned, were to be nationalized. Given the country's desperate need for investment this act of mass disinvestment seemed to me economic madness.

A quarter of a century later Julius Nyerere's economic policies were generally discredited. The country had also absorbed more in overseas aid than any other English speaking country in Sub Saharan Africa but remained one of the world's poorest.

In November Ian Smith's government in Rhodesia declared itself independent from Britain. The countries of the Organization of African Unity called upon Britain to take immediate steps to suppress the rebellion and return the country to constitutional rule.

Julius Nyerere called a press conference to which representatives of the diplomatic missions were invited. The President said that although he did not believe that other African countries would follow his example he intended to comply with the terms of the resolution of the OAU. How otherwise would anyone ever take such resolutions seriously? Unless Britain took measurable steps to return Rhodesia to the rule of law he would break off diplomatic relations with the former 'mother' country. Archbishop Huddleston travelled to Dar-es-Salaam to speak to Nyerere and Malcolm Macdonald also flew out to see him. Both encouraged the High Commissioner to believe that a way would be found to avoid a diplomatic rupture. I never doubted that Nyerere would do exactly what he said that he would do and break off diplomatic relations.

The fundamental difference between members of the colonial and diplomatic services was soon brought home to me. The latter exercise no executive responsibility themselves but try to influence those who do. An anti-British demonstration was organized by the governing party. The demonstration was to march down the main street and demonstrate outside the British High Commission. I rang the Commissioner of Police and was assured that the procession would not trespass on diplomatic premises. What in fact happened was that the demonstrators marched through High Commission property to the car park at the rear of the building where they proceeded to attack the High Commissioner's Rolls Royce and burn the Union Flag. To my annoyance all telephone lines to the Commissioner of Police suddenly became mysteriously engaged. When finally I did get through and reminded him of his duty to protect diplomatic missions he claimed that help was on its way. Since the journey was all of two blocks this was not plausible. I promised the Commissioner a formal complaint. I cannot say he sounded perturbed. When the last threads of the Union Flag had burnt themselves out, a few Tanzanian police made a leisurely appearance and the demonstrators dispersed.

We never did sign the £7 million loan agreement. Some on the liberal left argued that the disruption of diplomatic relations should never have been allowed to affect the disbursement of aid. I did not agree. The loan had been offered and accepted under a bilateral agreement between sovereign states. I thought it absurd to argue that we should leave the money behind as though it were a note for the milkman. I do not think that Julius Nyerere would have respected us if we had acted in that way.

So just before Christmas we had to pack our bags and return home. For the Kennedy family this was particularly inconvenient because we had let our house in Foxgrove Road and our American tenants refused to leave, even when we offered them an alternative, and we argued, equally attractive rented house. Also inconvenient was the fact that our car and heavy luggage remained in Dar-es-Salaam. Because the High Commissioner, Sir Bob Fowler, believed optimistic predictions that 'it would all be over by Easter' the Foreign Office, with a logic I thought reminiscent of Norman Mailer, refused to allow me to bring the car back on the grounds that I would soon be returning to Tanzania. I never did return to Tanzania. During a visit to the US, President Nyerere once asked me why my stay in his country had been so brief. When I explained, he chuckled: 'Oh *that* little, local difficulty'.

CHAPTER 14

1966: Scott's Emulsion

Towards the end of 1967 the Foreign Office telephoned to say that I was to be posted to Kuching as First Secretary and Head of Post. I confess that I did not know where Kuching was. I thought that it must be somewhere in China. I was reminded that it was the capital of Sarawak in Malaysia. I was also told that to be offered a position as Head of Post on only my second posting was something most people would jump at. But I said that I did not wish to go to another former colony. I did not wish to be tagged a Colonial Service re-tread. Also I wanted to do commercial work. The head of Personnel Department at the time was Ewen Fergusson (who went on to do great things and whom many years later my daughter Ruth did business with when Ewen was Chairman of the Savoy group of companies).

Ewen rang back the following day to say that the government attached much importance to our export trade with Sarawak. But I had looked up the figures. I replied that our exports the previous year had been worth less than £3 million and the biggest single item had been Guinness. The second biggest had been Scott's Emulsion. I did not think that the Borneo Company would need my help in selling stout and cod-liver oil. A few days later Ewen called back again. The office still wanted me to go to Kuching but would do a deal. First, the posting would be only for two years with a UK leave after one year. Second, my next posting after Kuching would be to a foreign language speaking post and would have a large commercial component. I said that there was a fourth condition. Ewen raised an eyebrow. I said that I wanted it all down in black and white in my file because by the time I came back from Sarawak he, Ewen, would be elsewhere. We shook on the deal.

Despite its problems and relative poverty Sarawak was and I understand is still a happy country. The Ibans and other indigenous tribes lived along the rivers and had preserved many of the features of their ancient cultures. The Chinese and Malays lived for the most part in the towns. The Chinese were the driving force in commerce and finance but the constitution ensured the political ascendancy of the Malays. In 1968 there were serious race riots in Kuala Lumpur between the Malay and Chinese communities and many of us believed that the Chinese were very much the victims in the disturbances. But despite much provocation the riots did not spread to Sarawak and the communities continued to live together, not always without tension, but peacefully and in mutual respect.

It was a wonderful experience to eat at the open market next to the bus station in the centre of Kuching. The food was cooked in little stalls round the periphery and the diners sat at little metal tables in the centre. Each stall specialized in a particular dish and the customers would go from stall to stall making their choice and chatting about the topics of the day. Everyone, rich and poor, ate at the open market. The food was delicious, the cost negligible and the atmosphere relaxed. Sunday night was our favourite time to go to the open market. The Governor's Rolls Royce would often be parked by the kerb and the Governor would be tucking into his chilli crabs and barbecued duck like everybody else.

The children loved Kuching as much as we did. We had a marvellous Chinese housekeeper cum cook. Mary had two children called Bing Seng and Poh Soon. Mark became a close pal of Poh Soon. They both got into all sorts of mischief when their parents were away. Mark once came close to serious injury when he and Poh Soon were setting off fireworks. Ruth and especially her young brother Jonathan spent a great deal of their time in Mary's kitchen. Jonathan preferred eating with Poh Soon and Bing Seng to eating with us.

Sarah and Mark. Kuching, 1969

The only shadow across our stay in Kuching was when the time came for Sarah and Mark to go to boarding school in England. Sarah was ten when she started at St Leonards Mayfield but Mark was only eight when he went to Avisford and although he was happy at this excellent little prep school I have always regretted that I let him go at such a young age. We were living a peripatetic life and it seemed important that the children should enter the English educational system. The Americans never missed an opportunity to tell us how barbaric they thought the practice. Maybe they had a point. Fortunately, my mother was still alive at that time and neither my brother Jack, nor sister, Dorothy, were themselves married. They became proxy parents for Sarah and Mark during half term and Easter holidays. My children are still very close to their Uncle Jack and Auntie Dorothy and we are all deeply indebted to them for the love they showed to our children. They still show it and it is returned in full measure by all our children and grandchildren. Later when Mark went to Ampleforth Anne's brother, Michael and his wife, Anne who were at that time living in Yorkshire, were equally caring.

One of Sarawak's unusual characteristics was its reluctance to surrender its colonial status. I often used to think how bizarre this would seem to my friends in Nigeria. Sarawak had been granted to Rajah Brooke in the nineteenth century to rule and administer as an independent country. The last Rajah spent the period of Japanese occupation during World War II in Australia and although he returned in 1946 he was persuaded by the British Government that the eccentric arrangement of rule by the Brooke family was no longer viable. That was not how the people of Sarawak saw things. They were loyal to their Rajah and happy to continue under his rule. But the Rajah's own administrative officers toured the country explaining that their future should be as subjects of the king in a Crown Colony. The subjects agreed but only by the narrowest of votes. In 1962 the people were told that their future should be as members of an independent Malaysian Federation. The people reminded the British officials that they had reluctantly agreed to colonization. They were now happy to be subjects of the Queen and wished so to remain. This was not what London wanted at all and Sarawak was pressed into membership of the Federation. Brunei refused and Singapore first agreed and later withdrew from the proposed Federation. The Federation has been a success and Sarawak's member-ship of it has been a success. But that does not alter the fact that Sarawak did not seek independence from the colonial power but had it thrust upon it.

Everybody who goes to Sarawak visits the longhouses. Anne and I made the trip to Kapit on the River Rejang. After the elaborate ceremonies of hospitality the head of the house enquired about the Queen and the weather in London. The Ibans seemed particularly fascinated by the idea of snow, which they could not quite imagine. The Chief then enquired whether we fancied a game of blind man's bluff. At first I thought that the interpreter had misunderstood what the Chief was saying. But it turned out that twenty years earlier Malcolm Macdonald, when UK Commissioner for South East Asia, had been a frequent visitor to the long houses and had introduced Victorian nursery games like Blind Man's Bluff, Pass the Parcel and Tail of the Donkey that were still being played in the long house.

Malcolm, for whom I had worked in London, had so fallen in love with the Iban community in Kapit that he had become an adopted son of the then paramount Chief, Temmengong Koh. He came to visit us in Sarawak and I arranged for him to make a nostalgic trip up the Rejang River. It took much longer of course to travel up river than down and my friends in the Malaysian Army generously offered to fly us to Kapit in a helicopter. We flew up the great river at tree-top level. When we got to Kapit, waiting patiently on a little wooden jetty and garlanded with flowers were the three daughters of old Koh, the adopted sisters of whom Malcolm was so fond. Two had travelled long distances to be present. It was a beautiful scene and a very moving moment. But later that evening one of Koh's daughters, Segura, said that she was sad and wished that Malcolm had not come. When Malcolm had been with them before, she had been young and those had been the happiest days of her life. But now she was a widow and her life was over. That morning I received a telegram from the *Daily Mirror* offering to pay me £200 if I could get a photograph of Malcolm with a topless Iban girl.

Malcolm Macdonald had played an important role in the transition from colonial status to independence in South East Asia and in Kenya. In both of these countries he had been the last colonial Governor and the first High Commissioner representing the United Kingdom in the newly independent country. He had also been the first High Commissioner in India. I enjoyed working for Malcolm Macdonald but did not agree with his theory of diplomacy. He tended to think that political problems could always be resolved by personal relationships. I did not believe this at all. Although his friendship with Nehru in India and especially with Jomo Kenyatta in post Mau Mau Kenya had been important politically, I did not think that his work as a roving ambassador in East and Central Africa had achieved any significant results.

Although he had been Britain's Secretary of State for the Colonies in 1939 Malcolm's sympathies were all with the colonized and not the colonizers and he was not always popular with the British expatriate communities of the countries in which he worked. He took a poor view of memoirs written by former colonial officers:

> autobiographies which a lot of pompous asses have written about themselves and their official work.

This did not stop Malcolm from writing – which he did beautifully – about his own experiences in India and South East Asia and Kenya. Writing can be a risky business. Whilst he was in Singapore Malcolm agreed to write a foreword to a novel which a young friend had written under the pseudonym, Han Suyin. It was only when the book had been published that Malcolm began to read it and only then did he realize that he was commending the story of a love affair between the author and an Australian journalist friend of his who had been killed in Korea. The journalist's wife was living in Singapore still unaware of what had been happening.

I talked to Malcolm Macdonald several times about two of the books that he did not write: his autobiography and the biography of his father, Ramsay Macdonald. There had always seemed something of a mystery about parts of Ramsay Macdonald's personal life and political career and I argued that Malcolm had a duty to write the books because no one else was in a position to do so. Malcolm never disagreed with the arguments but never wrote the books. Perhaps the prospect was too painful; perhaps the risk too great of revealing more of himself and his father than he wished to do.

I lived to regret the deal that I had made with Ewen Fergusson. Kuching was a wonderful posting and after two years I said that I would be glad to extend my tour of duty. But the FCO were not having any. The message was clear: 'Come in No 3, your time is up.' I was told that at my own insistence I was to be pulled out of Kuching after two years. The undertaking had been engraved in my personal file. What had been written, had been written.

The Office had been right about Kuching. Not only was it a marvellous place to live in, it was a particularly interesting time to be there. The 'confrontation' with Indonesia was ended but across the China Sea the US war with Vietnam was moving towards the climax of the Tet offensive. In 1969 South East Asia was one of the world's strategically important areas. The politics were far more interesting than the export statistics.

I was succeeded in Kuching by my friend and first Colonial Service boss, Toby Lewis.

CHAPTER 15

1970: The arithmetic of failure

I F I WAS SORRY TO LEAVE Kuching I was not sorry to arrive in Istanbul. The four years that we spent in Turkey were among the most exciting and satisfying of my career, not just for me but for Anne and the children and I think the many relatives and friends who came to visit us. We lived in a wonderful house, with congenial neighbours, in Ayaz Pasha on the shores of the Bosphorus. Each morning when we awoke we drew the curtains on one of the world's most famous views; we looked eastwards across the great waterway towards Leander's tower and the Asian shore. No city has a richer history or is more magnificently situated. Shortly after we arrived, the British Ambassador, Roderick Sarell, and I were passengers on a tug boat that eased its way through the dawn mist towing a steel cable that united Asia and Europe for the first time since Darius the Mede put in place his bridge of boats in 500 BC. We stayed in Istanbul long enough to see the first car drive across the completed suspension bridge, designed by Freeman and Fox and built by a consortium of British, German and Italian companies.

It was not by accident that Constantine and Mehmet the Conqueror made this town on the Bosphorus the capital of their Byzantine and Ottoman empires. As the citizens of Istanbul hurry to work, they glance up at a skyline defined by the profiles of Aya Sophia and Top Kapi and the Mosque of Suleiman the Magnificent: all architectural masterpieces with a history that stretches back almost two thousand years. Today the beauty of the Bosphorus has been further enhanced by the two graceful suspension bridges and the stunning new views of the city that they afford.

The biggest threat to the quality of life in Istanbul is its exploding size. The city is now said to have a population of 12 million. Even so, the little towns along the Bosphorus like Bebek and Tarabya seem little changed except for the prices commanded by property there. You can still enjoy the delicious seafood restaurants along the waterside that we used to patronize thirty years ago. With the Black Sea to the north and the Mediterranean to the south, Turkey has a rare variety of climatic conditions and the people of Istanbul enjoy excellent fruit, vegetables, meat – and one should add – wine, made possible by those conditions.

Jonathan, Sarah, Mark and Ruth in Istanbul, 1970

My enthusiasm for learning Turkish was not shared by my four-year-old son, Jonathan. Sarah and Mark were by now in boarding school in England but we enrolled Ruth and Jonathan in a French speaking school called Notre Dame de Sion. This long established school was run by an order of French nuns and though the great majority of the pupils were Turkish the medium of instruction was French. I thought that Ruth and Jonathan would benefit from learning French and Turkish from such a young age. Ruth was enrolled in the first class and Jonathan in the kindergarten run by a very nice young French girl. After a few weeks I called to ask the teacher how the children were getting on. The young French teacher said that Jonathan was a charming boy. Pause. I waited for the shoe to drop. The only problem was that he never spoke. Never? I asked. Never! said the young French girl. At least, she elaborated, never spoke to most of the fifteen other children in the class. The first day at school, apparently, Jonathan had teamed up with a young American boy named Tom. They were later joined by a young Canadian. The three 'Anglo-Saxons' commandeered the sandpit. All day they played in the sandpit. They spoke only to each other and only in English. We struggled on to the end of the first term. I went to see the young French teacher again. No change. A most charming boy. But never spoke to any other French or Turkish child. Only to Tom and only in English. I gave

Ruth painting. Istanbul, 1971

up. The following term I enrolled Jonathan in the English High School for Girls.

With Ruth, for whom our pet name has always been Looby, the problem was different. The problem was Mère Norbert. Looby played happily with the children of our next-door neighbour, Omar Tashkent, and chatted away in Turkish. Her French also came on in leaps and bounds. Mère Norbert, my five-year-old daughter carefully explained, was a dragon. All my attempts to persuade her to the contrary failed. I would take her to school. Everything would go smoothly until we reached the door of the classroom when Looby would burst into tears. Anne said that it was cruel to keep the child in a school she so disliked. I went to see the Principal and said that we did not mind how much or how little Ruth was taught at Notre Dame de Sion but what they must not do was to teach her to fear school. I was assured that Mère Norbert loved the children but we agreed that this was not something that should be kept secret. From then on Ruth said that Mère Norbert was very kind to her. As it turned out the problem was taken out of our hands at the end of the school year when Notre Dame de Sion discontinued the class to which Ruth's group would have been promoted. We transferred her to another French school, the Papillon. When I dropped her off in the morning on my way to work she always insisted on being dropped at the school gate. One day I said that I had to see the teacher. Before we reached the classroom Looby stopped and said, 'Daddy, you know French people cannot say 'Ruth'. So here they call me 'Anne''. Her mother did not mind and in fact Anne was Ruth's second name.

I thought that in later life it would be of value to have learned another language at an early age but I used to worry whether it was worth all the pain. I knew that my little daughter would always forgive me because she knew that I loved her to bits, but that did not make it any less of a worry. Today Ruth has forgotten most of her Turkish but she does speak French confidently and with an excellent accent. I hope that she thinks that even from Notre Dame de Sion some benefits came.

At weekends we would go on family expeditions to the Belgrade Forest or Kyria on the Black Sea Coast. Sometimes we had picnics at the Polish Village on the Asian side of the Bosphorus and during half term we made longer trips to Bursa and Cankaya. I dragged Sarah and Mark once to the site of Hannibal's grave. They were unimpressed. Once we went to Troy and looked down on the windy plain. There also unimpressed. But summer was a magical time when families from Istanbul would go to their summer houses on the Princes Islands. For several seasons we rented a house in the seaside resort of Kumburgaz from our friends Sevim and her husband. In the evening we would listen to their stepson Donat sing magical French ballads to his own guitar accompaniment.

With Ruth and Jonathan. Kumburgaz, Turkey, 1971

Then of course there was work. We worked in the magnificent surroundings of the former embassy in Tepebasi, the building that was so savagely attacked in 2003. The Consul General who tragically lost his life in that attack was a young information officer in Ankara at the time of my service in Turkey. He was a regular visitor to Istanbul.

In 1971 the Queen paid a state visit to Turkey accompanied by the Duke of Edinburgh and Princess Anne. I tried to persuade the Palace that on Saturday afternoon the Queen should watch a soccer match at the stadium of Galata Sarayi where she would be seen by seventy thousand people. My advice was overruled. Instead Her Majesty attended an exhibition by cavalry of the Turkish army. But the visit was a great success. One of the highlights was the reopening of the Royal Harem suite of rooms at the Top Kapi palace.

Istanbul was full of tourists in the summer months and the British amongst them kept the Consular section busy. Drug trafficking was punishable by severe penalties but despite strong and repeated warnings many young people still attempted to smuggle cannabis and other drugs from Afghanistan through Turkey to Western Europe. One of the sad duties of the Consular staff was visiting British nationals serving long prison sentences for offences involving drugs. One of the most notorious cases during my time was that of Timothy Davy, a fourteen year old boy who was sentenced to seven years imprisonment for trafficking in drugs. Timothy's mother, Jill, had driven into Turkey from the east in a mini van with her boyfriend and five children of whom Timothy was the eldest. They had buried a large cache of cannabis near Istanbul's airport. Although the danger was obvious because by now her boyfriend had already been arrested and was in prison awaiting sentence, Jill sent her young son to dig up some of the cannabis to finance the next stage of their journey. He was arrested trying to sell the drug to a dealer who was in fact a government under-cover agent.

In the early seventies the Cold War was very much part of the political landscape. Turkey had an army of some 400,000 men and was the lynch pin of Nato's southern flank. There was much espionage and counter-espionage between the two sides. The Chairman at that time of the Turkish football team, Galata Sarayi, was a friend of ours, Selahatin Beyazit. More recently we have stayed at his beautiful summer palace on the shores of the Bosphorus. That summer Galata Sarayi were invited to the Soviet Union to play a match against Moskow Dynamo. Selahatin invited me to watch the match and I very much wanted to accept the invitation. Selahatin suggested that I could carry a towel and claim to be an assistant trainer. (The team coach at the time was former Manchester

United player, Brian Birch.) But I was afraid that if I attempted to travel incognito I might be 'shopped' by one of the Soviet intelligence agencies. So I told my ambassador, Rod Sarell, of the invitation and asked him to give tacit permission to a private journey to Moscow. But Rod dithered and said in the end that I ought to send a telegram to the Foreign Office asking for permission. I knew that this would meet only with a refusal, and it did. So sadly I told Selahatin that I could not accompany the team to Moscow on Friday. He did not disguise how wimpish he thought me. The following Monday British newspapers and newspapers of several European countries carried headlines reporting the expulsion by Britain of over one hundred Soviet diplomats. I shuddered to think what would have happened if I had been in Moscow 'incognito' whilst all that was going on.

It took me some time to realize that despite the Duncan Report business could only be done by businessmen and not by diplomats. What businessmen needed from diplomats was primarily information and guidance on the political and economic context in which they sought to do business. When the businessman had one customer only in the foreign country, namely the government itself, then indeed the businessman and the diplomat became one.

Turkey in the early nineteen seventies was a good example of a country where the official services could make a material contribution to Britain's export trade. The country's economy was expanding and demand for imports rising. British exports were rising more rapidly than in most other markets but they were not rising, I believed, as rapidly as Turkey's demand for imports. But Turkey was in a difficult financial situation and had a complicated set of commercial regulations. My first responsibility was to be able to offer reliable guidance to British businessmen on the risks and requirements involved in doing business in Turkey. To do that effectively I needed sufficient Turkish to be able to read the financial press each morning before the first customer came knocking on the door. A second task was to offer guidance to British businessmen in the selection of Turkish companies who would represent them in that market. The best agents often secured the greatest market share but in practice many of the principals had been selected by the agents rather than the other way round.

I reorganized the commercial department of the Consulate General in Istanbul and brought in a new team of well-educated local Turkish staff, skilled in different sectors of the economy. I told them that they were the best commercial team in the world. They were certainly very good and morale was high.

With limited resources every target cannot be attacked and I considered for some time where to make a major effort in export promotion. One problem was that the official Turkish statistics covering the country's imports and exports were usually published only two or even three years in arrears. The official UK statistics were up to date but covered only exports. They did not indicate what share of the Turkish market the UK commanded in the various commodities and manufactures and whether that share was expanding or contracting.

I decided to make a study of the textile market and specifically of the market in Turkey for spinning machinery. I chose this area because (a) there was only one major British supplier of spinning machinery, Stone Platt Industries, and a large but limited number of textile factories in Turkey and (b) it was clear from even a cursory examination of the figures that a huge expansion was taking place in Turkey's textile industry. The fact that Stone Platt were the only UK player meant that I did not have to worry about helping one UK firm at the expense of another.

We had a friend in Istanbul, Ken Arklie, who was the sales representative for ICI's dyestuffs division. In that capacity he visited virtually every textile company in the country. Ken invited me to accompany him on his sales tours round these companies. When he had made his pitch on dyestuffs I was free to ask questions on spinning capacity and any plans the business might have for expansion. We toured companies in Western Turkey. On another trip we visited firms in the Aegean area and finally we made a marvellous trip to Mersin and the Chukurova plain in eastern Turkey. At the conclusion of these travels I compiled a report on Turkey's spinning industry for the Department of Trade and Industry. I estimated that spinning capacity in Turkey had increased in the last three years from approximately one million spindles to two million spindles. I listed the textile companies who had ordered the additional equipment and the manufacturers who had supplied them. The principal suppliers had been Ritters of Switzerland and Ingolstadt of Germany. The United Kingdom had secured only one order for, if I remember aright, something less than 20,000 spindles. The report concluded: 'When all the necessary qualifications have been made, this is the arithmetic of failure.' I learned later that the report had been read out at a meeting of the board of directors at Platt Industries. Shortly afterwards the company carried out a drastic overhaul of its marketing operations in Turkey and the Middle East.

From both a professional and a personal point of view Turkey was a happy posting. Despite the advice of friends and evidence of the primacy of the political in successful diplomatic careers, I persisted in seeking postings that were commercially oriented. In letters to the Personnel Department I argued that for my next posting I needed experience in the world's largest market. The Office did not disappoint. I was promoted and sent to Atlanta Georgia as Consul General.

CHAPTER 16

1973: Enough to make a Marxist wince

OUR TIME IN ATLANTA was enjoyed by all the family. We lived in a pleasant suburb on the outskirts of the city. I dropped off the children at Lovett School on the way to work and Anne collected them in the afternoon. Anne did all the cooking and catering with only occasional help at special events. I mowed the lawn and tried to grow tomatoes. We became members of the Capital City Country Club where Jonathan demonstrated his developing skills at tennis and I played golf. Every Saturday morning I played in a foursome with Walter Wattles, Bob Oppenlander and Charlie Stone. Walter was in insurance. Charlie was a doctor and Bob was the Finance Director of Delta Airlines. None of us were particularly good at golf but we were the best of friends and had wonderful times together.

We had arrived during the Christmas holiday period and the people of Atlanta could not have been more hospitable. Wiley and Marilyn Obenshain invited us to dinner with their family on New Year's Eve. Whilst dinner was being prepared their other guest tried to explain to me the mysteries of the American football game that we were watching on television. The guest was Judge Griffin Bell who later became the US Attorney General. Marilyn still writes to keep us informed of what is happening in their lovely city.

Billy Pfiffner and her husband also went out of their way to introduce us to prominent citizens that they thought we should know. Soon after our arrival she took Anne to eat at the Hungry Club which met every week in the Butler Street YMCA. The Hungry Club was a meeting place for politically active members of the black community and a platform for prominent black speakers. That evening Anne said that she had had lunch with Andrew Young and Julian Bond. I was quick to visit the Butler Street YMCA.

In the nineteen fifties Atlanta had had a population of less than 200,000 people. By the nineteen seventies the city was over a million and still growing at an explosive rate. I always felt that we were very fortunate to live in Atlanta when it was still just possible to claim that the people in Atlanta who made things happen all knew each other. Martin Luther King had been murdered in Memphis, Tennessee, only six years earlier. The city had not erupted in violence as many had predicted. The reason that

Consul-General. Atlanta, 1973

it had not done so was that Civil Rights leaders on one side, and civic
leaders such as Mayor Ivan Allen and Coca Cola Chairman Robert
Woodruffe on the other, went to great pains to see that it did not do so.
I reported in a despatch: 'It is enough to make a Marxist wince. Behind
Martin Luther King looms the shadow of Coca Cola.'

Andrew Young had just been elected to Congress. I invited him to
lunch at the Commerce Club of which I had been made an honorary

member. It was only when we got to the delicious Commerce Club ice cream that it dawned on me why we were receiving curious glances from the other tables. A few years later Mayor Maynard Jackson refused to have any dealings with the Commerce Club until it threw open its doors to black members.

Andy Young had been made a member of the Congressional Committee on Banking. I wanted to talk about the deepening economic recession but even more about black politics. But Andy insisted on talking about Africa. He was very concerned that Secretary of State Kissinger was about to order an invasion of Angola to evict the Cuban army that had recently arrived to shore up Angola's Marxist government. Towards the end of the meal Andy said: 'Look, I know that you want to ask me about black politics in the South. If you want to understand black politics there is one thing that you must do: go to the black churches.' I followed this advice. I became a frequent visitor to the Ebeneezer Baptist Church where 'Daddy' Martin Luther King preached and I also attended services at the churches of the Presbyterians and other denominations. I was always grateful for Andrew Young's advice.

The President of Atlanta City Council during Maynard Jackson's time as mayor was a young Atlantan, Wyche Fowler. When Andrew Young became Ambassador to the United Nations Wyche Fowler won the vacated seat in the sixth congressional district and later still was elected to the Senate. Wyche became a friend of the family and close to all our children. Mark worked for him in his law firm in Atlanta and Jonathan served for a time on his staff in Washington. Wyche was later appointed by President Clinton to be the United States Ambassador to Saudi Arabia.

The area of responsibility of the British Consul General extended to the seven south eastern states, from North Carolina to Florida and from Georgia to Mississippi. I always enjoyed visiting the other states and paying courtesy calls on their governors. The Governor of Alabama was George Wallace who had been paralysed from the waist downwards in an assassination attempt. George would always lean across the desk, clutch my arm in a grip of steel and tell me that his ancestors had come from Scotland. Tennessee was a state in which I always felt particularly at home and we made very good friends in Nashville. We already felt at home in Florida because two of Anne's brothers both lived there and still do: Tom, a gastroenterologist and Brendan, a specialist in diabetes. We spent many happy holidays in Sarasota with Tom and his family and later on would also visit Tampa where Brendan had settled.

Anyone from Lancashire feels an affinity with the small towns of North Georgia and the Carolinas because of our joint roots in the textile industry.

Jonathan fishing. Atlanta, 1974

By the nineteen seventies the growing of cotton had migrated from the old South to new fields in Texas and across the border in Mexico. But cotton was still spun and cloth woven in the mills of north Georgia, Alabama and the Carolinas. The quayside in the old harbour at Savannah is paved with stone brought in ballast by the ships that had unloaded their bales of raw cotton in Manchester and Liverpool. The 'special relationship' has many strands but if you come from Lancashire and address a Rotary Club in Greenville, South Carolina, or Spartanburg, North Carolina, you will soon be reminded of one of them.

In a developed country such as the United States, diplomatic 'commercial' work had another dimension to that which I have described in Turkey or Malaysia. As well as the promotion of exports *from* the United Kingdom we promoted the export of capital *to* the United Kingdom. To encourage this 'inward investment' the Consul General would call on the leading 'Fortune 500' companies in his district. Textile giants such as Burlington Industries and Roger Milliken's group already had subsidiaries in the United Kingdom but we tried to assure their senior management that Britain was still an investor-friendly environment. One of the foreign competitors that I had struggled against in Turkey was Platt-Sacco Lowell, the manufacturer of spinning machinery. By the time that I arrived in

Atlanta the company had been bought by Britain's Stone-Platt Industries. Instead of competing against the American company I found myself in the curious position of explaining to its puzzled CEO the mysterious ways of his new proprietors.

One of the obstacles to investment in the United Kingdom that we tried to overcome was the terrorist threat in Northern Ireland. We used to argue that put in proper perspective the disruptive effect of the IRA's operations on the economy and life of the Province was negligible. We sponsored a first visit to Britain by one Atlanta businessman. He arrived in London one Saturday morning and went for a meal in the evening to Scott's restaurant in Mayfair. He had not finished the main course when an IRA bomb crashed through the window of the restaurant. The businessman arrived back in Atlanta on crutches. But the bomb seemed to have been more effective than our propaganda. From then on the businessman was passionately pro-British and an outspoken opponent of the IRA and its allies.

We had arrived at what was a painful time for America and a painful time for Britain. After the emotional upheaval of the civil rights reforms the United States was struggling to come to terms with the trauma of Vietnam. It was also struggling to come to terms with a price of oil that had quadrupled in a year. People stared in disbelief as filling stations chalked up gas prices of 65 cents a gallon.

Across the Atlantic, Britain in 1974 was in a state of outright crisis. Wrote Peter Jay in the London *Times*: 'We are a confused and unhappy country.' The stock market had collapsed; inflation was running at over 20%; industrial relations were in tatters. In retrospect it is surprising how rapidly recovery came in both countries.

I was surprised at the attitude of the American public towards its own military at this time. Like most British people I had disagreed with American policy in Vietnam. This did not alter the fact that the United States remained Britain's principal ally and Western Europe's main defender against what was still a potent threat from the Soviet Union. The US armed forces had important military bases in the Southern States. Fort Macpherson outside Atlanta was such a base. I tried to include the officer commanding Fort Macpherson in diplomatic events and receptions for visiting British dignitaries and in general to give some recognition of the importance of his office to America's Nato allies. General Bernard Rogers later became Chief of Staff of US Armed Forces and Supreme Allied Commander in Europe. He lives in retirement in Kansas with his dear wife Anne. We have remained friends and still keep in touch. Each Christmas we exchange news about our ever more numerous grandchildren.

I was even more surprised by the treatment of Dean Rusk. It is true that Dean Rusk undoubtedly *had* been a prime architect of the doomed policy in Vietnam. Nevertheless he had served his country under two Presidents with loyalty and distinction. He had been a Rhodes Scholar and was a good friend of Britain. At a reception for Harold Macmillan shortly after John F. Kennedy's inauguration the British Prime Minister had called Rusk over. He said: 'Rusk, the President tells me that in cabinet you were the one most strongly opposed to the Bay of Pigs operation and yet you have been going around since as though it had been your idea. You are the sort of feller I can do business with.'

Dean Rusk was living with his wife in a modest little house in Athens and teaching a course in international law in the University of Georgia. When he stepped down from the post of Secretary of State he found it difficult to get an academic post. Leading universities across the States had been too afraid of student reaction on the campuses to offer him a job. In the Rotary Club of Atlanta we raised cash to buy the Rusks an automobile. I thought it a scandal.

In the controversy surrounding Vietnam most of the other protagonists wrote their apologia: Robert Macnamara, George Bundy and the others set out what by now were their heavily qualified positions. Dean Rusk was especially bitter at the duplicity of colleagues who a few yards away

Sunday afternoon in Atlanta. At home with Dean Rusk

from his office were collecting what would come to be known as the Pentagon Papers. But he remained true to the principles commended by Macmillan. Dean Rusk never defended in print or in the media his part in the war in Vietnam. He never wrote an autobiography or memoir defending his own part in the formulation of US policy on Vietnam. He went on to become a special adviser to President Carter and played a leading role in the establishment of a Southern Centre for International Affairs. But he declined all the lucrative opportunities to excuse or explain away his part in the tragic war. Whatever his misjudgements Dean Rusk was a man of rare integrity.

On one memorable occasion I arranged a small dinner party for Dean Rusk to which I also invited Julian Bond, the former civil rights activist, and General Kroesen, who had succeeded General Rogers at Fort Macpherson. The three men in public but very different positions had all been caught up in the same tragedy. Julian challenged Dean Rusk to tell him what was contained in the file that the FBI had kept on him and Dean challenged Julian to justify the burning of his draft card. Fritz, who, as an 'Eagle' Colonel, had led his men through the carnage of Vietnam, looked from one to the other. The conversation was serious but good humoured. A few years earlier it could not have taken place. One day when Dean Rusk dropped in on his way to see his sister, who lived in Atlanta, our sixteen-year-old son asked him whether there was anything that he wished that he had done differently as Secretary of State. 'Mark,' said Dean Rusk, 'I made a big mistake in overestimating the willingness of the American people to support such a war.' I once asked him which was the ablest of the Kennedy brothers. Dean's reply was, 'Oh, John, by some distance.'

When Prince Charles visited the South in 1977 I took him to Athens where he met Dean Rusk before watching the Georgia Bulldogs play Kentucky at football. Although until that match Georgia had been unbeaten that season they managed to get thrashed by Kentucky that afternoon. Later that year Dean Rusk was made an honorary KBE by the Queen.

One afternoon in 1975 I received a telephone call from Harry Pfiffner. 'Be at the 11th Street Holiday Inn five o'clock.' I cannot make five, I replied, I do not leave the office before five. '11th Street, Five o'clock,' Harry repeated and rang off. I turned up at five at the Holiday Inn in an unfashionable part of down-town Atlanta. There were about forty people present, mostly local journalists or officials of the local Democratic Party. Then Governor Jimmy Carter turned up and after a few minutes moved across to a little podium that had been rigged up in the centre of the room.

In those days the Governor was anything but impressive as a public speaker. After some nervous coughing Jimmy stumbled through a short speech, at the end of which he declared that he was going to run for President. I could hardly believe it. I turned to Harry and said, 'This time you have gone too far!'

To have what amounted to a ring-side seat in a US presidential race was a rare experience. It did not do my career any harm either. Carter's campaign team, mostly young Atlantans like Hamilton Jordan and Jody Powell, were all very friendly and approachable as were his close friends and advisers like Charlie Kirbo and Bert Lance. As the campaign progressed and victory became a real possibility I received from London and Washington an increasing number of requests for interviews with the campaign team.

Each year the Ambassador held a conference in Washington with his Consuls General from all over the United States. There were I think ten of us. It was customary on the last afternoon of the conference to invite the Washington representatives of the British media to join the meeting for a general discussion. That year the main topic was obviously going to be the campaign for the Democratic nomination, although we were still at a very early stage of the Presidential race. Most of the people who would be present at the conference had hardly heard of Jimmy Carter and none of them would have given him the ghost of a chance of winning. On the other hand I had come round to the view that there was just the glimmer of a possibility of our peanut-farmer Governor pulling it off.

The Sunday evening before the conference I went in search of a friend, Hal Gulliver, who was deputy editor of the *Atlanta Constitution*. Hal was not at home but I eventually tracked him down drinking with friends at a house in Ainsley Park. After several beers I managed to get him to one side. I explained that I was going to an important management conference and would be asked to give an estimate of Presidential prospects. I said that I was going to put my money on Jimmy Carter. If I was wrong no one would remember in a few months time what I had said any more than they would remember the failed predictions of the other Consuls General. But if they turned out to be right my words would be remembered for a long, long time. However, to carry conviction I needed to support my prediction with plausible arguments and that was where I needed Hal's help. Hal said, 'I'm your man. Come to the office tomorrow morning. We'll sock it to these guys in Washington'.

The following morning Hal stood before a large map of the United States and took me through the Carter campaign strategy, State by State. He called the odds in each constituency, indicating the threats and the best hopes in each. He identified six or seven key States that Carter had to win if the strategy were to succeed. One of them was Pennsylvania. When he had finished I said, 'Is it going to work?' Hal said, 'You know, it just might. Jimmy has the best chance of any candidate in the ring so far.'

The conference proceeded as expected. The media representatives were called in. The Ambassador went round the room and asked each Consul General in turn to give an assessment as seen from his part of the country. The consensus was that at that stage the race was too early to call. Few of my colleagues knew any of the candidates personally or rated the chances of the local man. My colleague from Boston offered a few diffident comments on Edward Kennedy but thought it unlikely that he would run.

As luck would have it I was the last person to be called. I began with what may have been unseemly bravado: 'Gentlemen, I am going to give you the name not only of the Democratic nominee but of the next President of the United States. It is James Earl Carter of Plains, Georgia. This, (pause for effect) is how it is going to happen.' Following the strategic plan outlined to me by Hal Gulliver I then took the audience through the electoral map, constituency by constituency. I named the states which Carter was confident of winning and those which he expected to lose. I identified the handful of key states that might go either way. The Carter campaign team would make their big push in those marginal states that would determine the result of the election.

And that, to everyone's surprise, is more or less how it did happen. Crucially, however, Jimmy Carter failed to take Pennsylvania. Charlie Kirbo told me that he and Carter's other backers had been determined not too charge up huge debts in a failed campaign that would leave them financially crippled for the rest of their lives. It had been imperative to generate by early success enough momentum to attract the additional finance that would fund the later stages of the campaign. They had set limits to the aggregate expenditure they would allow by each stage in the race. If one of these benchmark limits was reached or if one of the key constituencies was lost, Jimmy Carter would pull out of the race. By the time of the Pennsylvania election the team had reached their ceiling on expenditure for that stage of the race – they were overspent by some $230,000 – and by previous agreement Jimmy Carter should pull out. Charlie said that he went to see the Governor to give him the bad news. He found Carter in his room in the Holiday Inn, slumped before a television set. He had kicked off his shoes and taken off tie and jacket and looked exhausted and despondent. Charlie said that he just did not have the heart to tell his friend at that moment that it was all over. So he tiptoed out of the room and closed the door.

The rest we all know. During the inauguration celebrations the President said to Kirbo: ' Charlie, you remember when you came to see me in that room in the Holiday Inn in Pennsylvania?' 'Yes, Mr President.' 'I knew what you had come to say to me, you know.' 'Yes, Mr President.'

I never fully understood the position of the *Atlanta Constitution*. This was Georgia's one nationally recognized newspaper but it never gave unequivocal support to the Carter campaign. The editor, Reg Murphy, was implacably hostile to Jimmy Carter for reasons that went back to an earlier election when Carter had first run for office in the Georgia Senate. Carter had lost by a narrow margin and wanted to challenge the result in court on the grounds that there had been irregularities in the polling in some of the up-country constituencies. On the advice of a friend,[1] he went to see a lawyer named Charlie Kirbo and with the help of Kirbo's court room skills Carter won the case. Carter went on to defeat Carl Sanders in Georgia's next gubernatorial race and Bert Lance[2] always maintained that had it not been for Kirbo's intervention it would have been Carl Sanders and not Jimmy Carter who would have become President of the United States.

The *Atlanta Constitution* was owned by Cox Communications. Anne Cox Chambers, one of the wealthiest persons in America and a major shareholder, was one of Jimmy Carter's principal financial backers. She was appointed Ambassador to Belgium after his victory. But the views of his paper's proprietors did not alter Reg Murphy's stance one bit. The stance made no sense to me. Whatever the past disagreements and present reservations, Jimmy Carter was the only chance to elect a President that Georgia was likely to have for the rest of the century. I thought it was absurd that the State's leading newspaper should devote most of its editorial space to relentlessly undermining their candidate's chances. The Deputy Editor, Hal Gulliver, shared that opinion and that is why I approached him for the briefing.

On one occasion I was lunching in the Commerce Club in Atlanta with Bert Lance. Reg Murphy was sitting at a table in a corner of the room when in walked Jimmy Carter. Bert said: 'Well, we just might be able to make a little bit of history, today, Frank. Let us see if we cannot get these two together.' After greeting Carter, Bert said 'Come and say hello to Reg Murphy, Jimmy.' Carter agreed and the three of us went over to Murphy's

[1] Judge Griffin Bell viz p.142.
[2] Carter's controversial Director of Management and Budget who resigned after being investigated on charges of financial irregularities in his management of a bank in Atlanta and one in Calhoun, Georgia.

table. 'A friend here wants to say hello to you, Reg,' said Bert. 'Hello, Reg,' said Carter in the friendliest manner possible. Murphy looked up and uttered a sort of grunt. He could not have been ruder. After a couple of futile attempts at conversation we walked away. So much for our 'little bit of history'.

As the Carter campaign moved towards its successful conclusion, I became, for a few brief weeks, one of Her Majesty's more important overseas officials. I was peppered with requests from colleagues trying to brief ministers on the incoming administration. Downing Street wanted to know if I could possibly arrange for the Prime Minister to make an early call on the President Elect. I graciously indicated that I would see what could be done. In fact, in anticipation of such a request I had already made sure that a message of congratulations from Jim Callaghan was the first from the head of a foreign government that Jimmy Carter received. I had typed a letter saying – with only slight exaggeration – that I had been instructed by my Prime Minister to convey his warm congratulations etc etc. I had then sent my Vice Consul to Plains to deliver the letter in person. He was to make quite sure that it was the first such message that the new President received. Otherwise, I hinted, a return trip might be superfluous. How was he to do this, the Vice Consul asked. I said that he was to drive to Plains and with the car radio tuned to the news channel he was to drive round and round the Carter farmhouse until the radio announced that Gerald Ford had conceded. Then he was to dash up to the front door and deliver the letter.

All ended happily. Jim Callaghan's message was the first to be received in Plains and the Prime Minister was the first head of a foreign government to be received by the President Elect. The morning after the President's arrival in Washington he entertained the Prime Minister to breakfast. (Some people used to say that Jimmy Carter's breakfasts were rather mean affairs but there were no complaints from Jim Callaghan.)

The period between Carter's election victory and his assumption of office was an exciting time to be in Atlanta. Friends like Andy Young, Bert Lance, Griffin Bell, Anne Chambers and Philip Alston were leaving to take up positions in the new administration in Washington or ambassador- ial posts abroad. Dean Rusk chaired a selection committee that vetted all nominations for overseas appointments. Philip Alston, a respected lawyer, soon to be Ambassador in Australia, used invite me round to his office or home and we discussed again and again the life and work of a diplomat.

Stu Eisensat, later US Ambassador to the European Union, headed the transitional team and worked on policy issues for the incoming President. Charlie Kirbo acted as general confidant, adviser and wise man. He would telephone me and ask what I thought of such and such a book, say of correspondence between Roosevelt and Churchill. 'Mmm,' Charlie would say, 'I think I'll tell Jimmy to read it.' Often he would invite me to his office for a more structured discussion on a particular topic, say of the situation in Northern Ireland. These were valuable opportunities to get across our views on issues important to Britain. One topic we discussed more than once was South Africa. To stir things along Charlie said one day, 'Mmm, I have been talking to the South African Ambassador in Washington. What the feller says makes a lot of sense to me.' One day in January 1978 as Anne and I were preparing to leave Atlanta I received a call from the Ambassador. Pik Botha said that he had promised Charlie Kirbo that he would get in touch with me so that we could discuss together some of the important issues concerning South and Southern Africa. He was full of apologies for not doing so but had been recalled by his President to take up the post of Foreign Minister. I never imagined that the next time that we came into contact with each other I would be the UK's Ambassador to Angola.

During the transitional period Dean Rusk used to claim that the appointments to the new government had been the most rigorously screened of any incoming administration. I said that that might be true of the appointments to external posts but how could it be true of the domestic appointments. Many of the leading members of Carter's young campaign team were given White House or government posts. Surely there were people better qualified or with more varied experience for some of the posts. Ah, said Dean, to start off, the President needs around him people he is comfortable with. But most of these people will be replaced as the new administration beds down. That proved not to be the case.

The first term of the Carter Presidency ended in disappointment and there was not to be a second. The person to whom Carter was closest and whom he probably missed most in Washington was Charlie Kirbo. Unfortunately for Jimmy Carter, Kirbo declined to move to Washington.

Charlie Kirbo was a remarkable man. A partner in one of Atlanta's most prestigious law firms he affected the style and manner of a simple country lawyer. Living on a little farm some thirty miles from Atlanta and driving a battered old 'kit car' he might have been the prototype for the lawyer played by Gregory Peck in the film *To Kill a Mockingbird*. But behind the folksy manner and Southern drawl was a sharp mind and a wise head.

Some people made the mistake of thinking that because he came from Plains and taught Sunday School, Jimmy Carter was a simple peanut farmer. This was far from the case. Carter was and is highly intelligent.

On the other hand I did feel that he was often the victim of his own cleverness. Carter was an avid consumer of information. He appeared to think that if he worked long enough, studied closely enough and, perhaps, prayed hard enough, he could master any brief and understand any problem. I thought that this was a big mistake. Like some of our own ministers, he could be drowned in detail. Carter was every bit as clever as Charlie Kirbo but not, I thought, as wise. Carter's performance as President, especially during the early months, might have been more sure-footed if he had been able to have Charlie Kirbo at his side as White House Chief of Staff.

Jimmy Carter was very helpful to me both intentionally as Governor and unintentionally as President. Along with the other members of Atlanta's little Diplomatic Corps he invited us to his Inauguration in January 1978. It was a great privilege to have had a ringside seat from which to watch the fascinating progress from Governor to President.

Just as Jimmy Carter had approached Charlie Kirbo for help with a lawsuit so had another person, an Englishman, with a lawsuit on his hands, sought out Kirbo. That person was John King, later Lord King of Wartnaby. John King was suing a former employee in up-state Georgia. 'Ain't but one man can handle a jury in North Georgia, specially if the feller doing the suing is a foreigner.' King was told, 'Feller by the name of Kirbo.' I knew Charlie as Jimmy Carter's guru and campaign manager. John King knew him as his lawyer. It was through Charlie Kirbo that we met and because of Charlie that I was to spend such happy years working with my friend John King at British Airways.

Shortly after the Presidential election I visited Harry Horne, the Canadian Consul-General in San Francisco. We had been friends since his time in Atlanta. His office was in a high-rise building overlooking the Bay. The view was truly magnificent. I was asking Harry what one had to do to wangle such a posting when the phone rang. Harry said that it was for me – from London. I picked up the receiver. The Chief Clerk in the Foreign Office, Mark Russell, said that I had been posted to Lagos, Nigeria.

CHAPTER 17

1978: Fish shoup

THE SCENE IN LAGOS HARBOUR in 1978 could hardly have been more different from that in San Francisco Bay. Very different it was too from that we had remembered from sixteen years earlier when Anne and I and our two children had sailed from Lagos on the French ship, the *Jean Mermoz*. Now hundreds of ships rode at anchor waiting to enter port and unload their cargoes. Some had been waiting for months. Many were rusting old hulks whose cargoes would never be unloaded. The sheds and warehouses on the dockside were crammed to overflowing with goods waiting to be claimed and cleared through customs. In all the chaos clearing agents and officials spent days searching for particular consignments.

The chaos was not confined to the port of Lagos. Roads were in appalling condition and during rush hours traffic was often brought to a standstill. Telephones were frequently disconnected. It could take hours to secure a line to make an overseas call. Power cuts by NEPA, Nigeria's Electric Power Authority, were a daily occurrence. Commercial companies and private citizens alike were forced to import their own generating equipment.

The doubling and then quadrupling of the price of oil had entailed a dramatic shift in purchasing power from the oil-consuming to the oil-producing countries of the world. As sixth largest oil producer, Nigeria should have been a major beneficiary. Oil revenue accounted for some 80% of Nigeria's foreign currency earnings and over 90% of its government's revenue. But what should have been a boon for a country producing more than 2 million barrels per day had turned out to be more of a calamity.

The government had failed to control or even anticipate the tidal wave of inflation released by the economic boom that had followed the end of the civil war. An overvalued currency fuelled the demand for imports. The proliferation of construction projects had created a demand for cement far in excess of local production and far in excess of the capacity of the ports to handle the volume of imports that would have been required to make up the short-fall. Opportunists were quick to exploit the resulting bottle-necks. If you could fill an old tub with cement and tow it to

Nigeria you could make a tidy sum in demurrage just by leaving it to rot in the harbour. Others went even further. Why go to the bother of moving across the ocean ancient ships and deteriorating cargoes? Why not just simulate such transactions by forged documents conjured up by fraudulent suppliers and their Nigerian partners in crime? For years afterwards the Attorney General of Nigeria was tracking down such criminals and pursuing them in foreign courts.

Although I was later promoted to Minister and Deputy High Commissioner I arrived in Lagos to take up the post of Commercial Counsellor and in that capacity my immediate responsibility was the promotion of British trade with Nigeria. Exports were running at record levels and in the previous year had exceeded 1 billion pounds sterling. To cope with demands of British businessmen the commercial department of the British High Commission had expanded rapidly. There were eleven UK-based commercial officers each supported by Nigerian or locally recruited staff. The chaos in Lagos harbour was matched by the chaos inside the High Commission's commercial department. Because of the lack of working telephones officers spent hours in traffic jams just trying to reach Nigerian companies to set up meetings with the representatives of UK companies with whom they were trading. Every desk overflowed with paper. To retrieve a file – and in those pre-electronic days a file was still a key tool – might take days. For three consecutive days I sat with our Nigerian Head of Registry to try to understand the mess.

The High Commissioner was an old friend, Sir Sam Falle, for whom I had worked in both Malaysia and Tanzania. Sam asked what I wanted to do. I said that I wanted to reduce the number of UK-based staff. Sam, who liked to regard himself as a radical, was shocked by such bureaucratic blasphemy. '*Reduce* the number of staff?' he muttered, 'when we have fought tooth and nail to increase them!' I argued that the bottlenecks inside the office were partly of our own making and that in any case one or two of the UK-based staff were out of their depth in the chaotic conditions of Lagos 1978. Reluctantly Sam agreed that I might reduce the establishment of UK officers by two.

The First Secretary immediately in charge of the Commercial Department was a marvellous officer named Greg Faulkner. I told Greg that all the UK officers should work an additional hour's overtime each evening, weeding files of unnecessary paper. Greg said that I might have had experience in other parts of the world but I obviously had no understanding of life and work in Lagos. He could not possibly ask his long-suffering UK staff to work overtime every night. I said 'OK, then you and I will do the work. We'll work half an hour each evening and as many hours as necessary each Saturday and Sunday until the job is done.' After a moment's pause Greg stopped just short of outright defiance. After a few days first one and then another of the UK Commercial Officers joined Greg and me in the chore of weeding every file in the department and shredding a large number of them. The job was completed in a surprisingly short time and from then on work in the department was less frenetic and more productive.

In any case external pressures were slackening. The price of oil had risen and sales had fallen. General Obasanjo's government had cleared the docks at Apapa and in the 1978 budget had begun to address the problem of inflation by tightening the money supply and other measures. By the end of the year we looked out across the harbour at an amazing sight. The ships had gone.

If commerce between Britain and Nigeria at the beginning of 1978 was thriving, political relations had plummeted. Two years earlier the previous Head of State had been assassinated in Lagos. The attempted coup had failed but in the dramatic moments following the assassination the leader of the coup, Col Dimka, had visited the British High Commission and requested that a message be sent to General Gowon in London. In fact no such message had been sent but Britain was accused of being implicated in the plot and the High Commissioner was declared *persona non grata*. In the stress of the moment, when the future governance of the country and the personal safety of Ministers hung in the balance, it may have been tempting to make a scapegoat of the old enemy. In any event relations between the two countries sank to rock bottom.

In such an atmosphere normal political work was difficult. Contact between the High Commissioner and Nigerian ministers was minimal. Some ministers and officials were nervous about meeting representatives from the British High Commission. We were supposed to make all appointments through the Ministry of External Affairs. The only time some of the UK diplomats met their Nigerian counterparts and business-men was at meetings of the Metropolitan Club in Lagos. I found all this very unsatisfactory and determined to break out of the diplomatic purdah into which we seemed to have been cast.

It was much easier for me than for my colleagues. It was not that I had very many friends from the past in Lagos. There were some: our good friend, former Attorney General, Nabo Graham Douglas; my old boss and family friend, Jerome Udoji; Sir Ademola Odemegu who had lectured to us in London on the Devonshire Course; Fred Anyaegbunam, a friend from bachelor days in Onitsha and now a judge; Chief T.O.S. Benson who had been a minister in the first post independence government; Chief

Jonathan riding Kawasaki. Lagos, 1978

Chanrai with whom we had played the incredible hands of bridge in Port Harcourt; and so on. My old comrade-in-arms, Albert Osakwe, for some reason drove all the way from Onitsha each month to attend meetings of the Nigeria Manufacturers Association. We used to sit next to each other and talk about Udoji and our time together in the Premier's Office, Enugu.

The number of such long-standing friendships was less important than the fact that Anne and I and the children, despite all the problems, felt at home in Nigeria. We enjoyed being back in the country in which we had begun our married life and spent so many happy years. This sense of security made it much easier to develop new friendships. It also gave us the confidence to have disagreements and even, when circumstances made them unavoidable, diplomatic rows, without undermining personal friendships.

I had not been in Lagos three weeks before I found myself embroiled in a row. In their annual report the Chairman of Barclays Bank

International had declared that his bank intended to remain in South Africa but would work for the end of apartheid. We had tried without success to persuade the Chairman to qualify the statement, which we thought bound to provoke an angry response from Nigeria. I also tried to lobby members of the board of Barclays Nigeria. The Nigerian government ordered the withdrawal of all government accounts from Barclays and reduced the overseas shareholding to 20%. The two sides were unrepentant and both disregarded my arguments. Barclays made it pretty clear that their South African business was a good deal more valuable to them than that in Nigeria. My argument was that the smart thing was to preserve both. To Nigeria's Head of State the clash was part of a wider battle. The policy of indigenization was less about the transfer of wealth than the transfer of power. To win the battle of the boardroom, as he put it, the transfer of shares was not enough. Management agreements needed to be monitored as well. In my opinion what Nigeria needed – as had Tanzania in 1965 – was foreign investment, not disinvestment. But the thinking of the day was against such views. In Britain people like Wedgwood Benn still wanted to 'occupy the commanding heights of the economy'. A few short years later attitudes had reversed. Not indigenization but privatization became the battle cry. Even in 1978 I was struck by the fact that Chancellor Schmidt in a public speech in Nigeria could proclaim Germany's intention to continue trading with South Africa without provoking censure from Nigeria's government or press. He was even complimented on his candour. But then Nigeria at the time was concerned to obtain the Chancellor's support for a DM1.2 billion loan for a steel plant in Warri.

Personal friendships brought their own demands. Although immigration controls were not my responsibility I received a constant stream of requests and complaints about the Visa and Immigration Section of the British High Commission. On one occasion my old friend Fred Anyaegbunam stormed into my office in full legal regalia followed by a breathless and bewildered Clerk of Court. He had come straight from his Judge's bench to complain of the behaviour of a British Immigration officer.

There were undoubtedly occasions when a member of the staff of the Visa and Immigration Department of the British High Commission would be impatient or rude in dealing with a visa applicant. Such occasions were especially regrettable when the Nigerian applicant had become nervous and confused when required to answer simple questions. On the other hand it was also true that of all nationals attempting to enter the United Kingdom illegally a disproportionately large number were from Nigeria. Nigerians had been involved on a spectacular scale in increasingly ingenious attempts at fraud and smuggling. The volume of attempted forgeries and mendacious applications soon made cynics of many of the newly arrived Visa and Immigration staff. Sometimes I would find myself in cross-fire between Nigerian friends and my own colleagues.

The Permanent Secretary in the Department of External Affairs at the time – and in that capacity Head of Nigeria's Diplomatic Service – was John Ukegbu. John and I were near contemporaries. He was from east of the Niger and had joined the Nigerian Diplomatic Service in 1958. One day he telephoned me to appeal against the rejection of an application for an entry permit from a young woman who wished to visit Britain for two weeks. The applicant was sponsored by a distinguished businessman on whose word, according to John Ukegbu, I could rely absolutely. I said that I was not willing to rely on the word of the businessman whom I did not know. However, if he, John Ukegbu, gave me his personal guarantee that the lady would be back in Nigeria within 21 days I would have the case reviewed. John said that I had his word.

The immigration department of the High Commission was headed by a professional immigration officer seconded from the Home Office in London. He was not satisfied that the applicant was being truthful or intended to return to Nigeria on the due date. In his judgment it would be folly to issue a visa. He was unmoved by the support of the businessman or the Permanent Secretary and was equally unimpressed by my arguments. In exasperation I said that the word of the Head of Nigeria's Diplomatic Service might mean nothing to him but it did to me. I said that on overriding political grounds I was ordering him to issue the visa and that he proceeded to do but only after making clear that the consequences would be on my head.

A few weeks later the Head of the Immigration department marched into my office. It was clear from his 'told-you-so' expression what was coming. The lady had not returned. 'Are you sure?' I asked. He was sure. The Police had checked the address she had given in her application. She was not there. She could be anywhere in the United Kingdom. 'And,' added the Immigration Officer, 'there is nothing we can do about it.' 'You mean', I said, 'that there is nothing you can do about it. Let me show you what I can do.'

I rang John Ukegbu and told him that the lady had not returned. Was I sure? he asked. I was sure. Leave it to him, he said. Three days later a Security Officer in the High Commission reported that there was a lady in Reception who refused to speak to anyone but me and would not leave until she had done so. Our missing person had returned. When she entered my office the lady threw herself on the ground and in traditional style begged forgiveness. I said that it was not to me that she should apologize but the Head of the Immigration Department, for whom I sent. The bemused officer looked on in embarrassment as the lady went through her dramatic ritual of contrition.

A few months later I had a less satisfactory exchange with John Ukegbu. One afternoon shortly before the High Commission closed for customers a dozen or so Zimbabwean students managed to slip into the Reception area of the High Commission building. There they sat down and refused to move. They were demonstrating for the immediate grant of independence for Zimbabwe. Satisfied that they were carrying no weapons we tried to persuade the students to leave and continue the demonstration outside. They refused to move. We called the Police and the Protocol Division of the Department of External Affairs and received vague replies but no action. By four o'clock the majority of the High Commission Staff had left the building but we still had twelve sedentary students adamantly refusing to budge.

By six o'clock there was still no sign of action from the Nigerian authorities. As if by magic a British television crew had arrived and assembled their cameras and other gear at the entrance to the compound.

After several more fruitless telephone calls I went in person to see John Ukegbu. I told the Permanent Secretary that I was demanding that the Nigerian authorities remove the foreign trespassers who were illegally occupying part of the High Commission building. At first John took the line that I was making a fuss about nothing. Surely, I could deal with twelve *students*? Then he argued that if the students were in the High Commission building they were on sovereign territory of the UK and it was my job to get rid of them. I maintained that under the terms of the Vienna Convention the Nigerian government had a duty to protect the property of foreign embassies and I was asking him to discharge that obligation. I was also complaining that for the last several hours he had ignored my repeated requests for assistance. Finally, I said that if he, John Ukegbu, thought that I was going to be manoeuvred into a situation where the evening television news in Britain and in Nigeria were showing live images of black students being manhandled by white officers of the British High Commission in Lagos he could think again.

Around eight o'clock a grumpy Permanent Secretary followed by an Assistant Commissioner of Police and half a dozen Police constables marched into the High Commission. This was not John Ukegbu's idea of how to spend an evening. By now he would expect to be sipping his second whisky soda. After the Assistant Commissioner had addressed the students to no effect whatever the Permanent Secretary pushed forward.

'Oh, let me speak to them,' said John with the air of one forced by the incompetence of others to do every little thing himself. He spoke at length concluding with a straight command delivered in grand magisterial manner. From the little Zimbabwean students there was not a flicker. 'Get 'em out,' growled Ukegbu through clenched teeth. The Assistant Commissioner nodded. A constable picked up one of the Zimbabweans by an arm and a leg and pitched him through the door and out of the compound so fast that the ITV team failed to get the shot on their cameras. The other students hurried through the door without a murmur. With a scowl in my direction the Permanent Secretary marched towards his car. 'Now if only we had done that six hours ago . . .' I began, but Ukegbu did not wait for the end of the sentence.

The quickest way to wealth in Nigeria in the nineteen seventies was a contract for the production of a stated number of barrels of oil for a specified number of days, but lucrative returns were also made from capital projects which in many cases were executed by expatriate companies and financed by external borrowing. Because of its oil wealth Nigeria did not qualify for development aid from Britain but it did qualify for commercial credit and those of us with any involvement in the construction boom of those years must admit to some share of responsibility for the commercial debts which later escalated to such devastating figures by the inexorable working of compound interest.

Instead of the original three regions Nigeria was now divided into nineteen states. That meant nineteen legislatures, nineteen state develop-ment plans and nineteen capital budgets. Nigeria's trading partners competed for the contracts to execute the capital projects approved in those budgets. Sometimes they competed also for the supply of credit to finance the projects. Young merchant and investment bankers would comb through the State and Federal development budgets for projects with reasonable import contents and then on behalf of the legislators would seek to obtain insurance cover from one of the export credit agencies. Once such cover was obtained the bank would offer to finance the project or part of it and expatriate contractors could then be invited to bid for the execution of the project. Politicians, contractors, consultants and bankers all prospered in the business. It was widely believed that legislators benefited from the award of contracts in ways not dissimilar – though on a much greater scale – to those I had witnessed so many years ago in the Port Harcourt Planning Authority.

In time the Central Bank did begin to exercise a more rigorous scrutiny of capital projects submitted by State legislatures and other Departments and those bodies were required to obtain guarantees of the availability of the foreign exchange that would cover the subsequent loan repayments. The European export credit agencies also began to cooperate more effectively in restraining bidding competitions between themselves. But so far as I could see no one was effectively monitoring the risk implicit in the growing mountain of debt. Unquestionably this was the responsibility of the Central Bank of Nigeria, but in my layman's view it ought to have been also a collective responsibility of the lending banks. In practice the bankers seemed to regard the situation as one more credit boom. There was a feeling that the process could not last but in the meantime the profits were too great not to take some.

Nigeria was an important market for British goods, much larger in real terms than it is today, and Britain commanded an exceptionally large share of the market. But I was concerned that the share was under threat from other trading partners, particularly from France, Japan and Germany. I did not believe that British trade was keeping pace with the competition in the sectors of the market that were expanding most rapidly. My Nigerian friends in government and in commerce and industry told me that British firms were not assertive enough and that however negative the politics we should take a higher profile in the market place. An obvious example was the construction industry in which UK firms had once been dominant. Whereas twenty years earlier British construction firms had been business leaders, by 1979 they were minor players compared to a firm like Julius Berger, who in a few decades had expanded from a business in a small German town to one in which they were raking in profits at a rate of more one million dollars a day. So far as I could discover, no British firm had executed a contract worth more than $100 million. I believed that if the expatriate firms did not compete at the higher end they would gradually be pushed out of the market altogether as Nigerian firms took an increasingly large share of the lower end. The truth of the proposition would not have been easy to demonstrate but that was my theory and I determined to do something about it.

I waited patiently for a suitably large project to come on to the market which on the face of it was within the capacity of British firms to execute. Eventually one came with the announcement that the Federal Ministry of Transport were going to build a new port at a place called Onne in eastern Nigeria. The cost was expected to be around £130 million. By a neat coincidence Onne was situated just a few miles from my old stamping ground Okrika. When British firms lost contracts they were quick to complain that they did not receive the close support from their government that Japanese and French competitors enjoyed. The fact that

Onne was a public sector contract gave me an opportunity to demonstrate that we could match the competition when it came to official support. I was helped also by the fact that the Board of Trade in London had persuaded their colleagues in the Treasury and Overseas Aid Administration to establish a new type of financing called project aid that could be used to support British bids for large overseas projects. I thought that the Onne project would qualify admirably for help from the new fund. Although the new port was to be an industrial facility serving primarily the oil industry I argued that it would relieve the congestion at the nearby port of Port Harcourt and even the more distant port of Lagos. The experts in London accepted the economic case for the project.

My next problem was to find a British firm willing to bid. I advertised the project through the Export Opportunities service but little interest was expressed. One well known firm said that their board would not allow their Nigerian subsidiary to undertake any project worth more than £25 million. Given the size of their business they judged the risks too high and preferred to expand their exposure to the residential property market in Florida.

Eventually we managed to put together a consortium of UK firms led by Costains and supported by Balfour Beatty and Cementation. I became a frequent visitor to the office of the Permanent Secretary, Ministry of Transport. I also spent much time in the market place trying to find out what the competition was doing. I learnt that some thirteen firms had bid and with a bid in the region of $140 million my best guess was that we were about fourth from the bottom in the pecking order. With one of the other laggards we persuaded the Nigerian Ministry of Transport to extend the period of the bidding.

The consortium pruned its estimates of cost and we improved the terms of the supporting finance. Market intelligence told me that we had moved up strongly in the batting order and were now in about fourth position from the top. That was still not good enough. One of the four contenders was a Japanese group and they were believed to be supported by an offer of finance on concessionary terms. If I remember correctly the sum was around $30 million. I told our colleagues responsible for the disbursement of Project Aid that we had to improve on the Japanese offer. We had to win the confidence of the Nigerians by showing them that the British firms had official backing as strong as that enjoyed by any competitor. We had to show the Nigerian government that we could compete in the big league. And having chosen Onne Port as the battlefield on which we were going to demonstrate our prowess we had to win.

I was pleasantly surprised when the Department of Trade in London bought into these arguments and came up with an exceptionally generous offer of financial support. I think that the total figure was $50 million but what made it special was that a large chunk of this of this was to be in the form of a grant. In other words this sum would be an outright gift which the Nigerian government could put towards the cost of the project. The grant element was the silver bullet in our armoury. Nominally ours was not the lowest bid but overall it was the cheapest. The Japanese withdrew from the bidding. We submitted our revised bid and I was confident that we were on to a winner. Then came the bombshell.

In 1979 efforts were continuing to negotiate an end to Ian Smith's illegal regime in Rhodesia and bring the country to independence under a democratically elected government. The Commonwealth had imposed sanctions on Rhodesia. It was left largely to Britain to enforce the sanctions and several African and Caribbean countries, though making little practical contribution to the process themselves were loud in their complaints against Britain's failure to enforce a solution. Zambia, which continued to import from South Africa throughout the period of UDI, was one of the most vociferous and was strongly supported by Tiny Rowlands's company, Lonrho, which had lobbied frantically to be allowed to continue operating their oil pipeline from Beira to Rhodesia at the beginning of UDI. The British government eventually appointed a commission to enquire into the allegations that Britain was allowing oil to reach Rhodesia. The Bingham enquiry found that British oil companies had devised elaborate schemes to bypass sanctions.

As Zambia was to be host to a meeting of Commonwealth Heads of Government later in the year a lively session was expected, the more so as Britain had just acquired a new Prime Minister. Margaret Thatcher had already displayed a robust determination to fight for what she regarded as her country's interests. To the dismay of the Foreign Office she seemed disinclined to continue sanctions against Rhodesia and disposed to recognize the interim government of Bishop Muzorewa. She was rumoured to regard the Foreign Office as being staffed by a bunch of 'wets'. The Nigerian government was fiercely opposed to the recognition of the Muzorewa government and had already made clear its readiness to use oil as a weapon in support of its policies in Southern Africa.

At the beginning of the summer Mervyn Brown, who later became Sir Mervyn Brown, who had succeeded Sam Falle as British High Commissioner in Lagos, was on leave and I was acting in his place. Anne had flown to England to collect the children from school. I was quietly enjoying the unaccustomed distinction of high office when the contenders for the Onne Port contract were summoned to the Ministry of Transport for the announcement of the award. The representatives from Costain, Balfour

Beatty and Cementation trooped out of my office. I looked forward to their return, confident that this was going to be our red letter day. They had hardly been gone ten minutes when they were back. Before the other tenders were read out the British Consortium had been called to approach the podium and told that on the order of the Presidency the British Consortium was asked to withdraw from the bidding. No reason had been given. An embargo had been placed on the award of Federal contracts to British companies. I was furious. I was also uncomfortably aware that the Nigerian government might not have focused their attack on the Onne Port contract if I had not made such a hullabaloo about it. I told the morning staff meeting at the British High Commission that once there had been a beautiful princess called Onne whose father was a wicked giant who lived in a remote castle with walls higher than anyone could scale. The giant had said that he would give the hand of the princess in marriage to the first knight to bring him one hundred bags of golden treasure. Eventually the fairest knight in all the land arrived at the castle and laid down one hundred bags of golden treasure. But the wicked giant looked down from his tower and said that he had changed his mind. He would not allow the knight to marry his daughter after all because he was involved in a quarrel with the family of the knight.

When he had stepped down from office President Obasanjo would sometime invite me to lunch at his home in Abeokuta or at his farm. We would discuss the political situation in Southern Africa and Europe and domestic politics in Nigeria and the UK but usually at some point he would work the conversation round to the subject of Onne Port. He relished raking over the subject. 'Mmm,' he would say with a chuckle, 'You weren't too happy were you, Frank, with my handling of that contract?' There was obviously nothing wrong with the President's sources of intelligence.

The Onne Port fiasco was the beginning of what turned into quite a long, hot summer. One morning I picked up the daily newspaper. 'BP Oil Tanker seized in Bonny', screamed the headline. I almost dropped my cup of coffee. It seemed that on 30 April a tanker chartered by BP had collected a cargo of oil and was about to sail when the port authorities belatedly discovered that the ship's previous port of call had been Durban and that a large number of the crew were South Africans on South African Seamen's passports. The ship was arrested and its captain placed in detention in Port Harcourt. Some days later the ship's cargo was confiscated. BP pointed out that the ship was a chartered vessel and did not belong to their company. The Nigerians retorted that although it was under charter to BP and registered in Panama the MT *Kulu* was operated by SAF Tankers and owned by a subsidiary of the South African Marine Corporation. A representative of BP told the Nigerian National Petroleum Corporation that that the incident was the result of an unfortunate error on the part of one of his company's tanker scheduling officers. He denied that his company had any intentions of breaching Nigeria's restrictions on the destination of oil shipped from Nigerian ports. The NNPC said that the explanation was not good enough.[1]

The Nigerians argued that if BP planned to sell the cargo of crude oil on the spot market in Rotterdam whilst delivering to South Africa a cargo of similar size from another 'non-embargoed' source, this was no more than an attempt to disguise what was the equivalent of a shipment of Nigerian crude to South Africa. The controversy was further complicated by the suspicion on the part of the Nigerians, one that we were never quite able to dispel, that BP was not acting independently but under instructions from the British Government. The belief was strengthened when in answer to a Parliamentary Question tabled by a former Foreign Secretary, David Owen, Lord Carrington confirmed that he had recently informed BP that the kind of back-to-back shipments just described were permissible under the regulations laid down by HMG provided that in all cases the oil shipped to South Africa was from a country that did not operate an embargo against supplies of oil to that country. He repeated that there should be no shipment either of Nigerian crude or North Sea crude to South Africa. Britain respected similar embargoes that had been put in place by Israel, the Arab states and other countries.

Although Shell and BP were responsible, through the jointly-owned company Shell-BP, for the greater part of the production and export of Nigeria's oil, the operating partner was Shell. As a result Shell had a large staff in Nigeria whilst BP had few. Even so the company were well aware of the Nigerian government's position on Rhodesia and South Africa and on the prohibition to ship oil in any vessels that were involved in trade with South Africa. They had before them the examples of what had happened to Barclays Bank and the embargo recently placed on contracts to British firms. Although BP could argue that no Nigerian oil reached South Africa through the shipments which they had arranged, they knew that the South African connections of the chartered vessel put them in breach of their contract with the NNPC. I never doubted that in the absence of any initiative on our part President Obasanjo would take drastic action against BP. His government had been angered by an *Economist* article that suggested that Nigeria, because of the dependence of its oil

---

[1] BP Archive no 126998 1979.

industry on expatriate expertise, was more bark than bite; and here was an opportunity to disprove the suggestion. I was concerned that he might also seek to penalize British interests more generally, although I thought that Shell would be safe because of their key role in the production of Nigeria's oil. Unfortunately I failed to persuade BP of this view. When the crisis broke a director of BP's main board, Q. Morris, took over responsibility for the company's tactics. 'Q' had a background in finance but, I believed, little sense of the realities of Nigerian politics. He decided that the best policy was to 'let sleeping dogs lie' and to follow the adage that if in a hole, the best thing to do was to stop digging. I disagreed strongly. I argued that the dog was not sleeping; on the contrary, it was preparing to bite and we would be its victims. I urged BP to seek an interview with the President. I believed that we should engage the Nigerians in dialogue, try to establish what was their bottom line and then seek to modify it. I knew that BP's area manager and Nigerian manager agreed with me but they seemed to have little purchase on the views of 'Q'. He pointed out that a cargo of oil had been seized. They had been given a dressing-down. That might be the end of the matter. The trouble was that with every day and every week that passed it began to look as if Q might be right and I wrong.

It used to be said that if the British saw a queue they joined it before they knew what they were queuing for. When some Nigerians see a queue they join it on the chance that they might be able to sell their place later at a profit. I spent much time in the Secretariat in Lagos getting to know secretaries and private office staff so that if I needed to see a Minister in a hurry I had a reasonable chance of doing so and if I received the time-honoured reply, 'Not on seat', there was a chance that it might be true. But the man I most needed to see at that moment, the man whose next move I was trying to guess, was the President and he, like the giant in the story, was locked behind the high walls of Dodan Barracks.

The Friday before the Commonwealth Heads of Government were due to meet in Lusaka, I received information from sources that I thought reliable that President Obasanjo was preparing to announce punitive measures against BP that would include the seizure of their assets in Nigeria. The measures would probably be announced on Monday, 31 July. It was not clear whether other British companies would also be attacked. Nigeria's Foreign Minister, Major-General Adefope, had already arrived in Lusaka but President Obasanjo had delayed his departure because he had as his guest that week-end the Australian Prime Minister, Malcolm Fraser.

I spent the weekend trying to mount a desperate, last-ditch stand against the approaching onslaught. I submitted a formal request to the Protocol

Division of the Department of External Affairs for a meeting with the acting Minister. I received no reply. I drew up a list of twenty leading British companies in Nigeria and lobbied each of their Nigerian chairmen. All of them were prominent in business and society and regarded as persons of influence. I warned each one of the danger that I believed threatened not only BP but their companies as well. I urged them to approach the President and try to head off the danger to our common commercial interests.

The Chairmen looked at me in a mixture of surprise and alarm. They enjoyed the dignity and perks of office but the idea of going into bat in what promised to be a bruising dispute with the Nigerian government was one that they found singularly unattractive. I did not get one positive response. I remember in particular my discussion with the Chairman of BP Nigeria, the late Chief S.L. Edu. He was a prominent and highly respected member of the business community and I had always found him very friendly. He had accepted the post of Chairman only a few weeks earlier. I knew that he enjoyed ready access to President Obasanjo and I urged him to see the President before the measures were announced. It soon became clear that he would do no such thing. He gave me the impression that he was not going to endanger his good relations with the President by fighting what would be an unpopular and probably losing cause. The Chief said that he did not believe that the company was in imminent danger. I should not worry so much. Everything would blow over. We should all relax and have a nice weekend. In the light of my conversation with their Chairman it was hardly surprising that my arguments should have made such little impact on the men from BP in London. I made a mental note of the fact that there was a battle of the boardrooms to be fought with objectives quite different from those that President Obasanjo had in mind.

I waited all Friday for a response to a request for a meeting with the Acting Foreign Minister but by evening I knew that the clock was ticking away and that an Acting Minister would not be able to deflect the President from a course of action had already been decided and presumably approved by the Supreme Military Council. It was very unsatisfactory that I had failed to register the opposition of my government before the axe fell. Next to the President the most senior members of the Supreme Military Council were his Chief Minister, Major-General Shehu Yar'Adua and his Minister of Defence and Chief of the Armed Forces, Lt-General T.Y. Danjuma. General Danjuma and I later became good friends but at that time though I had met him once or twice could hardly claim to know him well. Nevertheless I risked calling on him at Flagstaff House on the

Sunday afternoon. Despite the invasion of his leisure time General Danjuma received me in a relaxed and gracious way. I explained how seriously my government viewed the developing crisis and went over the whole saga. I summarized the arguments of the two sides and recalled the huge contribution made by BP to the development of Nigeria's oilfield over a period of forty years. I argued the importance to both our countries of finding a mutually acceptable solution to a problem that should not be allowed to threaten our relationship. General Danjuma listened attentively to all that I had to say and asked me to clarify one or two points. He gave no assurance that any of my representations would be accepted but said that he would see that they were made known at the most senior levels of government.

The following morning the Nigerian Government announced the nationalization of the shares of BP Nigeria. President Obasanjo said that the action was Nigeria's gift to the Commonwealth and flew off to join his fellow Heads of State in Lusaka. Lord Carrington denounced the action as totally without justification and warned of the damage that it would do to Anglo Nigerian relations. According to some press reports he had been involved in a bad-tempered exchange with the Nigerian Foreign Minister at an official garden party. I was instructed to seek an appointment at the highest level and make known in the strongest terms the objections of Her Majesty's Government. I submitted a formal note to the Department of External Affairs seeking an urgent appointment with the Chief Minister. I asked my Head of Chancery, Duncan Slater, to take the note in person and to stress to the Permanent Secretary its urgency and importance.

By seven o'clock in the evening we had still received no response to our formal note. Duncan and I had a long discussion. What were we to do? I had informed London and Lusaka of my discussion with General Danjuma but I had not carried out my instructions to register with the Nigerian Chief Minister the strongly held views of my government. I was very anxious to have such a meeting not for its effect on President Obasanjo's government, which I expected would be slight, but for its effect on our own government and especially my Foreign Secretary. We all loved working for Peter Carrington. We thought him an excellent Foreign Secretary who exercised a moderating influence on the Prime Minister's wilder impulses. But on this occasion it seemed to be the Foreign Secretary and not the Prime Minister who had lost his cool. I worried whether Lord Carrington had been given a full and frank briefing by BP on the sequence of events which had led up to the seizure of the assets. I could understand his anger. But surprise? It was not as though the

Trying to persuade Foreign Secretary, Lord Carrington, that it is time to leave.
Lagos 1980

Kulu incident had come out of a clear blue sky. There had been a series of incidents since the beginning of the year involving tankers of various nationalities which had called previously at South African ports. The NNPC had issued ever more strident warnings threatening to revoke the contracts of the offending oil companies. On 23 April the managing director of Shell-BP, Nigeria, had warned his partner, BP:

> I must ask you to redouble your efforts to ensure that no ship calling previously in South Africa reports for cargo at our terminals. It seems possible that the MT *Ervikan* (a foreign owned tanker) may even have discharged crude at Durban.
>
> I have today instructed both terminals that any ship which shows a South African Port as its previous port of call will immediately be turned away. The risk of this kind of incident escalating into a major political row simply is not acceptable.

A BP director said that the MT *Kulu* incident had been an unfortunate error. The claim was somewhat undermined when the captain of that vessel asked from his place of detention what the fuss was all about as this was the tenth time that he had made the trip from Durban and had never had any trouble before.[2]

As it happened I lived in the same area of the city as Major-General Shehu Yar'Adua. We lived next door to the Commander of the Armoured Brigade, Brigadier-General Babangida. General Babangida had a tank on his front lawn, for whose presence we were grateful because we never had to worry about being burgled. On the other side of General Babangida's house, down a little side-street, was the residence of General Yar'Adua. There was a check point at each end of the side street. Duncan Slater and I discussed whether I should try to get an interview by going unannounced to the General's residence. I pointed out that it was now pitch dark and the house was certain to be heavily guarded. I might get nowhere near the entrance to the house. I might be arrested or declared *persona non grata*. Duncan reckoned it was worth taking the chance. I agreed.

I changed into a dark suit and walked the few hundred yards to General Yar'Adua's residence. I must confess that it seemed a very long few hundred yards. I told the sentries at the outer gate that I was the Acting British High Commissioner and had come to see the Chief Minister. I was waved on. I repeated the ritual at the next barrier with the same result. I asked one of the sentries if he would tell the General's domestic servants of my arrival. The Corporal kindly rang the front door. A steward smartly dressed in white came to the door. He said that Master was still at evening prayers. I gave the steward one of my calling cards and said that I would return at 8.30 p.m. to ask whether the General was able to see me. When I returned I smiled at the sentries who waved me through as an old friend. The steward opened the door and said that Master would be pleased to receive me.

General Yar'Adua, who came from a part of Northern Nigeria that had supplied many of the country's leaders, received me with great courtesy and invited me to speak my piece. I began by refuting the Nigerian claim that the arrangement by which BP with the approval of the British Government had supplied North Sea oil to a 'non embargoed country' whilst that country had supplied a similar amount of oil to South Africa was a subterfuge to hide the delivery of Nigerian oil to South Africa. But I also stressed the long history of BP's service to Nigeria's oil industry and the overriding importance to both our countries of preserving the close and long-standing relations that existed between us. My government strongly objected to the action taken against the British company and

[2] BP Archives no 125325 and 127418.

urged the Nigerian government to reconsider its decision. General Yar'Adua listened to it all in a relaxed and polite manner. He had kicked off his sandals and was reclining at the end of a long working day. He gave me the impression that the melodrama of recent events was not necessarily to his taste. He said that he understood the strength of feeling of my government and the seriousness of my representations but Nigeria's action had been taken after a careful consideration of all the facts. His last words were: 'However, although we have closed the door we have not thrown away the key.'

I returned to the High Commission where Duncan and I composed a telegram reporting my conversation with General Yar'Adua. I also sent a covering telegram to Lord Carrington. In this I said that the Prime Minister had every right to be angry over the action of the Nigerian Government, which was totally unjustified. However, I believed that the game was far from over and that substantial British commercial interests were still at risk. I made three points. (1) In a tit for tat contest we had few cards to play. We commanded some 23% of Nigeria's import market but because of North Sea oil we accepted only some 4% of Nigeria's exports. (2) Nigeria was not only one of the best markets in the world for British exports, it was composed overwhelmingly of middle technology goods that were at the heart of our economy. They were labour-intensive and if we lost the Nigerian export market our unemployment figures would suffer. (3) The experience of the last few days had convinced me that if they were seen to be political footballs British companies would find it increasingly difficult to attract the best Nigerian candidates for appointment to their boards and the best Nigerian companies to appoint as their agents. This would damage our longterm export performance. I concluded that there was a great deal still to play for.

In Lusaka the Prime Minister made a restrained and skilful speech. She reiterated Britain's commitment to black majority rule in Rhodesia and to bringing the country to legal independence on a basis that the Common-wealth and international community would find acceptable. Some ob-servers reported that behind the scenes President Obasanjo of Nigeria among the black countries of the Commonwealth and Malcolm Fraser among the white had acted as mediators. The conference unanimously approved the final communiqué.

Whether my advice made any difference I do not know although Lord Carrington sent me a message thanking me for it. Q. Morris said that Nigerian attitudes to the UK changed dramatically after the Lusaka conference. On his return from Lusaka General Adefope said at a press conference that it had been made crystal clear that Nigeria could bite as well as bark but it was not the intention of his government to nationalize other British interests or to drive out other British nationals. Before the end of the year Lord Carrington had signed the historic agreement with Zimbabwe's ZANU-PF at Lancaster House and by early 1980 Duncan Slater was in Rhodesia as part of the team preparing the country for the elections that would mark the beginning of what turned out to be Robert Mugabe's inglorious reign.

The nationalization row seriously strained relations between Shell and BP. When BP withheld payments that were outstanding on two earlier cargoes of crude oil, Shell insisted that BP's contractual obligation was to Shell-BP and not directly to NNPC. With the help of funds supplied by Shell, Shell-BP settled the account and demanded repayment from BP. I sympathized with BP. Withholding the two payments was one of the few counterstrokes available to them. It seemed to them that Shell was prepared to stab its colleague in the back to save its own skin and the peremptory language used by the managing director of Shell-BP[3] suggested that it had no compunction in doing so. On the other hand I did not believe that Shell could be blamed for refusing to allow its company's interests to be put at risk by what it saw as the political ineptitude of its former partner, especially in the light of its repeated warnings to BP.

In Lagos we had a marvellous old cook whom we called Baba. Baba made a most delicious fish soup, clear and spicy. The day after my nocturnal meeting with General Yar' Adua I had gone home for lunch and was sitting alone at the dining-room table eating a bowl of 'fish shoup', as Baba called it. Suddenly the door flew open and in stormed Baba Kingibe, a young man who at the time was head of the European Department of the Ministry of External Affairs. You could almost see the steam coming out of his ears. 'What the hell do you think you're playing at?' he shouted. 'Meeting the Chief Minister without the permission of the Department of External Affairs! This is outrageous!' I asked whether he would care to have some fish shoup. No he certainly would not. I had broken all the rules of protocol and his department were not going to tolerate it. I had no right to set foot in a Nigerian minister's residence without permission. When he paused for breath I said: 'Don't talk to me about protocol.' I had been submitting requests for a ministerial appointment for three days and his dysfunctional department (I think that the word that I actually used was 'useless') had not even had the courtesy to

---

[3] The late Sir Peter Holmes who went on to become Chairman of Shell Transport and Trading Company.

reply. The function of diplomats was to facilitate communication, not to obstruct it. I had been instructed by my government to deliver urgently a message that was important to both our countries. If his department chose to block normal channels then I would find other ways of carrying out my instructions. Anyway, I said, I had asked and received General Yar'Adua's permission before entering his house. He had received me with great courtesy and propriety. Come to think of it, I added, if we were talking trespass, I did not recall inviting him to enter a residence that was the property of Her Majesty's Government and I would be obliged if he would kindly remove himself. After further exchanges in similar vein, Kingibe flopped down in a chair at the far end of the table. But he still would not accept any fish shoup.

After the return to civilian rule some of the protagonists in the little drama that I have described became and have remained good friends. (Talking to General Adefope a little while ago I discovered that we both had grandchildren at the same school in England.) I once told General Danjuma that what still puzzled me about the BP affair was the length of time that had occurred after the *Kulu* incident before the nationalization decree had been issued. The general said that the answer was simple. He and his colleagues had been nervous about taking such a drastic step in case Britain retaliated with damaging counter-measures. The Supreme Military Council had therefore commissioned outside consultants to assess the risk. The consultants reported that the effect of any counter-measures on the Nigerian economy was likely to be slight but it had taken them a few weeks to prepare their report.

In the short run, because the rupture came shortly after the company had lost its first and greatest source of crude oil in Iran, the impact on BP was significant. But after some months the shortage was made up and the company recovered. Compensation was eventually paid in the form of crude oil. Three months after the row the embargo on Federal contracts was quietly lifted. As for Onne, I made a point of visiting the place some years later. I found the docks empty and the project still unfinished. I was told that the Netherlands firm that had won the contract after the withdrawal of the British had been driven into insolvency by cost overruns and disputes between principal and client. So perhaps Costains and their consortium colleagues were fortunate to have escaped the consequences of a successful bid. But that did not alter the fact that General Obasanjo had swatted us away like a troublesome fly.

President Obasanjo is now serving a second term as Nigeria's democratically elected President. He is sometimes criticized for the failings and deficiencies of his government. Some of the criticism is justified.

Some is from people who have not the slightest conception of the difficulty of governing a country as large and complex as Nigeria. But what no one can take away from President Olusegun Obasanjo is that of all the military rulers in Africa he is the only one to have voluntarily relinquished power and returned his country to civilian rule.

Etched in my memory are two events from the 1970s that in their way are symbols of the democratic process. The first was that clear, frosty morning in Washington DC in January 1978 when Jimmy Carter was inaugurated as President of the United States. After the inaugural ceremony on the steps of Congress the cavalcade moved slowly down Pennsylvania Avenue. After a few yards the President stopped the procession and alighted from the limousine. Jimmy and Rosslyn from Plains, Georgia, walked hand-in-hand down the Avenue waving to the crowd on each side. In the evening we dined with Bernie and Anne Rogers in the lovely house of the US Chief of Staff of the Armed Forces with its marvellous view of the illuminated Jefferson Memorial.

The second memory is of the ceremony in the Independence Stadium in Lagos on 1 October 1979 to mark the return to civilian rule. The retiring President, General Obasanjo, and the newly elected President, Alhaji Shehu Shagari, stood side by side in an open Landrover, President Obasanjo on the outside, waving to the crowd. After one circuit President Obasanjo stopped the procession and exchanged places with Shehu Shagari. The cavalcade moved off and the new President waved to the crowd, timidly at first, then more confidently. Before the lap of honour was finished Shehu Shagari was waving madly, as Presidents do, to all sections of the crowd.

CHAPTER 18

1981: Dundee cake

F OR MY LAST POST in the Diplomatic service the Office had offered me
that of Director-General of United Kingdom Trade and Development
in the United States and Consul-General, New York. This was regarded
as the senior commercial post in the service and I was delighted to accept.
But first the Office asked me to do undertake a tour of Angola, a country
torn by a civil war that had been raging for fifteen years and an east-west
ideological conflict between the Soviet bloc and the West led by the
United States. The MPLA government was sustained by Soviet military
aid and a Cuban army of some 50,000 troops. Units of the South African
Defence Forces had invaded and occupied the southernmost province of
the country and defended the Namibian frontier against infiltration by
guerrilla fighters of the South West African Peoples Organization. The
United Nations had demanded the withdrawal of South Africa from
Namibia and had established a 'Contact Group' of diplomatic representatives from the United States, Canada, France, the Federal Republic
of Germany and the United Kingdom to act as mediators in the
negotiation. Because the United States was not in diplomatic relations
with Angola's Marxist government the British embassy was in
unusually close and regular contact with Washington. Our objective was
to negotiate the withdrawal of the Cubans from Angola and the South
Africans from Namibia as a precursor to democratic elections in each
country but in the process to deny any direct link between the two. It was
a fascinating job. Pik Botha, the ambassador whom Charlie Kirbo had
been so anxious that I should meet before leaving Atlanta, was now
South Africa's Foreign Minister. I worked closely with my French and
German counterparts and with successive US Assistant Secretaries of
State for African Affairs, Chet Crocker and Frank Wisner. Chet had
been a professor at Georgetown University whilst Frank was a career
diplomat. Both were untiring in their efforts to find a compromise
acceptable to half a dozen warring factions in the region and both had
behind their backs at least as many warring factions in Congress and
the business lobbies of Washington. Things were no easier in Luanda.
An Angolan minister, Kito Rodrigues, told Chet Crocker: 'In Angola,
there are many kinds of wolves, and there is a wolf on every hill.' In his

Leaving for Buckingham Palace, HM Ambassador, Luanda. London 1981

book[1] on the decade-long negotiations for the withdrawal of Cuban troops from Angola and South African from Namibia, Chet Crocker paid warm tribute to the assistance the US had received from British diplomatic posts in Africa. The British, he said, 'had been our secret weapon', which of course is what our Allies in the Contact Group had suspected all along. Lord Carrington once asked me what he could do to advance our negotiations in Angola. 'Have a public row with the Americans,' I suggested. 'Ooh, I could not do that,' Peter replied.

There is no space here to tell the story of our experiences in that beautiful but tragic country 'where every prospect pleases and only man is vile'. That will have to wait for another occasion, perhaps another book. Blessed with a benign climate, diverse agriculture and mineral wealth that included diamonds and oil in abundance Angola was not only one of Africa's most beautiful countries, it could also have been its richest. Instead, when we were there, the roads were mined, the shops closed, the land no longer farmed. We imported food by air and Anne would barter a bottle of whisky for prawns or crayfish or, occasionally, pork brought in from the countryside. But we lived in a house that on one side looked out over the bay towards the city and on the other to the Atlantic Ocean.

---

[1] *High Noon in Africa* by Chester A Crocker p.460.

Livingston had stayed in the house at the completion of his epic journey across the continent from Mozambique. There was a tree in the garden under which he is said to have rested. A little farther up the road from us lived Sam Nujoma, the President of SWAPO.[2] Sam and his lieutenants would sometimes drop into the residence to read the English newspapers. Anne used to serve them tea. On his first visit the future President of Namibia asked as he took his cup, 'Do you by any chance have any Dundee cake?'

We witnessed the South African attack on Luanda's oil refinery and attended the macabre press conference at which the Angolan Minister of Defence, as though he were a conjurer producing rabbits from a hat, laid out on a table before him the dismembered limbs of commandoes killed in the explosion. We were in Angola when the Falklands War broke out and tried to persuade Sam Nujoma that we were all Freedom Fighters now. But there were happier things too. Everyone, communist or capitalist, African or European joined us in celebrating the wedding of Prince Charles and Princess Diana. We saw the beginnings of perestroika and I used to slip copies of the *Economist* and the *Tablet* to keep my Polish colleague up to date with what was happening in Warsaw and Gdansk. I managed to catch a glimpse of an earlier and more gracious way of life when I attended the 200th anniversary celebrations of an old mission centre near Huambo. On the way to my morning swim I would jog past the great fortress that the Dutch had built in the seventeenth century. Sometimes I would pop in, still jogging on the spot. The courtyard was full of giant figures in stone or marble or concrete. They were statues of the great Portuguese explorers and poets of centuries past: Vasco da Gama and Camoes and the rest. They were all packed together higgledy-piggledy. They had been taken down from plinths in Luanda's parks and squares and waterfront and had been replaced by heroes of the 24th of November and other drab ikons of the revolutionary age. But the guardians of the past – unlike the countless effigies of Stalin and Saddam Hussein – had not been destroyed. They still kept watch over their beautiful city, patiently waiting to resume their places as part of its cultural heritage.

One event that stays in the memory was the visit to the United Kingdom of the Angolan Foreign Minister. This was the first such visit by a minister of Angola's Marxist government. It was interesting to look at the British political scene and indeed the British countryside through the eyes of Paulo Texeira Jorge. The Foreign Office had arranged a programme that turned out to be enjoyable as well as useful. After two

[2] The Namibian Liberation Movement, the South West Africa People's Organization.

days of official talks we travelled to Oxford where the Master of Balliol, Sir Anthony Kenny, entertained us to lunch. One evening the Parliamentary Secretary to the Foreign Secretary, Malcolm Rifkind, hosted a meal in the marvellous surroundings of the old Admiralty building. Another evening we took our visitor to see a performance of *Cats*. Paulo Jorge had repeatedly asked me what these Cats were that we were going to see and I had been unable to enlighten him, never having heard of the show before. He was welcomed at the theatre by Andrew Lloyd Webber and sat through the musical completely entranced. But the highlight of the visit was the masterly performance of the Prime Minister. The British press had been campaigning for the release of five Britons who had been taken prisoner some years earlier when they had been fighting as mercenaries in the guerrilla war that had followed the departure of the Portuguese. A number of MPs, including Cecil Parkinson, had in their constituencies relatives of the prisoners. Each of the MPs pleaded with the Angolan foreign minister for the release of their constituents but Paulo Jorge was careful to acknowledge the requests without making any commitment.

After lunch with Francis Pym, who had succeeded Lord Carrington as Foreign Secretary, we attended Prime Minister's Question Time in the House of Commons. Paulo Jorge was scandalized. When the Prime Minister stood up the Opposition benches erupted in such shouting and stamping that her answer was drowned in the din. He shook his head in disbelief. A little while later we received an invitation from the Prime Minister to meet her in Downing Street. Paulo Jorge was thrilled. We were shown into the Prime Minister's private sitting room. The only other persons present were a Private Secretary, the Angolan Ambassador, who doubled as Ambassador to Paris, and myself.

Margaret Thatcher could not have done more to put the Angolan visitor at ease. It was a chilly February afternoon and she began by apologizing for the weather. 'We brought this in but it is not very good,' said the Prime Minister, pointing to a wretched two-bar electric fire that you would expect in the proverbial flat in Bayswater Road. I thought at first that she was having us on. Maybe she was. Paulo Jorge went into a long speech saying how pleased he was to have attended a session in the famous House of Commons. But he had to say how shocked he had been at the lack of respect shown to the Prime Minister by members of the Opposition Party. That would never happen in Angola where comrades were free to criticize the government but were expected to listen courteously when another comrade was speaking. 'Oh,' said the Prime Minister, 'that was a big mistake on the part of the Opposition. The more din they made the further I lowered my voice. I was able to get through my answer and on to the next question before the silly people knew what was happening. Now, Foreign Minister,' she said, leaning forward in her most engaging manner, 'tell me about Angola. How is the economy doing? Is agriculture recovering?' Paulo Jorge was off. He had got as far as the latest production figures for coffee when the Prime Minister interrupted him. 'Coffee! Oh do forgive me, Foreign Minister, I forgot to offer you coffee.' Oh no, no Prime Minister. Oh yes, yes Foreign Minister. This went on for some time but of course the Prime Minister insisted on making us coffee. She said that she would put the kettle on and disappeared into a tiny little kitchen next door. I was open mouthed at the whole performance when the Prime Ministerial head popped round the door: 'It's only Nescafe, I'm afraid. Will that do?' In the course of forty minutes conversation there was not the remotest allusion to the issue of prisoners. Finally, the Private Secretary reminded his boss of her next engagement. By now she and the Angolan Foreign Minister were old friends. She was reluctant to let him go. They carried on their chat as she accompanied him down the staircase and through the hall to the door. After a final farewell and more vigorous hand-shaking she said goodbye and turned away. Then, as if suddenly remembering a minor point, she turned and murmured with an affectionate smile 'And Foreign Minister, I know that you will do what you can over that business of the prisoners.'

When we got back to the official car, Paulo Jorge bounced up and down on his seat. 'Iron Lady'! he snorted. 'Just wait till I get back to tell Lucio.'[3]

The ex-mercenaries were released three months later.

---

[3] Lucio Lara, a senior member of the MPLA, regarded as one of the party's doctrinaire hard-liners.

CHAPTER 19

1983: And the Brits ain't one of them

THERE IS A SPECIAL EXCITEMENT about New York. Whatever our nationality and background, New York seems to have been a part of all our lives. When we first visit it we all feel that we have been there already; the famous skyline, Central Park, the view down Park Avenue as it dips and rises again before the Crown Building, Grand Central Station and the Public Library, the steam rising from underground mains, the street-smart drivers in their battered yellow cabs, the Rockefeller Centre and Metropolitan Opera House and the greasy joints serving coffee, eggs and bacon and pancakes with maple syrup. We have seen these things so many times in films and on television that they are as familiar to us as many of the sights and sounds in our own hometown. When you live in New York all your friends and relatives, including some that you did not know you had, come to visit you. In Angola the only official visitor that I remember receiving was Richard Luce, Minister of State at the Foreign Office.[1] In New York, members of the Royal Family, ministers and members of Parliament were all frequent visitors. Every member of the Cabinet found it necessary to make frequent visits to New York.

Such visits sometimes played an important role in the formulation of government policy. If the government were preparing a new framework for the regulation of financial services they could not sensibly do so without considering the practices and opinions in the world's largest financial market. When a Secretary of State for Trade and Industry considered how best to regulate the new value-added networks and emerging information technology it was prudent to consider US practice and listen to what US giants like ITT and IBM and Microsoft had to say. When the Secretary of State for Health visited New York the heads of the giant US pharmaceutical companies were all anxious to see him because the British National Health Service is one of the world's largest consumers of health products.

A newly arrived British Director of Trade and Investment is immediately struck by how closely interrelated the commercial structures of the

---

[1] Lord Luce, PC, currently Lord Chamberlain of the Royal Household, and a former Minister in Margaret Thatcher's government, has the rare distinction of having begun his career as a member of the Colonial Service when he served as a District Officer in Kenya in 1960–62 and having resumed that career thirty years later when he was appointed Governor of Gibraltar.

With Mayor of San Francisco (later US Senator) Dianne Feinstein and Ambassador Sir Oliver Wright. New York, 1985

two countries have become. It is a process which appears set to continue. In the year 2003/4, of all US investment in the European Union almost half went to the United Kingdom.

My ambassador in Washington and friend, Oliver Wright, was always anxious that I should not allow my duties as Director General of Trade and Investment to distract me from those of Consul General, New York. New York is the nation's commercial and financial capital as Washington is its political capital and in general the work of Ambassador in Washington and Consul General in New York were complementary. In practice, we worked harmoniously, and I think, effectively together. The supervision of the commercial work of the other Consulates meant that in the course of his tour the Director-General had opportunities to travel the length and breadth of the United States and to meet many of its commercial and political leaders. I never visited Hawaii or Alaska but did get to most of the other States. Once, after repeated reminders from its Governor that I was also accredited there, I managed to fit in a visit to Bermuda.

The office of the Consul General was at number 845 Third Avenue. On the other hand the Director General of Trade and Investment occupied an office several blocks away on Fifty Eighth Street. This arrangement had been in place for many years but seemed a potty idea to me. I tried at first to spend the mornings in one place and the afternoons in another but in practice you have to make one or other your principal base, with one Personal Assistant who reconciles competing claims on your time and develops one final programme of the day's activities. Since the office of Trade and Inward Investment was staffed from the Department of Trade and Industry but that of the Consulate General from the Foreign and Commonwealth Office there were those who thought the physical separation of the two an admirable arrangement. Such arguments only strengthened my resolve to scrap it. Once they saw the figures, London could not resist the savings in rent and overheads that a merger of the two offices would yield. As soon as space became available I moved the commercial operations into 845 Third Avenue. The biggest savings in my opinion were in improved efficiency.

I had seen in Atlanta how terrorism could negatively affect the plans of US companies to invest in Northern Ireland. In New York the problem was much more immediate because New York, along with Chicago and Boston, had one of the largest Irish-American populations in the country. Some of the funding for the IRA and its sister organizations came from these populations. Activists urged action against companies whose Northern Ireland subsidiaries failed to comply with what they called the MacBride Principles. These were modelled on the Sullivan Principles that had been used successfully against the apartheid government in South Africa. They laid down criteria by which to judge what they defined as fair employment practices of companies operating in Northern Ireland. They urged State legislatures and municipal corporations not to invest in shares or bonds of companies that failed to meet the requirements of the MacBride Principles. Since the States of New York, Pennsylvania and New Jersey and many of the municipalities in those states operated pension and retirement funds valued at many billions of dollars, these were potent threats. I spent a good deal of time in the lobbies of the State legislatures and in correspondence with some of the State Treasurers. We had some success with the legislators but little with the average supporter of the Irish nationalist cause. It was not so much that these Irish-Americans were pro-IRA as that they were anti-British. The injustices of the Famine of 1848, the cruelties of the Black and Tans; the eviction of Irish peasants by Protestant landlords; these were not only part of the communal folklore: they were matters of faith. For many people they were among the reasons that their families had emigrated in the first place. Every evening from 5.00 p.m. to 7.00 p.m. a group of IRA supporters would demonstrate outside our Third Avenue Office, chanting through loud-speakers: 'Brits Out, Brits Out', 'Bobby Sands Murderers' and similar slogans. Our staff ran the gauntlet of the demonstrators each evening as they left the office.

I used to complain to my friend, the Irish Consul General, that he should keep better control of his parishioners. 'You should be so lucky!' he would snort. 'You are only the enemy. I am the bloody traitor.'

Northern Ireland was a topic that I frequently debated with New York's lively and colourful mayor Ed Koch. On one occasion the press reported that in a speech over the weekend the mayor had expressed sympathy for the aspirations of the oppressed, nationalist minority in Northern Ireland. I telephoned the mayor to complain. 'Look, Consul-General Francis,' said Ed, who for some reason used to address me in those terms, 'let me tell you something. Noo York is composed, 93 percent of ethnic minorities. And,' he added, 'the Brits ain't one of 'em. When I want to speak to my voters I don't have to get the permission of Her Majesty's Consul-General.' I said 'Fine. In that case I shall not feel constrained from publicly disagreeing with the mayor of New York when he criticizes the actions of my government in a Province of the United Kingdom.' 'Feel free,' said Ed. On another occasion a member of the IRA leadership had been nominated as parade marshal for the annual Saint Patrick's Day Parade. This was regarded as a prestigious appointment. The mayor, the Catholic Cardinal and other dignitaries would walk alongside the Marshall at the head of the Parade (which would pass below the window of our apartment in Fifth Avenue). I went to see the mayor to urge him to refuse to march alongside a man who was a declared enemy of an ally of the United States. 'Francis,' said the mayor, 'when the US faces the Soviet Union and our Warsaw Pact enemies I salute Great Britain, our closest ally and best friend. But when the Irish march down Fifth Avenue on St Patrick's Day I see a quarter of a million votes. On the 17 March I am an Irishman. When the Greeks have their national day I am a Greek; when the Poles march I am a Pole.' 'What about the Turks?' I asked. 'Yes, them too,' said Ed less certainly. The primacy of ethnicity in US politics is something we foreigners sometimes forget.

I also called on Cardinal O'Connor, the head of the Roman Catholic Church in the United States, to object to the St Patrick's Day arrangements. It was interesting to go from Ed Koch to the Cardinal because at the time they were in the middle of a ding-dong public row over abortion clinics. The Cardinal was much more reticent than the mayor but on Northern Ireland his position was not all that dissimilar. The Cardinal would listen carefully as I urged him to distance himself from the murderous activities of the IRA and to discourage the support given to the IRA by many Irish Catholics. He would reply in guarded terms hinting at difficulties he experienced in dealing with the various factions in the Irish Catholic community.

For many years the British Government and its diplomatic mission in the United States opposed American involvement in the affairs of Northern Ireland on the grounds that these were the internal affairs of the United Kingdom. The Irish National Caucus in Washington characterized the policy more crudely as 'Mind your own business'. So long as the United States had an Irish American population of some 38 million people this policy was never going to be very productive. British governments came to accept that not only was there an American dimension to the problem of Northern Ireland but that the US government could make a positive contribution to its solution, as of course could the government of the Irish Republic. In New York I started to hold monthly lunches of a small group of former US ambassadors to Ireland and Governors and other distinguished public figures with an interest in Irish politics. These were reasonable men and women attuned to the political realities of the situation and open to valid argument by either side. Indirect pressure from them was usually more effective than direct pressure from us in influencing opinion in the Irish American community. It was surprising how few Americans took seriously or even knew of the undertaking of the British government that if at any time a majority of the people of Northern Ireland voted for union with the Republic of Ireland, Britain would make the necessary constitutional changes. At the time of writing (October 2005), the peace process in Northern Ireland has still not been brought to a successful and definitive conclusion. But great progress has been made thanks to the sustained efforts of many of the parties involved. As well as Tony Blair and his predecessor, John Major, and Bertie Aherne and his predecessors, those parties include also the former President of the United States. How far we have travelled from the situation that I have been describing was demonstrated by the warmth of the welcome accorded to President Clinton by people on both sides of the Northern Ireland divide when he made his historic visit to Belfast.

Northern Ireland was by no means my only preoccupation. In support of our export promotion and inward investment efforts I called frequently on the movers and shakers of US industry both in New York and elsewhere. I remember calling once on Jack Welch, Chairman and CEO of the great General Electric conglomerate. At that time, in the mid eighties, General Electric was the biggest manufacturing conglomerate in the world. The company is valued at some $500 billion; its annual turnover exceeds the national budgets of most of the countries of Africa. I asked the great man where he saw Britain's competitive advantage in the US import market. He didn't. 'I don't buy things from Britain,' said Jack. 'You guys don't make anything I need. When I go to UK I don't buy

Anne chatting with Duke of Norfolk. New York, 1984

things, I buy *brains*. Maybe I'll pick up a dozen maths graduates or a few Cambridge PhDs. They are very good, very cheap.' Warming to his theme, Jack went on, 'I bet you can't name one single thing that's worth my buying. Go on, name one.' I fell headlong into the trap. Jaguar cars were selling particularly well in the first part of 1985 so I said confidently: 'Look at Jaguars. Brilliant cars. You should buy one.' 'Huh! Jags!' said Jack, pressing a buzzer on his desk. 'Send Bob in, please, Margaret.' Into the office came one of Jack's Senior Vice Presidents. 'Bob, tell the Consul General about your Jag.' 'Broke down last week in the middle of Manhattan. Overheating,' said Bob. When I got back to New York I rang Graham Whitehead in New Jersey. Graham was the Managing Director of Jaguar Motors in the United States. I begged him to fix the car of the Senior Vice President of General Electric and see that it remained fixed. I told him that we were being crucified by Jack Welch's bad-mouthing of the brand. It did not do any good. Four weeks later I was in a meeting when my secretary announced an urgent telephone call from a Mr Jack Welch. A voice in gleeful tones said, 'Broken down Eighty-ninth and

Fifth. Air conditioning.' and rang off. On another occasion I got a call early in the morning, 'Jack, here. Bob's stuck in garage. Car won't start.' You had to hand it to Jack Welch. He not only had a sense of humour; when he was on to something, he did not let go.

All the family enjoyed New York. Sarah was married and visited us with her two children, Emma and Kate. Mark was working with the Hong Kong and Shanghai Bank but found time to visit us from the Middle East. Ruth and Jonathan were at university and during the vacations found temporary jobs in New York. Amongst other jobs Ruth worked for the designer Joseph and this I think may have been the first step in an exciting and successful career. We engaged two young girls whom Anne trained to be excellent servants. Anne supervised all the catering and hospitality. It was a happy household.

Of the many dinner parties, receptions and lunch parties the most memorable was a dinner that we gave for the Prime Minister. Margaret Thatcher loved the United States. This was not surprising because the Americans loved Margaret Thatcher. On this occasion she was to make a speech in the United Nations and I offered to give a dinner in her honour the evening before. I suggested a guest list of businessmen and bankers.

With HRH the Duchess of Kent in JC Penney's. New Jersey, 1985

Back came a telegram from Downing Street: 'No businessmen, just bankers.'

As well as the heads of the two British-owned banks in New York I invited the chairmen of the four largest 'money centre' American banks, as we used to call them in those days. Oliver Wright, our ambassador, came from New York as did Tim Lankester, a senior British Treasury official who was our Finance Minister at the embassy in Washington and UK representative on the IBRD and IMF. But I also invited Paul Volker, the Chairman of the Federal Reserve Bank, and several investment bankers and monetary experts including Alan Greenspan and the former Treasury Secretary, Bill Simon. Because the guest of honour was Margaret Thatcher all those invited accepted, even if for some it meant flying up from Washington for the event.

It was an extraordinary evening and fascinating to listen to the discussion of these leading experts of Western capitalism. The Prime Minister revelled in the adulation. 'We are your supporters,' said Bill Simon. 'This is your College of Cardinals.' 'Look here,' said Margaret, 'I have done everything that you people told me to do. I have tightened the money supply. I have lowered taxes. I have abolished exchange controls and freed the markets. I have reformed industrial relations. And yet growth is sluggish, inflation is too high and what is more my ratings in the opinion polls are still down. What am I to do?' 'Keep the faith,' said Alan Greenspan. Greenspan, who was the star of the evening, then gave a masterly summary of the recent history of the UK. What had been going wrong since 1925 and perhaps since 1914, he said, could not be put right in two years or even ten. But the Prime Minister had made a start. She had done all the right things. She must continue as she had begun. The conversation moved on to US domestic politics and Paul Volker and Bill Simon asked the Prime Minister if she would speak to her friend the President on some current issues. He was more likely, they said, to listen to her than to them.

After dessert, Nigel Wicks, her Principal Private Secretary, made frantic signals that the Prime Minister must leave because she still had work to do on the speech that she was to give the following morning. But the Prime Minister had no intention of leaving. Taking Alan Greenspan on one arm and Bill Simon on the other, she said, 'Now, Consul General, let's all go next door and have a nice drink.' We did all repair to the drawing room for whiskies and soda but not before Margaret Thatcher had been back-stage to thank each of our servants, and Anne, for what she described as a lovely evening.

Our time in New York came to an end all too quickly. It seemed no time at all before I was going to Washington for a farewell dinner at the embassy given by Oliver Wright. He kindly asked me to suggest one or two friends that I would like invited and I remember suggesting Dean Rusk and Wyche Fowler from Atlanta and James Schlesinger from Washington. Wyche was now a member of the US Senate He was later appointed by President Clinton to be US Ambassador to Saudi Arabia. I had been a fan of Jim Schlesinger since my days in Atlanta. He had been Defense Secretary in the Nixon Administration and Head of the Department of Energy in Jimmy Carter's and had a wonderfully sharp mind. Among other guests Oliver invited was the current Defense Secretary, Caspar Weinberger. Weinberger, who was later to take a hammering in the Arms for Iran inquiry, was a devoted supporter of Ronald Reagan. He was also a great anglophile and was later made an honorary GBE (Grand Knight Cross of the British Empire). In 1941 before the United States had entered World War II he had volunteered for service with the RAF. It was a relaxed and enjoyable evening that typified in more ways than one the 'special relationship'. One reason that I remember it so clearly is because it was the evening that US Air Force carried out the bombing raid against Ghadafi's palaces in Libya. Half way through the dinner, to the surprise of the rest of us but not of course to Caspar Weinberger, our host stood up, tapped his glass and said: 'I have to tell you, gentlemen, that the planes took off thirty minutes ago from their base in East Anglia. Please join me in wishing our boys a successful mission and safe return.' During a 'comfort break' before dessert Jim Schlesinger took me to one side. 'What is it with your man?' he asked. 'You guys are supposed to get some sense into our feller in the White House, not make him worse.'

We left New York on the QE2. The ship sailed one Sunday afternoon in April. Anne's brother, Tom, had flown up from Florida to say good-bye and Mark had joined us for the return trip to England. We had had a lovely farewell dinner the evening before and had packed and sent on our luggage to Cunards. At eleven o'clock we went to St Patrick's Cathedral in Fifth Avenue and attended High Mass. As it happened, Cardinal O'Connor was the preacher that day and at the end of the service he announced that the British Consul General and his family were in the congregation. He said a few gracious words and wished us bon voyage. So finally I did get to hear him speak in more than a monosyllable. I was wearing my favourite flat cap, which of course is an important part of any Lancastrian's wardrobe. As we were leaving the cathedral, several people came up to Anne's brother to wish him and his family well. When he pointed them in my direction they said that they had thought that I was the driver. John, who *was* our driver, took us back to 4, East 66th Street where we said good-bye to our servants and then drove across Manhattan to pier 44 on the Hudson River and climbed up the gangplank of the QE2. It seemed a perfect way to leave the wonderful city. At the top of the gangplank the first person that we ran into was an old friend from Lagos, Bank Anthony. Bank took Mark under his wing and throughout the voyage gave him serious advice on the dangers of spending too much time in the casino. Bank died a few years later but a bronze statue of him has recently been erected in the centre of the dual carriageway that leads to the Murtala Mohammed airport in Lagos. So now when I drive to the airport after a visit to Nigeria, Bank Anthony's statue brings back happy memories, including that of our trip together from New York on the QE2.

In Southampton my sister, Dorothy, and her husband, Peter, and two dear friends, John and Hilary Lowe, were waiting on the dockside. We climbed into their cars and they drove us back to Chorley, where our travels had begun thirty years before.

Postscript

IN THIS BOOK I have not tried to write the story of my life. To do so would have taken more volumes than I would wish to write or anyone would wish to read. I have just tried to write down a selection of stories that are typical of a Diplomat's life and were typical of a District Officer's. I hope that the stories convey something of the flavour of how it felt to be involved in the things described, at those particular places and times.

Eliot's phrase is a little misleading. The dust suspended in the air, marks the end not of the story but of one particular telling of the story. The story itself goes on developing, changing, evolving, as long as there are people to tell it or remember it or relive it. Every narration is a translation. Organizations like the Virgil Association and the Biblical Institute exist for the purpose of telling and retelling a single story.

Our story did not end with retirement from the Diplomatic Service. Two months earlier I had been waiting for a plane at Los Angeles Airport when my name was called and I was asked to go to the nearest phone booth. The call was from Lord King in London. He was the Chairman of British Airways, soon to be privatized. When was I going to retire from that diplomatic job? he wanted to know. 'Come and see me when you get to London,' he said. Thus began what for me was an exciting new career. After years of assisting businessmen by what in the Diplomatic Service we called commercial work, I now had the satisfaction of actually doing business.

I was very fortunate. People in retirement often look back nostalgically on their working life and spend time recalling and even recounting the rich experiences of younger days. You may say that that is what I am doing now, and you would be right, but I have never felt the need to look back nostalgically on earlier experiences. The stories that I have lived have gone on evolving, developing new twists and further turns. Two years after I joined British Airways the company bought British Caledonian Airways. Among the routes served by the expanded carrier were the London-West African routes. I found myself making regular visits to Nigeria as a director of British Airways and of course renewing old friendships. I met Clara Jack again, and then again. I became Chairman of British Airways Regional and of the UK subsidiary of Fluor Daniel Corporation, whose engineering and construction division in Greenville, South Carolina, I used to visit

*With Lord King welcoming HRH Princess Alexandra to British Airways Terminal,
JFK. New York, 1986*

Welcoming Dr Mahathir, Premier of the Federation of Malaysia. London Heathrow, 1993

235

With Lord King and Governor of Georgia. Atlanta, 1992

from Atlanta twenty years earlier. I joined the boards of Smith and Nephew and of the Brunner Mond chemical company and its subsidiary, the Magadi Soda Company of Kenya. Each quarter we attended board meetings in Kenya. From Nairobi we would drive through the Ngong Hills to Lake Magadi in the Rift Valley, through the scenery made famous in the film, *Out of Africa*. We would drive past the junction where the road from Karen meets the road to Magadi, the spot where Joss Errol of the notorious Happy Valley set had been murdered in 1941. The case was the subject of the film White Mischief.

As well as business there were other things to do. In 1989 I became a member of the board of governors of the Lancashire Polytechnic and a few years later when the institution was granted a charter as the University of Central Lancashire I was honoured to be appointed the university's first Chancellor. It has given me great satisfaction to be involved in the growth of this successful educational institution, now one of the largest in the country, with more than 25,000 students, of whom 15,000 are full time. The school that I attended in Preston so many years ago no longer exists but of course I still remember my Jesuit headmaster and our battle over the respective merits of scientific and classical educations. I was particularly pleased to attend recently the ceremonial opening of the University's

Receiving Masai ceremonial staff from Chief of Magadi. Kenya, 1999

splendid new Science Wing. At a time when some other universities are closing science departments, the University of Central Lancashire has announced its intention to resume the teaching of chemistry.

Looking back on my early career, it is remarkable how young we were when we took on substantial responsibilities. I was twenty seven when I arrived in Nsukka and thirty one when I took over as District Officer, Ahoada. Of course, those were simpler times. We painted on a small canvas. Just a few years later Lt-Col Yakubu Danjuma was in Nsukka with the division of the Federal army that went on to capture Enugu. He was thirty one. The General Officer Commanding the Third Marine Commando Division, Lt-Col Olusegun Obasanjo, fought his way through Ahoada. He launched the offensive that ended the civil war and accepted the surrender of the Biafran army. He was thirty two.

Since Independence Nigerians have endured hardships and tribulations that would have reduced less resilient nations to anarchy or revolution. By 1996 even the stoutest of hearts had been brought to the brink of despair by the unspeakable Sani Abacha. Corrupt, unprincipled and unpredictable,

Chancellor of the University of Central Lancashire, 1995

his regime seemed a reversion to the tyrannies of centuries past. The former president, General Obasanjo, was languishing in prison. General Shehu Yar'Adua, his Chief of Staff, who had told me during our nocturnal meeting at the time of the BP incident that Nigeria had closed the door but had not thrown away the key, was less fortunate himself. He had been rushed from prison to hospital where he died of undisclosed causes. Nigeria had been suspended from the Commonwealth. To his great credit, Chief Emeka Anyaoku, the Secretary-General of the Commonwealth and himself a Nigerian, had led the Commonwealth in maintaining pressure on the government of his own country. He may well have saved the life of President Obasanjo; in the process he certainly enhanced the standing of the Commonwealth in world politics.

President Nelson Mandela said in a message to his Nigerian counterpart that when he had been in prison on Robben Island he had been visited by only one Commonwealth leader. That leader had visited him not once but twice. His name was Olusegun Obasanjo. He, Nelson Mandela, could not sleep comfortably knowing what was happening to his friend.

With the Mayor of Preston in procession to the Guild Hall, Preston. 1997

From time to time, with the help of friends, it was possible to get messages and reading material to the former president. I was always aware of the risk involved. On the one hand I wanted to help in a small way a friend who was enduring suffering on a scale difficult to imagine; on the other hand I was conscious of the danger of Abacha's security services intercepting a message and alleging that their distinguished prisoner was in touch with the agent of a foreign power. The last thing that we needed was accusations of a Dimka-style[1] conspiracy. In the event no such crisis occurred. Our friend seemed to endure his ordeal with a serene courage and confidence. In one message he wrote:

> I have no doubt whatsoever that we will have those lively and instructive conversations again.

After his release President Obasanjo said that three things had kept him strong during his imprisonment: first, he had kept fit by regular exercise; second, he had been able to do some physical work. Once he had persuaded the warders that he was not attempting to dig an escape tunnel

---

[1] See p.151 above.

they allowed him to grow vegetables in a little plot behind his prison cell; and third, he had rediscovered his Christian faith.

In 1996 I was invited to give the annual lecture of the Nigeria-Britain Association. I agreed because it was an opportunity to visit Lagos and express solidarity with friends at a difficult time. I was circumspect in my remarks. I tried to censure the regime obliquely by recalling the words of the Roman poet, Horace, after years of civil war and the chaos that had followed the assassination of Julius Caesar. But I did venture to commend the virtues of a stable currency, open markets, a strong civil service and higher standards of probity in politics and commerce. Prime Minister Margaret Thatcher had rarely missed an opportunity to disparage the civil service and perhaps even more so, the foreign service. But in Nigeria the position was far worse. It was heart-breaking to visit friends who, thirty years earlier, had been colleagues of the same rank and seniority, working in the same office, and find that they were now living in penury. Unless an officer had acquired property or had found other ways of earning money, he or she found it impossible to survive on the official retirement pension. Roaring inflation had wiped out much of the value of a civil servant's pension: teachers, doctors, police officers as well as administrators all suffered disastrous financial loss.

People can argue about what has gone wrong in Nigeria in the last forty years and who is to blame and how much of the blame should be laid at the door of the British and how much at the door of the politicians who succeeded them. Many of the arguments are impossible to resolve, but I do think that the progressive impoverishment and demoralization of Nigeria's public services has been egregious folly. It has been a tragedy that those in government should so often have seen the bureaucracy as opponents rather than as an essential instrument of policy. There have been exceptional periods such as that between January 1967 to August 1968 when Ministerial government was suspended and Permanent Secretaries were seen as wielding more power than the Military Government wished them to have. But the process goes further back in time. Nnamdi Azikiwe in the then Eastern Region publicly undermined and humiliated his own Chief Secretary, and the Biafran leader, Ojukwu, did pretty much the same. Zik was determined to wrest power from an administrative structure inherited from the British that in fact was only too ready serve him and carry out his policies. Twenty years later 10,000 civil servants were dismissed in President Murtala Mohammed's purge of 1975. The effects were felt for years to come.[2]

---

[2] For an excellent survey of the problem see *The Nigerian Civil Service in 2010* by Izoma, PC Asiodu, 12 August 1997.

In May 1997 I found myself embroiled in yet another row between the British and Nigerian governments with a commercial company being used as a football between the two. Unfortunately the company was British Airways, of which I was a director. A privately owned Nigerian cargo plane had landed in Britain despite repeated warnings that the aircraft did not comply with internationally accepted air safety regulations. When the Nigerian plane again landed in Britain with the defects still not rectified the British Minister of Aviation banned all Nigerian aircraft from British air space. This caught not only the cargo plane but a newly refurbished DC10 of Nigeria Airways which had finally been insured and cleared for service after an expenditure of several million dollars. The Nigerian government retaliated by banning all British aircraft from Nigerian air space.

The reaction of the Nigerian government, some of us believed, ought to have been anticipated but the British Minister of Aviation, the former actress and film star, Glenda Jackson, had been in office barely two weeks. She had little knowledge either of the airline industry or of Nigeria but she did know of Ken Saro-Wiwa[3] and had strong views on Nigeria's human rights record. She denied that her decision had been influenced by any considerations other than those of air safety. Since the flights to Nigeria were among British Airways' most profitable routes whilst those operated by Nigeria Airways had been making a loss, the Nigerian dictator concluded that the ban must be hurting Britain more than it was hurting Nigeria. At the level of airline revenue this was certainly true. At the deeper level of cost to the economy and to Nigeria's international political standing it was probably untrue.

After a short time the British Government raised the ban but the Nigerian government did not follow suit. By then Abacha had decided that he was on to a good thing and ordered that the ban be kept in place. The ban was lifted only after the death of Sani Abacha in 1999. We were staying in Florida with Anne's brother, Tom, when this happened. Very early one morning the telephone rang. It was Chief Anyaoku, the Commonwealth Secretary-General, with the good news. When the first British Airways aircraft flew into Murtala Mohammed Airport in Lagos thousands of people turned out to welcome the flight. The warmth of the welcome showed how keenly people had felt the isolation imposed on them by the Abacha regime. It showed also, I think, how much Nigerians value their connection with London.

---

[3] Artist and leader of the protest movement of the people of Ogoni in South Eastern Nigeria, Saro-Wiwa was executed by the government of Sani Abacha, despite huge international opposition.

If 1996 was a low in the history of Anglo-Nigerian relations 2005 must be one of the highs. In July 2005 at the conclusion of the G8 Gleneagles Conference, President Olusegun Obasanjo, President of Nigeria and of the African Union, stood side by side with the British Prime Minister and condemned 'in no uncertain terms' the terrorist attacks that had taken place in London the day before. The two leaders announced the decisions of the G8 leaders on aid to Africa. The debts of the world's 18 poorest countries, of which 14 were African, were to be cancelled. The G8 countries pledged to double their aid within 5 years: by 2010 aid would rise by $50 billion per year. The meeting also welcomed the agreement of the Paris Club to write off $17 billion in commercial debt.

Of course, some people have said that the results of the conference were too slow in coming and insufficient in scale. What about pollution? What about Iraq? What about presidential election results in some constituencies in Nigeria? What about them? There are always buts and progress is never fast enough. But President Obasanjo was surely right to describe the outcome of the conference as a success. The British Prime Minister, Tony Blair, has moved Africa up the international agenda and up the agenda of his own government and whatever activists may claim that is not an inconsiderable achievement.

The beautiful but desolate waterways of the Delta region that I used to travel as DO, Degema, are now stained with oil and, in places, with blood. Weapons have poured into the area through illegal channels. Ancient quarrels, like that between Ijaws and Itsekiris, have broken out into open fighting as they did so many years ago in Okrika between Koniju and Tuboniju. I would have thought that the first people to blame for such outbreaks of violence are not the Federal Government or the multi-national oil companies or the 'international community' but the leaders of the local communities themselves. But if the unemployed youth of the Delta are so alienated that elders and traditional rulers no longer exercise any influence or control, what then? It seems that in the Delta things may be in danger of falling apart in a sense more terrible than that imagined by Chinue Achebe in his famous novel. If some reports are to be believed, the threat of 'mere anarchy' being loosed upon this rich but mismanaged world is by no means fanciful. Sadly, 'the ceremony of innocence' has long since been lost.[4]

Some experts say that 50 thousand barrels of oil are stolen every day in the Delta. Some put the figure much higher, but even at the lower figure the scale of the 'illegal bunkering', as it is euphemistically called, is

----

[4] WB Yeats: *The Second Coming.*

With Anne, Ruth and Jonathan after investiture. London, 1986

alarming. If the smuggling and sabotage and racketeering are releasing as much as $2 million per day in the Delta area that is a frightening figure in a population said by many observers to have a per capita income of less than a dollar a day.

As this book goes to press (2006) the Federal Government is wrestling with these appalling problems. The Finance Minister has introduced greater transparency and accountability in the allocation and expenditure of oil revenue. Agreement on a more acceptable share of revenue between central government and the oil-producing states is under negotiation – still. The President continues to press forward his campaign against corruption. Two State Governors have been arrested. The self-appointed leader of one of the Delta militias (Mujahid Dokubu Asari) has been taken

Anne in 2005

into custody. The network of newly constructed highways makes the villages and settlements of the Niger Delta far more accessible than they have ever been in the past. As well as bringing economic benefits they must surely make the task of policing easier and more effective.

Mark and his wife Virginie in Tokyo, 1993

Six of the grandchildren, 2004

Dust Suspended. Two retirees

Gabriel Marcel said that the purpose of travel is to enlarge the area in which we feel at home. Today everybody travels. We take our holidays in Spain or Florida or Phuket and we benefit from the change of scene as well as from the sun and the sea. But working and living in another country as those in the Colonial Service did and those in the Diplomatic Service do, is a different thing, a special privilege. It is a privilege to be immersed in the customs and culture of another country and to deal on a daily basis with those who are responsible for the government and the commerce of that country. Such careers can be an antidote to envy and curiosity unsatisfied. Admittedly, they bring with them their own dangers. They can turn perfectly normal people into crashing bores; of which there is none more deadly than the returned expatriate. But on balance I think that when you have lived abroad you are more likely to appreciate the values of your own country. You are less likely to fret about what lies on the other side of the hill. Moreover, it is the job of a diplomat to put himself in another's shoes (if only thereby to oppose him or her more effectively) and that can help to correct those unattractive distortions of national prejudice to which we in this country seem at present especially prone.

I am fortunate to have a wife and four wonderful children who have put up with the rough and enjoyed the smooth of overseas life. We have enjoyed returning to England and I have greatly enjoyed my later business career. There is much satisfaction to be found in activities whose results are measured by a bottom line. I had a fascinating diplomatic career in which we made good friends all over the world and in which our lives have been enriched by cultures other than our own. And I was fortunate to spend ten formative years in the Colonial and Overseas Services where results were as satisfying as any measured by a bottom line. We may not have aspired to 'the spotless glory of Elphinstone', as Macaulay described it; but we could certainly agree with the view expressed by Monro in his letter from Madras two hundred years ago, that the chief reward of the job was having done it. When Mr A.O. Diribe took me in hand in the Resident's Office, Onitsha, in 1954, and said, with only the slightest of sighs, 'This, Kennedy, we call a file,' I knew that I was apprenticed to a decent trade.

Index

Rivers State in 2000